REA

ITALIAN
POETRY
1950--1990

Translated and edited by

Gayle Ridinger

Co-edited by

Gian Paolo Renello

(A bilingual edition of the Dante University Press)

© Copyright 1996
by Dante University of America Press

Library of Congress Cataloging-in-Publication Data

Italian poetry, 1950-1990 / translated and edited by Gayle
Ridinger, Co-edited by Gian Paolo Renello [edited by
Adolfo Caso]
    p. cm.
English and Italian.
Includes bibliographical references.
ISBN 0-9378-3234-0 (pbk. : alk. paper)
1. Italian poetry--20th century--Translations
    into English. I. Ridinger, Gayle. II. Renello,
    Gian Paolo. III. Caso, Adolfo.
PQ4225.E8R53 1996   96-742
851'.91408--dc20   CIP

DANTE UNIVERSITY OF AMERICA PRESS
17 Station Street
Box 843 Brookline Village
Boston, MA 02147

ACKNOWLEDGEMENTS

T he editors would like to thank all the poets who have retained the copyright to their work, as well as the heirs of Antonio Porta and the following publishers, for authorizing the inclusion of the original poems in Italian: Einaudi Editore (Franco Fortini, Milo De Angelis, Patrizia Cavalli); Guanda Editore (Angelo Lumelli, Tiziano Rossi, Gregorio Scalise, Milo De Angelis, Giancarlo Majorino, Cesare Greppi); Garzanti Editore (Pier Paolo Pasolini, Tiziano Rossi, Mario Luzi, Amelia Rosselli); Feltrinelli Editore (Edoardo Sanguineti, Valerio Magrelli, Edoardo Cacciatore); Arnoldo Mondadori Editore (Giancarlo Majorino, Maurizio Cucchi, Eugenio Montale, Giovanni Raboni, Andrea Zanzotto); Campanotto Editore (Giulia Niccolai); Edizioni Prova d'Autore (Silvana Colonna); All'Insegna del Pesce d'Oro Scheiwiller (Patrizia Vicinelli); Marcos Y Marcos Casa Editrice (Alessando Ceni); Editoriale Jaca Book (Alessandro Ceni); Corpo 10 /Michelangelo Coviello (Silvio Giussani, Giusi Busceti, Michelangelo Coviello, Ivano Fermini); Coliseum Editore/ Nanni Cagnone (Giampiero Neri, Emilio Villa, Nanni Cagnone).

The editors would also like to thank George Whiteside for his editing advice.

CONTENTS

THIRD GENERATION:
POETS BORN AFTER 1945

PREFACE

The job of compiling an anthology always signifies problems and difficulties as regards the ulterior aims and criteria that go into the selection of authors and their work. Difficulties that multiply when the literary currents of a country are many and wide-ranging, as is the case of Italian poetry in this century. And yet, as a consequence of this, twentieth-century Italian poetry has done much to rejuvenate, re-elaborate, and even "re-invent" both the Italian language and its linguistic possibilities in literature. (Not that this is so surprising given the illustrious precedent set by Dante.)

Without getting into a detailed history of Italian poetry over the last hundred years, it should nevertheless be stressed that this has been at times a tumultuous century of great receptiveness to new ideas: it's enough to think of the great contrast that existed at the start of the 1900s, with the poetry of Giovanni Pascoli on the one hand and the rise of Futurist Tommaso Marinetti on the other. Though beyond the shadow of a doubt Marinetti the innovator inspired experimentalists for generations, not all great contemporary Italian poets, naturally, have tried to push the formal limits of language to an extreme; Montale comes to mind here, as does Fortini. That said, it must be admitted that this anthology reflects our belief that a number of the so-called experimental poets, not always included in "mainstream" anthologies, in fact represent some of the most interesting and original voices in Italy; it is our hope that their publication here will in some small way help to right the balance.

A consequence of our selection of some "difficult" poets keen on linguistic games and inventions was that we had to consider their "translation potential" in English, a language which does not usually allow for the same semantic distortions as Italian. Though much has been inevitably lost in these translations, if compared to those of other poets, we have tried our best to render as many layers of meaning as English will gracefully accommodate.

This anthology is divided into three sections representing three generations and attempts to give a fairly ample overview of contemporary Italian poetry. It is not exhaustive, and clearly there were problems as to who to include and exclude, as well as how to decide what the term "generation" meant exactly. Whatever the defects of our approach, this grouping them by age effectively illustrates in how many different directions poets born around the same time have moved. Also, while we are fundamentally interested in presenting the poets as individuals, each generation intrinsically shares certain broad tendencies: for example, most first-generation poets (born before 1935) were much more into formal experimentation than those born immediately afterwards.

For this *Deus ex machina* presentation to work, certain significant poets of interest had to be excluded. This is the case of Vittorio Sereni and Giorgio Caproni, whose work is currently being reassessed. Then there are others like Elio Pagliarani or Nanni Balestrini, who, though working in very different directions today, played a decisive role in the Neo-Avant-garde of the 1960s, a movement that is represented here by Edoardo Sanguineti.

The translation of each poet's work is accompanied by a biographical note and a schematic bibliography of his or her entire production; readers wanting to know and read more will know where to go.

--Gayle Ridinger and Gian Paolo Renello

INTRODUCTION

Perhaps all anthologies of twentieth-century Italian poetry should carry the subtitle: "Avant-garde vs. Anti-Avant-garde: an Unconcluded Battle." Yet while that is undeniably true, it does not give a complete idea of what has occurred and is still occurring here. The term "avant-garde" usually denotes forward-looking experimentalism and a willingness to face and condense social reality, whereas "anti-avant-garde" conjures up reactionary backward glances to, say, the model of the lonely poet-hero of lyrical verse. What continues to happen in Italy, however, is that experimentalists may look to authors of the past (not just Italian) for inspiration and be quite 'hermetic' in orientation (Andrea Zanzotto comes immediately to mind here), while poets who are more "traditional" in approach may be intent on describing the hard social realities around them.

What the phrase "an unconcluded battle" does underscore, on the other hand, is poetry's strong corporate aspect in Italy and the heavy legacy of Petrarchan interest in style (put on a par with--if not placed before--content). This emphasis takes its toll on all poets no matter what their tendency. Indeed, the debate in Italian literary circles is more often than not on how a poet writes than on what he says. Does he (like Giovanni Raboni, Tiziano Rossi or Maurizio Cucchi) use everyday language and squeeze poetry from the ordinary objects of daily life? This might be seen as going back to certain tenets of Giovanni Pascoli, who urged poets to adopt a humbler voice and more prose-like expressions. (In Pascoli's time, that was revolutionary--poets were being "anti-literary," moving away from the influence of Gabriele D'Annunzio, whose poems pushed language towards its rhetorical limits of sophistication.) But what when the contemporary poet of today radically experiments with language (as do Emilio Villa and Edoardo Cacciatore)? Then--as is the case with two avant-garde groups, the historically important **Gruppo 63** of the sixties and the short-lived **Gruppo 93** of the nineties--he is thought to be continuing "the tradition" of innovation begun by the Futurists at the start of the century and to be disregarding (or snubbing) the Pascoli-inspired "neoclassical traditionalism" of his peers.

Does this feuding--not without its comic side--tell us that poetry in Italy is distressingly subordinate to its "schools"? That content-wise, it lacks in spontaneity, vitality, and originality? That most of the innovation is linguistic, involving largely untranslatable language games of little appeal to non-Italians? That is surely going too far. (Besides, there are quite a few good poets around who do not fit into any cubbyhole and who for this reason risk oblivion, an error that we have no desire to perpetuate.) True, there is no electrifying tension in Italian poetry to make international readers sit up in their chairs; there are only some strong, individual voices--or soft, curious voices--that are perhaps easier to hear and to appreciate if arranged by generation than into "currents" (or worse, into two warring factions).

THE FIRST GENERATION:
Poets Born Before 1935

Admittedly, the term "generation" is used very loosely indeed when referring to poets born as much as forty years apart. It seemed fitting, however, to to begin with the wide diversity of poets living through the Second World War. Furthermore, it seemed right to begin with Nobel Prize winner Eugenio Montale, the best known modern Italian poet, not so much to show the impact of his work on younger poets as to underline the *lack* of this molding influence.

The poems included here are not from *Cuttlefish Bones* but from the very last period of Montale's life, which is to say the seventies, the only part of his production contemporary with the other poets in this anthology. What emerges from these short poems, very much on the order of extemporaneous (and well-crafted) annotations and jottings, is Montale's long-standing fascination with meaning as revealed in the language of poetry. His principal conclusion, never so bluntly put as here, is that poetry expresses man's disillusion and discouragement at the sight of how everything in its essentialness is actually inessential.

The pessimistic conviction of futility in Montale is transformed into a more open-ended sense of man's contradictions in Pasolini. Pasolini the poet is drawn to a wide range of subjects, much like Pasolini the social-minded film-maker and essayist; moreover, the fundamental appeal of his voice remains the revelation of mankind's clashing inner impulses, which Pasolini dramatizes in situations that may take place at any hour of day or night. Pasolini considers the individual as an intrinsic member of a social collective--with all the alienation that this inescapable membership inevitably arouses. Poets, however, like Giancarlo Majorino, Giovanni Raboni, and Giampiero Neri conceive of the tension between the public and the private in very different terms. A political leftist like Pasolini, Majorino has explored (probably more than any other contemporary Italian poet, and in increasingly experimental ways) the impact of politics and society on the private, everyday life of people, noting the divergences but also the overlaps of the ideal with reality. Neri, who comes from a strongly right-wing background, writes principally *poesia della memoria* (poems exploring personal and collective memories of various decades, from prior to World War Two onwards) which are delicately dream-like both in content and wording. Raboni, on the other hand, seems to concentrate less on the language and more on a precise rendering of real situations in his unemphatic, soft-spoken style (baptized by critics *la linea lombarda*), which with its silences and careful details presents the reader with the anguish of existence.

The only other poet to attempt the same utopian mix of poetry and communist politics as Pasolini (hence becoming a sort of National Poet of the left) was the late Franco Fortini. As critic Cesare Garboli has written, Pasolini "went from A to Q to Z, taking the shortest route possible, while Fortini proceeded in zig-zag fashion and took hours." Difficult and complex as his poetry may seem at times--for in addition to everything else Fortini was fascinated by Brecht and his way of proceeding by reversal and paradox--, he was most famous for (and most proud of) "The Poetry of Roses" included here. Many of the contradictions in contemporary Italian poetry are embodied in Fortini: more left-wing than the Left at times, he nevertheless wrote powerful essays attacking the experimentalist movement, **Gruppo 63**. At the same time, he belittled the Hermetics while expressing affinity with Mario Luzi for writing poems that contained "universal messages" for humanity.

What Fortini was perhaps driving at is Luzi's ability to dramatize the relationship between individual and cosmic eternity; the formal aspects of this include a recurring use of analogy and the continual evocation of other (ghostly or absent) presences than man (like Baudelaire in *Correspondances*).

Luzi's early voice, almost always confined within the thematically closed and rhymed form of the traditional lyric, has over the decades developed more fluid and speech-like tones; it has, as it were, become the voice of human consciousness as it grows sadly aware of the lacerations of a civilization that it itself is part of.

Andrea Zanzotto, who like Luzi has been an important presence in Italian poetry for nearly forty years, threshes the most and best out of language until, in his dense multi-layered poetry, the present is rendered in its essence and fullness. Even Zanzotto's very first poems, while highly influenced by Hermeticism and full of elegiac effusions, contained small but important "stylistic lapses" that were indicative of the rich creative vein of experimentation to follow. It is to the utter discredit of the Italian Neo-Avant-garde that they were unable to see and embrace his innovations. Today Zanzotto has achieved an international reputation for his unique mix of refined language, foreign terms, scientific and technical forms, and (most importantly) allusions to psychoanalysis--a poetic vocabulary that successfully correlates the poet's outer and inner worlds.

Edoardo Sanguineti, one of the strongest voices of the Neo-Avant-garde (**Gruppo 63**), gained national fame very early on for his book, *Laborintus*, published in 1956. Written in an experimental style that back then passed for being revolutionary, these poems explored the ways in which the human psyche makes mental associations and elaborates thought processes. Though Sanguineti's work today is very different and infinitely more accessible, he has remained fundamentally true to his ideal of "militant poetry" and to his Marxist belief in mega-systems, though this theory no longer appears overtly in his work; rather, it is discreetly contained in those fleeting, seemingly insignificant moments of life that Sanguineti chooses to describe.

Edoardo Cacciatore was long ignored by an Italian literary establishment unable to fit his work into any orthodox scheme of classification. As in the case of Emilio Villa, another neglected giant, amends are being made only now. Like Villa,

Cacciatore has gone about his work in great solitude, studying and absorbing and incorporating much from cultures and languages and poetry from all over the world. The special poetic language Cacciatore has created is as refined as it is baroque. His *ars retorica* is not simply a stupefying embellishment of style, for his use of language powerfully enhances the imagery and reflections. As critics have noted, Cacciatore's work is "thought-poetry", like the equally solitary achievements of Giacomo Leopardi.

Many years before the Italian Neo-Avant-garde appeared on the scene, Emilio Villa, a polyglot poet and artist of vast learning and refinement, was already conducting similar (if not more fascinating) experiments with language and style. The tendency of Italian letterati to snub their cultural "fathers" and embrace--with much fanfare--their cultural "grandfathers" (in this case Marinetti and the Futurists, as well as the Dadaists) may explain the movement's failure to acknowledge Villa. But the breadth and scope of Villa's knowledge (which includes the mastery of ancient Mid-Eastern languages) is such that his poetry seems literally to burst with it. The myths he reworks, or invents, restore to language the strangeness and freshness, and the elaborateness and the necessity, of its origins--and it is language, or, more precisely, the authentic and explosive re-emergence of "content" as a consequence of the taut clashes between "forms of expression", that concerns Villa the poet most.

Giulia Niccolai and the late Amelia Rosselli are two women poets of exemplary bilingual backgrounds (Niccolai's mother was American and Rosselli's English), who have both written and published work in English and French, in addition to Italian. Niccolai's penchant for nonsense and Anglo-Saxon-like punning gives her work an apparent air of lightness and playfulness, fundamental to her making comedy out of certain small "mental events" and "linguistic coincidences" whose importance has been revealed by psychoanalysis. Rosselli takes these manifestations to heart in a different way, in the sense that "Freudian slips" and other verbal distortions become tell-tale characteristics of her poetic voice; indeed, poetry itself seems the subject of exploration, just as the patient is on his analyst's couch. Niccolai's work is rooted in experimentalism while Rosselli's is more attached to Italian poetic tradition (her allusions to Petrarch are evident and she tends to deal with "lyrical" themes like love).   Nonetheless, Rosselli is not one to camouflage feelings; Sappho comes to mind here, for these poems pulse with forthright sexuality.

SECOND GENERATION:
Poets Born Between 1935 - 1945

The schism created in Italian poetry--and in the publishing world--by the appearance of the Neo-Avant-garde (**Gruppo 63**) in the sixties was such that it is not going too far to say that poets who didn't belong to or clearly dissent from it risked not getting enough support or encouragement to properly get their careers off the ground. Perhaps this tells us why the up-and-coming young poets back then (those born between 1935 and 1945) were so relatively few in number; certainly, it explains why most of them are so little known to the general public, despite fine books of poetry to their credit.

Angelo Lumelli's work stuns the mind on initial impact the way a seemingly unrestrained, vehement rush of language always does, yet his tightly controlled choice of words in reality allows each poem--often about women or about couples--to expand with all sorts of perceptive and hallucinary connotations. Cesare Greppi, on the other hand, writes extremely brief, concise poems--rather like miniatures in their perfect formal construction--that resemble geometrically-balanced windows through which one sees the poet's experiences and vision of life.

Tiziano Rossi's work shares certain affinities with the poetry of Giovanni Raboni, most noted (as we've indicated) for his *linea lombarda*. Using everyday speech, symbolic household objects, and small events that prefigure rites of passage, Rossi's poetry aims to describe a world where even the poet's spontaneous actions and sensations become "things" to be noted each day.

Oftentimes a poem by Silvana Colonna may be read as a fragment of memory--one that seems to stem from a thought or dialogue whose beginnings lie in the distant past, or else which seems extrapolated from some other source (perhaps a diary or journal). She uses the same language to describe thoughts as she does gestures and bodies. The effect is that the internal workings of the mind are manifested to others with the same clarity as external actions.

Nanni Cagnone's work has evolved from an experimentalism close to that of the Neo-Avant-garde to the epic-narrative retellings of myths typical of the excerpts here, work which displays an evident speculative and philosophical intent. Of late, Cagnone has explored what critic Romano Madera calls "the drama of not-belonging", as well as those "eternal reminders of (what may be called) the opposing myth", in short poems of considerable linguistic difficulty. This complicated poetic language testifies to Cagnone's desire to re-invent *not* reality but *"the song that reality sings."*

Much like Cagnone, Gregorio Scalise wrote his first books of poetry under the influence of the Neo-Avant-garde, yet by the time of his major work, *La resistenza dell'aria* (Mondadori, 1982), Scalise, too, had found a style and a voice that no longer had anything flamboyantly experimental about it. There is a definite metaphysical cast to his poetry now and, in particular, a focus on what may comfort or perturb man in solitary moments--though also the consciousness that man, being "an amalgamation of elements", eludes even the most serious or *earnest* inquiry.

Antonio Porta (the one poet of our second generation to have been formally a member of (**Gruppo 63**) came to prefer what he called *la poetica della trasparenza,* a kind of poetic *glasnost* whereby all terms used in a poem should be simple, immediate, communicative, and easily recognizable; in contrast to much experimental poetry, everything now was to be measured in terms of a hypothetical reader. The specific aim that Porta set for himself towards the end of his life was to try to render intense moments of inner awareness in short poetic fragments.

The late Patrizia Vicinelli, after close initial contact with (**Gruppo 63**), and above all with Adriano Spatola, took off in directions of her own (though as regards her concrete and visual poetry, she herself acknowledged that she was working on the same wavelength as Emilio Villa). Vicinelli strove to free language from the constrictions of context, at the same time as she wanted to "train it along" interesting channels of sound, sense, and form. The reader can follow the pathways of meaning traced by constantly emerging and dissolving analogies and metaphors, or else immerse himself in what amounts to pure word play.

THIRD GENERATION:
Poets Born After 1945

E very so often in Italy an anthology of contemporary poetry is published with a curious or blazing title which gives critics the chance to thrust everyone included in it into a school or a movement, when they hardly merit such treatment. It is especially difficult to grasp "the unifying principle" behind *La parola innamorata* (Enamoured Language), which in the seventies established the reputation of many (but certainly not all) of the young poets represented here.

Mile De Angelis comes perhaps the closest to filling the shoes of the Poet that critics were determined to see. Up until the late eighties his way of writing (and his literary review, *Niebo*) exercised enormous influence both on numerous peers and on younger poets. With De Angelis there allegedly reappeared in poetry the evocative or delicate *language of revelation*; words and concepts like "fascination," "softness," "abyss", "danger", "enigma", "sacredness", "ritual," "desire", and "unveiling" came back into use again. What seems more important to us, however, is that this poet has his special way of writing mythical autobiography--an effect achieved as much in the style (mixing dialogue, impersonal observations, and symbolic details) as in the choice of theme and setting.

Included in the anthology *La parola innamorata* were very different poems by Michelangelo Coviello, Maurizio Cucchi, and Valerio Magrelli. Coviello's almost nonsensical rhyming poetry, and more recent efforts in prose poetry (which, by the way, is still considered a suspect genre in Italy, despite the fabulous results already obtained by Dino Campana decades ago), render the preciousness and ludicrousness of life above all in their frenzy; there is a driving whirling thrust to his work which seems to want to leave the reader breathless and yet revitalized, keeping him in a constant crescendo of tension even where there are repetitions or asides, and without the comfort of catharsis until the very end. Cucchi and Magrelli have somewhat unfairly been considered heirs of the *linea lombarda*. Certainly, elements of daily life and snatches of commonplace autobiography are to be found in both men's poetry, but divergences abound. Cucchi's work renders shifting existential feelings of uncertainty and hesitation in the concrete language of everyday speech. By contrast, Magrelli seems almost 'scientific' or 'technical' in tone as he strives for the most precise poetic description of mental states beginning at dawn and ending in that lingering reflective moment before sleep.

Biagio Cepollaro and Lello Voce were two founding members of now disbanded **Gruppo 93**. **Gruppo 93** received the blessing of the older Neo-Avant-garde at the international poetry festival *Milanopoesia* at the start of the nineties. Cepollaro and Voce (and others) have articulated a new *raison-d'être* for experimentalism: taking into consideration the developments of the 1990s in cybernetics, computer programming, and multi-media art, they attempt innovations in poetic style and content that have little to do with the concrete poetry of the past. In their poems represented here, words and syntax may be "compressed" or distorted enough to dissolve into the magma flow of strophes: a melting process--as it were--that allows the poet to reconstruct experiences and concepts differently. (Yet it is a reconstruction that does not imply new crystalizations; in fact, often there's no more than a streaming, mathematical-like series of co-ordinates, images, and overlapping worlds for the reader to orient himself by.) Their poems' structures show that man's existence has multiple layers of meaning at the same time that no meaning is possible.

, Light-years away from such concerns is a poet like Patrizia Cavalli, who writes downright conversational, gossipy poetry that just wants to set the record straight. Her disarming, self-ironic voice prods the reader out of any lackadaisical, conservative acceptance of the status quo that he or she might be guilty of.

Cavalli likes to play with bawdy allusions to male-female differences, and renders modern woman in all her restless physicality. The other woman poet included here, Giusi Busceti, does her wandering about in the opposite realm: that of dreams. The reconstructed passages fit together like pieces in a shiny mosaic of rational 'bits' which as a whole suggest the mysterious and visionary. Poems by Ivano Fermini, on the other hand, describe fragments of reality that refuse to stay glued together; the surrealistic combination (or unpredictable juxtaposition) of images express in their nervous tension the bewilderment, the throbbing hurt, or the whimsy of the poet's psyche. The light note in Franco Buffoni's poetry is more that of pervasive irreverence. The poet's spoofing--not always gentle by any means--takes to task the world for being all too similar to a puppet theater occupied by marionettes of little self-awareness. Generally speaking, Alessandro Ceni's poetry moves in the same direction as earlier work of mythical autobiography by Milo De Angelis. Ceni's tone, however, is one of greater, cosmic desperation; he tends towards a choice of stark vocabulary and towards unsettling pronouncements about the present and future--the world viewed in its progressive decline beyond appeal.

Finally, there are two poets who are, unfortunately, something on the order of a well-kept secret beyond the circle of their peers in northern Italy: Silvio Giussani and Dario Villa. Giussani, who writes prose poetry, maps the inward nature of us all--and at times even that of society, encompassing in his geography both our public gestures or routines and those irrational impulses that when suppressed make for queer explosions. We are given a sense of the violence inherent to things, to life, despite the poet's adherence to the role of objective onlooker. With a similar eye for understatement, Dario Villa manipulates shades of meaning and syntax to create atmospheres and predicaments, wherein the appearance of the first-person "I" is not the poet speaking but the voice of some other, casual presence--a device that adds considerably to the reader's identification with the poem. Villa's lexical precision and his inventive ability to engage the reader represent modern lyrical Italian poetry at its best.

A final word. There would seem to be little room for amazingly die-hard commonplaces on Italy, but it is all the same tempting to wonder if the cover-to-cover reading of an anthology of contemporary Italian poetry might help to foster a more accurate reading of the culture as well. That said, it's probably wiser not to let our imaginations run too much. As the English poet Charles Tomlinson has written, "(Italy) is an idea/ Neither the guidebook nor the imagination/ Tolerates. The guidebook half lies/ Of 'twenty minutes in a comfortable bus'/ Of rows of cypresses, an/ Uninterrupted series of matchless sights.'/ The imagination cannot lie. It bites brick;/ Says: 'This is steel--I will taste steel'..."

FIRST GENERATION:
Poets born before 1935

FRANCO FORTINI

F ranco Fortini was the pseudonym used by Franco Lattes, born in Florence in 1917. Fortini obtained his degree in law in 1939 and a second, Arts degree in 1941. Over the years he worked as a journalist, editor, copywriter, and editorial consultant. As a professor at the University of Siena, he also taught courses on the history of literary criticism. Fortini was well known for his ethical stand on political issues and for his frequent essays in Italian literary reviews, which have been published as book-length collections. He published important literary translations of such authors as Goëthe and Proust. Franco Fortini died in Milan in 1994 following a long period of illness.

Fortini's poetry reveals his progressive abandonment of the tenets of Hermeticism (the school of so-called obscure or "pure" poetry, stressing craftsmanship in writing and ivory-tower dedication to art in general), at the same time as it confirms his careful avoidance of both Neorealism and the Neo-Avant-garde. Fortini is one of the few Italian poets to deal directly and at length with the trauma of the Second World War (especially in his first book of poems, *Foglio di via*). If his experiences as a Jew under Fascism instilled in him that strong critical conscious-ness evident in all his work, his Marxist outlook on life fueled a conception of humanity's collective destiny in some potentially positive future. Given the blindness of our society, Fortini's poetry is caustic in these ethical regards. It can be noted how the poetic themes of current events and history at times lend themselves to the form of a diary; Fortini is not the only poet of his generation, in fact, to make an indiscernible mix of the public and private.

POETRY

Foglio di via (Exile Papers) 1946
Poesia ed errore (Poetry and Error) 1959
Una volta per sempre (Once And For All) 1963
L'ospite ingrato (The Ungrateful Guest) 1966, 1985
Questo muro (This Wall) 1973
Questo muro: poesie 1939-1975 (anthology) 1978
Paessaggio con serpente (Landscape with Snake) 1984

FICTION

Agonia di Natale (A Christmas Agony) 1948, revised in 1972 and
        published as *Giovanni e le mani* (Giovanni and His Hands)
Sere in Valdossola (Valdossola Nights--memoirs of the
        Underground) 1952, 1963, 1985
I cani del Sinai (Dogs of the Sinai) 1969

ESSAYS

Asia maggiore (Greater Asia) 1957
Verifica dei poteri (Power Assessment) 1965
Saggi italiani (Italian Essays) 1974
Questioni di frontiera (Border Debates) 1977
Insistenze (Times of Insistence) 1985
Nuovi saggi italiani (New Italian Essays) 1987

The Poetry of Roses

1

Roses, roses of dust, how much hardness
in stumps at night, roses bent over
with thorns like the sturdy sinews and
wasted muscles on the girl in the car who maneuvers
silk and leather but is softened when highbeams
hit her and is speckled down her throat
like roses bruised during the work of midnight and nettles.

Oh how sweet the toil of bees
against the flowers open to the haze
like hearts hoping that day will never come
but only headlights to winding bends
inflaming the theaters of rosebushes in the
huge dry Roman park!
For this reason "dust" as I called it, from burns rounding curves,
from cemetery vaults, gravel, ancient jars...

Dust on the ramparts; to godlessness
go the roses, thirst never ceases but heightens
with spurts of blood
where the dim-witted cockroach digs.
The lady lashes out with a kick, loses a sandal, demands
atrocity, gets grass-stained, drools.
Honey obstructs all triumphs, oh latin bee.
It leaves mouths satisfied, happy are the roses.

2

But you recognize this beginning. In grottos and fountains
immobile opposites breathe.
An opening rose is a declining rose

and the moment is one but the truths are two.
Come to the frost and the great heat. Here
at the edge, dare to hesitate. It will open branches
and penetrate the tangles. You appear
in the lightning: your lit-up temple

seeing that you were a laurel-like surge in the calm
and cypress arch, and you still,
with another name, and you'll be back with a different body.
Sister in heresy, intent on the waters' mirrors, stony-faced
[splendid
negation of future unity, forehead
stretching towards the emptiness and wounded...Now you are
[shaking,
I see this again, you cross through the ivy

and how you blacken and change,
I know, and when the rice begins to sway
you are already serpent scales needle nail blade
that sharpens the roses' tongue;
and the-half-living blow with the creaking wood as they
search the scene for as long as the artery floods,
and you divert the line to Hecate.
An old woman pats you on the hip.

3

The liberating body creates and debates even you,
immense, inhuman mouth. Fighting time: nothing but
the vile glory of your tongue. That performance by a
pack of slaves, straining to come together in one blood,
to live once more before daybreak.

Lower yourself to the trampling, then; choke, adore,
caress the deformed symbols of the future to the
point you can't see straight. You'll go blind from

staring at and wheezing with them! Oh my. How they
flay at their vital selves (like tetanus,
it sets off sharp pains), and how they venture forth in
rolling bunches to shriek in the arteries.
The rose which breaks up, tears up, its own flesh

will laugh intact come morning.
There's no other way of squandering--of showing the night--the
marvelous naked disgust that maliciously has kept you in its
gripe for years: the coat of arms that your elders have issued
                                                        [your brain,
and the canine anger of the dead, and here you nourish yourself
upon this meal of roses, animal, tearing them up.

4

And now the passion of the trees rises high again.
Desire and separation are about to end.
We'll know who we've been and it will be painless.
What seems like a fairy tale to you is already
coming our way, and it will, children of this century,
be full of ironies. We'll emerge from our dream
and live in one sole truth.

All perfect loves one sole love.
All glorious days one sole day.
Oh vanished bodies that we've loved:
from these miserable recreated remains
you will surely return, blessed with mercy,
amazed identical spirits mad with laughter,
hundred-leaf indivisible rose
that already dazzles the amazed brain.

It's a time that dries and curdles all liquids--
produces souls that seem crooked, dwarfish and ironed flat by
                                                        [the moon.

You can see the kingdoms in array now. Criss-crossing
the corridors of sky like empty sailing ships
come the shadowy Saints. Is it affliction? Judgment? Are they
poor women whose faces have been slashed
by soldiers? Small clearings in the heavens?

5

Far far away voices, wailing...
Must you always repeat the same scenes,
false consciousness?
Trifles dispelled, roses in decay,
space broken down to the rare molecule or two,
it seems these proportions breed peace.
And before the nesting begins, the shrieking:
these mythical dead of yours will return,
opaque men bound to go homeless.

And meteorites of mental steel
spin over the continents, invade the force-fields of
drowsy roses, bend the frequencies of created objects,
make every attempt to be of help. The plane
skimming the cathedral tops makes its attack,
rises, goes: it's not for us.
I live here, where one night of reducing the century to ashes
persuades me and kills me off slowly and I tremble.

6

So only one way, one phosphorus,
one worm through the carbons of
roses? To crypts, rooms, bowels,
after the show hang stacks of torn-off
abdomens, garden-snake manes and cables,
skinned-off masks, Sisyphus, Pirithoús, Thyestes,

and the Furies. To catacomb clay, where
under our walled-up larvae-to-be
an insect senate gesticulates.

7

But no. Go crashing down, you last rivers of
infernal mockery--fountains, waterfalls roar.
Can't just one--the true one--return? Fly off, allegories.
You should have known you'd return for the cold,
for the wanting and the thorn, for unambiguous words,
for a possible yet slow science, for the sun
that paints the Indus and the Nile,
for the imperceptible teeth of history.

But tomorrow how will I be able to recognize
the dead roses or the live ones?
I turn away from here where my madness has been
and feel it coming on again:
for it as well, I ask justice and love.
As for you who are still asleep: I don't
want you to miss anything. No matter if the mites
crush the lumps or the beetles fine-grind the
future with their tiny jaws, without
regard for the dawn sniffing out the lights of
large cars there below; if hope and guilt are
part of the same persistent wrong dividing us,
which rises to the tops of the weeping willows here
and mortifies them. The air is fine and black.
Long life to the spring rose. Long life to
the grass, to flowers, to kisses, to pain.

La poesia delle rose

1

Rose, rose di polvere, quanta durezza
nei ceppi a notte, rose arcuate
di spine quali i tendini robusti
e i muscoli disseccati della ragazza
che nell'auto seta manovra e cuoio
ma molle se un abbagliante la sbatte ma maculata
lungo la gola come le rose contuse
nel lavorío di mezzanotte e ortiche.

Ah contro i fiori aperti all'afa
com'è dolce l'affanno dell'ape,
come i cuori vorrebbero non venisse
mai giorno ma sempre i fari ai tornanti
a infocare teatri di roseti
nel parco immenso arido romano!
Per questo "polvere" ho detto, da ustioni
di curve, da colombari, ghiaie, anfore...

Polvere sugli spalti; delle rose
l'empietà ne gode, la sete si esalta
senza posa a colpi di sangue
dove scava balordo lo scarabeo.
Scalcia la dama, perde il sandalo, esige
immanità, si lorda tra erbe e bava.
Miele occlude i trionfi, o ape latina.
Lascia sazie le gole, beate le rose.

2

Ma riconosci questo inizio. Da grotte, fontane,
i contrari respirano immobili.

Dove si schiude una rosa decade una rosa
e uno è il tempo ma è di due verità.
Vieni al gelo e al gran caldo. Qui osa
sul limite esitare. Aprirà
i rami, le trame penetra. Appari
tu ai lampi illuminata tempia

che eri slancio d'alloro nella calma
e arco di cipresso e sempre sei
con altro nome e tornerai con altra salma.
Intenta a specchi di acque, sorella
d'eresia, impietrita negazione
splendida di unità futura, fronte
tesa al nulla e ferita... Ora tu tremi,
rivedo, traversi le edere

e come t'anneri e tramuti
so e all'oscillio del riso già sei
squama di serpe ago unghia lama
che la lingua delle rose affili
e per crepitio di stipe soffiano, frugano
la scena i semivivi sinché dilaghi
l'arteria e ne derivi la riga tu
a Ecate. Una vecchia ti liscia l'anca.

3

Ah che per essa contro il tempo immensa
inumana bocca, liberante corpo
che anche del tuo si crea e dibatte,
solo hai questa lingua di gloria vile,
questa recitazione di servi. Si cercano
per esistere in un sangue, per rivivere
prima di giorno. Affòndati allora
nel calpestio, ingòrgati, adora,

accarezzati i simboli deformi
dell'avvenire, sino a non più vedere,
tu che ti accechi se li fissi e rantoli
con loro! E come si scuoiano intrisi
di linfa, come il tetano scatena
morsi e oh come s'avventano a grappoli
rotolando e nelle carotidi gridi.
Smaglia le carni la rosa, si sbrana,

che al mattino intatta deriderà.
Non altro modo di profondere, di
denudare alla notte la delizia
del ribrezzo che tanti anni maligno
in sé ti stringe, stemma
che i vecchi diramarono per le meningi a te
e la rabbia dei defunti canina e qui sfami
a questo pasto di rose, bestia, stracciate.

4

E ora la passione degli alberi alta ritorna.
Il desiderio e la separazione
non ci saranno più. Chi siamo stati
sapremo e senza dolore. Già verso di noi
quel che vi parve favola viene e sarà,
figli di questo secolo, ironie.
Noi dal sogno usciremo per esistere
in una sola verità.

Tutti i perfetti amori un solo amore.
Tutti i giorni più belli un solo giorno.
Corpi spariti che avevamo amati,
dai miserabili resti ricreati
ritornerete di pietà beati
stupiti identici spiriti pazzi di risa,
centifolia rosa indivisa

che già la mente incredula abbagli.

È l'ora che i liquidi essica e accaglia
e queste emanazioni sono anime
ma storte, nane, sotto il ferro lunare.
Vedi schierarsi i regni. Varcano obliqui
per i cortei del cielo neri i Santi
vuoti come velieri. È l'assenzio? Il giudizio?
Sono le povere femmine ch'ebbero il viso
squarciato dai soldati? Le chiarine celesti?

5

Molto lontane voci, strazi... Le tue figure
sempre, falsa coscienza, così le ripeti?
Dimesse le frasche, tumefatte le rose,
in molecole rare lo spazio si divide,
le moli pare le allevii una pace.
E prima che inizino i nidi il gridio
queste tue favole di morti torneranno
uomini opachi avviati sui lastrici.

E meteoriti di ferro mentale
filano sui continenti, tangono
campi magnetici di rose sopite,
curvano frequenze di cose create, tentano
aiuto. L'aereo che grave le cupole rade
combatte, cabra, va; non per noi. Qui abito
dove una notte l'incenerirsi del secolo
persuade, e mi stermina lenta e tremo.

6

O tra carboni di rose un fosforo, un verme,
la sola via? A cripte, aule, visceri

dove a spettacolo spento pendono mucchi
di addomi stronchi, criniere di bisce e funi,
maschere scorticate, Sisifo, Piritòo, Tieste,
e le Erinni. A tufi di catacombe, dove
sotto le larve di noi futuri murate
un senato di insetti gesticola.

7

E no. Ultimi fiumi di un ironico inferno,
precipitate, fontane, gli scrosci.
Torna uno il vero? Fuggite, allegorie.
Dovevi saperlo, saresti tornato
a scegliere il gelo, il volere e la spina,
univoci i nomi, la scienza possibile
e lenta, il sole che imbianca Indo e Nilo,
il dente della storia impercettibile.

Ma come domani saprò riconoscere
le rose uccise, le vive? Mi volgo di qui
dov'è passata, e tornerà, la mia demenza:
anche per essa chiedo giustizia e amore.
Voi in sonno ancora: voglio che nulla si perda.
Anche se sempre, se senza pietà dell'aurora
che tanto deboli laggiù fa i lumi
di posizione dell'alte cilindrate,

gli àcari stritolano i grumi,
le cetonie triturano l'avvenire
con le minuscole branche; se colpa e speranza
sono un unico male che ci separa e ostina,
che da noi sale le cime dei salici
e le macera. L'aria è fina e nera.
Viva la rosa della primavera.
E viva l'erba, il fiore, i baci, il dolore.

"Perhaps the Time Of Blood"

Perhaps the time of blood is on the return.
There are men to be killed.
Fathers to be mocked.
Places to desecrate, cuss words to bawl out,
fires to arrange, crimes to approve.
But above all there's the getting back to another kind of
                          patience,
to the fierce science of objects, to that coherence
in dilemmas that we believed we could leave behind.
To the resolution of simply having to take and do.
Looking now for our equals, daring to recognize them.
Let them judge us; guide them, be guided,
want a world of good with them, do with them bad
and good and reality serve deny change.

"Forse il tempo del sangue"

Forse il tempo del sangue ritornerà.
Uomini ci sono che debbono essere uccisi.
Padri che debbono essere derisi.
Luoghi da profanare bestemmie da proferire
incendi da fissare delitti da benedire.
Ma più c'è da tornare ad un'altra pazienza
alla feroce scienza degli oggetti alla coerenza
nei dilemmi che abbiamo creduto oltrepassare.
Al partito che bisogna prendere e fare.
Cercare i nostri equali osare riconoscerli
lasciare che ci giudichino guidarli esser guidati
con loro volere il bene fare con loro il male
e il bene la realtà servire negare mutare.

Italy 1942

Now I realize that I love you,
Italia, that I embrace you,
necessary prison.

Not for your streets of sorrow, for the cities
lined like human faces,
not for the ashes of church passion, not for the
voices of your distant books.

But for these words
woven by common folk, which beat
like hammers in the mind,
for this pain which now
envelopes me as a foreigner inside you.

For this language of mine
that I'll speak to grave ardent free men
of the future, comrades in resilient sorrow.
At present, it isn't even enough to die
for your very old very vain name.

Italia 1942

Ora m'accorgo d'amarti
Italia, di salutarti
Necessaria prigione.

Non per le vie dolenti, per le città
Rigate come visi umani
Non per la cenere di passione
Delle chiese, non per la voce
Dei tuoi libri lontani

Ma per queste parole

Tessute di plebi, che battono
A martello nella mente,
Per questa pena presente
che in te m'avvolge straniero.

Per questa mia lingua che dico
A gravi uomini ardenti avvenire
Liberi in fermo dolore compagni.
Ora non basta nemmeno morire
Per quel tuo vano nome antico.

GIANCARLO MAJORINO

Giancarlo Majorino was born in Milan in 1928. After working in a bank, he taught philosophy and history at secondary school for over twenty years. Presently, he teaches courses on semiotics and literary analysis. Founder and editor of several small literary magazines and presses (his most recent review is entitled *Manocomete*), he has always tried to combine his interest in leftist politics and in literature (encouraging the same, meanwhile, in others) in the form of essays or organized public debates. Majorino has contributed a regular arts column to such newspapers as *Il Corriere del Ticino* and *Il Corriere della Sera* and has been a consultant for the Italian-Swiss Radio as well as for a private T.V. network. Besides poetry, Majorino has written for the theater and in collaboration (on multi-media pieces) with contemporary Italian composers, sculptors, and painters.

From the beginning, Majorino's poetry has shot off in multiple directions, ranging from early pieces written in hendecasyllabic and septenarius meter to recent work on the order of multi-lingual prose poetry. (His most innovative book, in terms of stylistic innovation, is commonly considered to be *Provvisorio*, published in 1984.) Often Majorino tries to give his poetry the feel of "discursive dialogue" with the reader. The poet attempts to describe as objectively as possible what he sees happeining in the world (though not necessarily what is going on right in front of his nose). Above all, history and politics become material for poems even of the most private nature.

POETRY

La capitale del nord (The Capital of the North) 1959
Lotte secondarie (Secondary Battles) 1967
Equilibrio in pezzi (Shattered Equilibrium) 1971
Sirena (Siren) 1976
Provvisorio (Subject to Change) 1984
Testi sparsi (Miscellaneous Works) 1988
La solitudine e gli altri (Solitude and Other People) 1990
Cangiate (Shifting) 1991
Tetralegro (Bleak-blithe) 1995

PROSE

Ricerche Erotiche (prose and poetry on Eros) 1986
Qui e altrove (Here and Elsewhere) 1992

ESSAYS AND CRITICISM

Passaggi critici (Critical Passages) 1984
Poesie e realtà 1945-75 (Poetry and Reality 1945-75,
    an anthology) 1977
Centanni di letteratura (A Hundred Years of Literature). 1984

THEATRE

L'uccellino meschino (The Petty Bird) 1979
Fanno notte del giorno (They Make Night of Day) 1987
Elektra (co-written with Cinzia Bauci) 1990
Castigo e delitto (Crime and Punishment--after the original) 1993
Io io io (Me me me) 1993

Mirrored

That's right, there's a clear spot in me, and in you--
sweet round round honeycomb--it's dark and equally active,
not proletarian in origin, from a childhood
not poor but imaginative, and higher up,
on that trunk of shrewd white conquests,
sharp sense of penetration, rapid, violent,
able shunting towards utility, cardinal
centralizing, rapacious, of stuff that
veils from us--exquisitely--
the poverty, the death of other people.

Specchiati

Già vi è un punto chiaro in me, in te
- rotondissima, dolce favo - scuro
e ugualmente attivo, di provenienza
non proletaria, d'infanzia
non avara, fantastica, e più sù,
nel tronco delle scaltre conquiste bianche,
pungente senso di penetrazione, rapido, violento,
abile smistamento verso l'utilità, un accentramento
cardinalizio, rapace, di panni che ci celano, squisita mente,
la povertà, la morte di altra gente.

Kisses

So many kisses. Kisses that have pulled me
free from stinginess and retention like a
butterfly from a wall.

Then comes the non-stop flight.

Sweet mother, niggardly wife

who roared like a bull in childbirth,
I sucked those breasts like honey.

My mother, in flashes, small and high-strung:
I was her triumph in public.

Then comes the non-stop flight.

I baci

Quanti baci. I baci m'hanno strappato
dall'avarizia e dalla ritenzione
come una farfalla dalla parete.

È che poi si vola ininterrotta mente.

La dolce madre, stata grama moglie,
e che ruggiva toro nelle doglie,
le succhiavo le tette come il miele.

Mia madre, a scatti, piccola, nervosa:
io ero il suo trionfo fra la gente.

È che poi si vola ininterrottamente.

Scene-script

Face, huge face on the screen
interior, reddening face, flooding with love

and student, already alone, afternoons
at the movies for that surrogate white
between the black rocks between the
coils of smoke

calling back, desperate man,
the constant laughing wide-open
face flooded with light

but half-veiled in brown.
and "soul," thinking, between the black rocks;
and "body," undressing, between the coils of smoke.

Copia di scena

Volto, grande volto sullo schermo
interno, colorato
volto intriso d'amore,

e studente, già solo, i pomeriggi
al cine per quel bianco surrogato
tra rocce nere tra fili di fumo

richiamando, uomo, disperato,
il continuo, ridente spalancato
volto intriso di luce

velettato di bruno.
E "anima" pensando, tra le rocce nere;
e "corpo" denudando, tra fili di fumo.

My Flesh in its Sweat

Dance, room, quiet,
bright clinic, dance and dance,
how fierce, you know,
solitude is.

Over there a sky-blue helmut, the frequent
television antennas: ironic, a small still rustling,

is my flesh in its sweat.

Salami-flesh which shivered
when linked up, now on the run on the run,
can't--so tender--be displaced by air.

La mia carne sudata

Balla, stanza, tranquilla,
ambulatorio chiaro, balla e balla,
ché feroce, sai,
è la solitudine.

Là un elmetto celeste, le frequenti antenne
televisive: ironica, una quiete
foglietta la mia carne sudata.

La salumosa carne che congiunta
rabbrividiva ora fuggitiva fuggitiva
non sostituita, tenera, dall'aria

Hints

   green sea clothes on
outfits with folds and careful tucks that pull
clothes which swamps of women descending
along furniture ribbons head-nod

or in the silence of the house: what should I do?

in the silence

I feel your specific points   you women descending
and clothes lowered   and rah-hah raised
I feel specific points aimed at us

spirits moan also in you, I believe; now that our sisters have
[made
a clean sweep of it, our brothers feel a new chill, our brothers
[who are sharp, who know about sharps.
Understanding changes which dirty the customary floors
[is semi-impossible,
yet necessary, yet a good idea, yet it hurts less to search through
[old
photographs, rise to the bottom.

bandwagon of musts?
end to the sparks?

From here precipitated the question of our differences:
[do your ghosts
also tremble, sister? I think so; though the right
[and authority to
negotiate has been for centuries ours, of the male mind.

I do as I please, however
no one can judge me
not even you
however
shut your mouths, however

even if invisible beaks lightly flutter
softly insinuating our thoughts to us?

silence
but, over here on the side, you what do you think?

we are both packed tight in the shelter
skin-masks over our face

silence

si-len-ce

Allude

mare verde addosso d'abiti
vesti con pieghe e punti curati che a sé tirano
vestiti che maremme di donne scese
lungo mobili nastri capochino

o nel silenzio della casa: che faccio?

nel silenzio

sento punti precisi   di te voi donne scese
e abiti discesi   e ri saliti
sento punti precisi che ci mirano

Gemono anche da te gli spiriti, credo; ora che le sorelle fanno
                                                            [piazza
pulita, i fratelli avvertono un brivido in più, i fratelli
                                                [acuti compagni delle acute.
Intendere mutamenti che sporcano i pavimenti consueti
                                                [è semimpossibile,
pure bisogna, pure conviene, pur essendo meno doloroso,
                                                [frugare tra le foto prece
denti, salire in giù.

              carro di devo?
              oblio delle scintille?

Di qui precipitava la domanda della differenza: gemono anche
                                                [da voi gli spiriti?
credo di sì, sorelle; tuttavia la delega e l'autorizzazione
                                                [a trattare è da seco
li nostra, della mente maschile.

              però faccio come mi pare
              nessuno mi può giudicare
              nemmeno tu

però
chiudete il becco però

anche se becchi invisibili aliano lievi
sofficemente insinuandoci i nostri pensieri?

silenzio
ma, discreto, tu che cosa dici?

siamo entrambi stretti nel ricovero
maschere di pelle sulla faccia

silenzio

si len zio si

Doing

space with figure who holds the newspaper
half-open and crumpled over his chest;
our fallen albatross could even be
the man with the paper, pages open like wings
though tattered and bound to dirty,

news, papers, of the moment:
the vastness of indirect experience,
up through the eyes in your head and back, the surface
that isn't the opposite of profundity but its assistant
many arms beyond these
two of mine, beyond yours
space can divide
and re-form like a vacant sea
the air of a thought
moves writing along and my arms?
the air of feelings?
helmet inside the skull and soil

from buried star paths
muck from the air, rows of booths
    rows of variations
      on the order of a main pipe, nothing more?

"the philosophic light round the window is now my joy"
yes, but the wavering
    of new trees, events, faces, and boulevards?

     questioning, beginning
     the child moves towards talking
   in a sweat, colossal, huge unwieldy
  crowd occupying sites and unrented apartments
  threatened child
 staring at you, parroting, angry stutter
the whirling crowd of crowds of crowds of singles all
or almost all

Fare

spazio con figura, che tenga il giornale
mezzo aperto e spiegazzato addosso;
l'albatros caduto   potrebbe anche essere
l'uomo con giornale, pagg. aperte come ali
benché un po' malconcie, sporcanti,

notizie, giornali, attimali:
la vastità   dell'esperienza indiretta,
tramite gli occhi in testa e ritorno, la superficie
che non è l'opposto della profondità ma la sua vice
sono molte braccia oltre queste mie
due, oltre queste tue
lo spazio può tagliarsi
e ricomporsi quale assente mare
l'aria del pensiero
muove la scrittura e le mie braccia?

l'aria dei sentimenti?
elmo interno al capo e da vie stellari
sprofondate terriccio i lineamenti
melme d'aria file di cabine
  file di varianti
  una conduttura, circa, poco più?

 "la luce filosofica attorno la finestra è ora la mia gioia"
sì, ma l'ondeggiare
  degli alberi nuovi, dei fatti, dei volti e dei viali?

  interroga, comincia
  pupo s'avvia a parlare
  sudato, colossale, gruppo enorme
  frastagliato occupando luoghi e sfitte case
  minacciato   il pupo
 fissandoti, imitando, furioso balbetta
il vorticoso gruppo dei gruppi dei gruppi dei singoli tutti
o quasi tutti

Say--So I'll Say

and yet, we have need as we tremble
the strong out there the strong out there announce
something's going to blow, galactic cash
fear forced etiquette voices voices voices voices voices voices
we have great need of palpitations and peace we have great
            [need
of palpitations, voices kicking off
    [millions of minutes   forests of those ferocious
the strong out there the strong out there announce
something's going to blow
      millions of minutes

nourished by peace

meal

one is nourished by peace

the trembling have need of everything
don't be astonished if I throw up a yell of paper
                nourished by peace/meal/one is nourished by peace
books and tables   listen gravely
the air--(d)ay--is a large unlaced body

                        the strong out there

                        yes

                        the strong out there

beveled pupils zerological galaxies
but also junk, shattered fragments of olive presses
of a struggle between two classes

                        out there the migh-
tee hee

        and yet

then sometimes, come May, swirls settle in the glass classroom
rains of flickering fire fell clinging to the clothed bodies
of hospital nuns, doctors, and to our sick, naked as they are
from my hiding place I tremble in the whirling wind out there
                        [and I tremble less

Di'--Allora dico

eppure, abbiamo bisogno, tutti tremanti
forti di fuori forti di fuori annunciano
esploderà qualcosa, galattici contanti

paura galateo coatto voci voci voci voci voci voci
abbiamo un gran bisogno di palpiti e di pace abbiamo un grann
                                                  [bisogno
di palpiti, schiattate
            milioni di minuti   foresta di feroci
forti di fuori forti di fuori annunciano
esploderà qualcosa
            milioni di minuti

nutre di pace

si

nutre di pace

di tutto abbiamo bisogno tutti tremanti
non vi stupite se lancio sto grido di carta nutre di pace/si/nutre
                                                  [di pace
tavolo e libri   gravemente ascoltano
l'aria--di'--è un gran corpo slacciato

                    forti di fuori
                    sì
                    forti di fuori

pupille smerigliate zerogiche galassie
eppure son quisquilie, cascami di frantoio
di lotta di due classi
                    forti di fuo
ri
   eppure

e poi qualche volta volute di maggio riposo nell'aula di vetro
cadevano piogge di fiamma leggera e tenace su corpi vestiti
di suore infermieri dottori e su nostri malati spogliati così
celandomi tremo nel vento che vortica fuori e tremo di meno

EUGENIO MONTALE

E ugenio Montale was born in Genoa in 1896 and died in Milan in 1981. Despite health problems he earned a diploma in accounting in 1915. He became increasingly interested in music and even took voice lessons; at the same time, he was also discovering literature, and by holing up in libraries he not only did his vast reading but also taught himself foreign languages. He worked as a librarian and personal secretary for several years down in Florence, only to lose his position for not adhering to the Fascist Party. He became a regular editor on the staff of *Il Corriere della Sera* in 1948, the same newspaper for which he later wrote music criticism. In 1964 he started writing poetry again, feeling that he "owed it" to his wife, who had died the previous year. In 1967 he became a senator for life of the Italian Parliament, and in 1975 he was awarded the Nobel Prize for Literature.

The poet Montale was active for nearly 60 years, during which time his work came to represent a turning point in Italian poetry. After the early poems, heavily influenced by D'Annunzio, Pascoli and the Hermetics, Montale began his search for a personal voice which would take him from the subjective sort of poetic narrative (favored by the Hermetics) to an "objective narrative", whereby every and any detail of concrete reality in the outside world could serve as the pretext or "occasion" for coming to terms with life's acute erosion over time.

The resulting style, which he became famous for, was a mix of elegiac sadness and extremely dry formulations and observations. Montale wavers between a direct rendering of sensations and their "noble", intellectual re-elaboration. A keen awareness of the metaphysical holds in check the poet's intrinsic narcissism. In the prose-like work of his last decade of life, Montale's elegiac tone became satirical and at times pointedly ironic and sarcastic.

POETRY

Ossi di seppia (Cuttlefish Bones) 1923
La casa dei doganieri (The House of the Customs Men) 1932, included then in
Le occasioni (The Occasions) 1939 and 1940
Finisterre (Land's End) 1943, included then in
La bufera e altro (The Storm and Other Poems) 1957
Xenia 1966
Satura 1971
Diario del '71 (1971 Diary) 1972
Diario del '71 e '72 1973
Quaderno di quattro anni (Four-Year Notebook) 1977

ESSAYS AND OTHER

La farfalla di Dinard (Dinard's Butterfly) 1956
Auto da fè 1966
Fuori di casa (Out of the House) 1969
La poesia non esiste (Poetry Doesn't Exist) 1971
Nel nostro tempo (In Our Time) 1972
Trentadue variazioni (Thirty-two Variations) 1973
È ancora possibile la poesia? (Is Poetry Still Possible?)--
Nobel Prize acceptance speech--1975
Quaderni di traduzioni (poetry translations) 1975 (2nd ed.)
Sulla poesia (On Poetry) 1976
Cronache in due tempi (Chronicles in Two Parts) 1982

Ours is group solitude,
a new fact in history and certainly
not the best, as some idiot
who lives on his own would surely say.
But it's not so bad really. I have
here on my table a collective individual,
a marbly coral harder than a boulder.
This must be his definitive form
for he's resilient to the hammer.
His big advantage there on the
counter of human beings is that
he doesn't speak.

Siamo alla solitudine di gruppo,
un fatto nuovo nella storia e certo
non il migliore a detta
di qualche Zebedeo che sta da solo.
Non sarà poi gran male. Ho qui sul tavolo
un individuo collettivo, un marmo
di coralli più duro di un macigno.
Sembra che abbia una forma definitiva,
resistente al martello. Si avvantaggia
sul banco degli umani perché non parla.

My Muse

My muse is distant: one could say
she's never existed (as most people think).
But if ever there was one,
she wears the clothes of a scarecrow propped up on
a chessboard of vines.

She flutters as best she can: she's weathered
monsoons remaining upright, only a little hunched over.
If the wind dies she knows how to move all the same,

almost to tell me: walk on, don't fear,
as long as I can see you I'll give you life.

Some time ago my muse left a
closet of theatrical costumes, and
whoever dressed up in her was of high rank.
One day she was filled by myself and
walked proudly about. She still
has a sleeve left now and with it
conducts one of her quartets of
paper straws. It's the only music I can bear.

La mia musa

La mia Musa è lontana: si direbbe
(è il pensiero dei più) che sia mai esistita.
Se pure une ne fu, indossa i panni dello spaventacchio
alzato a malapena su una scacchiera di viti.

Sventola come può; ha resistito a monsoni
restando ritta, solo un po' ingobbita.
Se il vento cala sa agitarsi ancora
quasi a dirmi cammina non temere,
finché potrò vederti ti darò vita.

La mia Musa ha lasciato da tempo un ripostiglio
di sartoria teatrale; ed era d'alto bordo
chi di lei si vestiva. Un giorno fu riempita
di me e ne andò fiera. Ora ha ancora una manica
e con quella dirige un suo quartetto
di cannucce. È la sola musica che sopporto.

I repeat I'm ready, but ready for what?
not for death, which I don't believe in, nor
for that swarming of robots called life.

Eternal life is an absurdity--that's what
life's ancestress, with all her defects, would say.
Afterlife is there in the ether,
the hospital air that the happy breathe
when they fall into the trap.
Afterlife exists in the time that
one nourishes himself on, so as to
remain fooled all the longer.
Being ready doesn't mean choosing
between two misadventures or two adventures
or even between all and nothing.
It's saying I have tried it out,
this is the Veil, if it's an illusion
it's one that can't be rent.

Sono pronto ripeto, ma pronto a che?
Non alla morte cui non credo né
al brulichio d'automi che si chiama la vita.
L'altravita è un assurdo, ripeterebbe
la sua progenitrice con tutte le sue tare.
L'oltrevita è nell'etere, quell'aria da ospedale
che i felici respirano quando cadono in trappola.
L'oltrevita è nel tempo che se ne ciba
per durare più a lungo nel suo inganno.
Essere pronti non vuol dire scegliere
tra due sventure o due venture oppure
tra il tutto e il nulla. È dire io l'ho provato,
ecco il Velo, se inganna non si lacera.

Bird-Shooting

You wonder why I sail along in uncertainty
rather than trying another route?
Ask that of the bird who turns round, unharmed
by the long shot and the oversized rose

of explosion.

Even for us without wings
rarefications exist,
made not of lead but of deeds,
not of atmosphere but of vexations.
If a weight loss may save us
remains to be seen.

Il tiro a volo

Mi chiedi perché navigo
nell'insicurezza e non tento
un'altra rotta? Domandalo
all'uccello che volta illeso
perché il tiro era lungo e troppo larga
la rosa della botta.

Anche per noi non alati
esistono rarefazioni
non più di piombo ma di atti,
non più di atmosfera ma di urti.
Se ci salva una perdita di peso
è da vedersi.

Murder's not my forte.
Not of human beings, maybe of a couple of insects,
a couple of mosquitoes crushed against the
wall with a house slipper.
For many years the window screens served the function
of protecting them. Then, for the longest time,
I myself became an insect--though an unprotected one.
Now I've discovered that life's not a
question of dignity nor of
any other moral category. It doesn't depend,

it didn't depend, on us.
We may exhalt in our dependency at times
but it never cheers us up.

L'omicidio non è il mio forte.
Di uomini nessuno, forse qualche insetto,
qualche zanzara schiacciata con una pantofola
sul muro.
Per molti anni provvidero le zanzariere
a difenderle. In seguito, per lunghissimo tempo,
divenni io stesso insetto ma indifeso.
Ho scoperto ora che vivere
non è questione di dignità o d'altra
categoria morale. Non dipende,
non dipese da noi. La dipendenza
può esaltarci talvolta, non ci rallegra mai.

The Story of Every Day
The sole science to remain standing--
eschatology--
isn't a science but a fact
of everyday life.
It's a question of crumbs that disappear
without being replaced.
Who cares about crumbs, mutters
the haruspex,
it's the cake that remains, even if chipped and
deflated here and there.
The secret lies in its aging,
and a hundred years rather than ten,
or a thousand years instead of a hundred,
will do much for the flavor.
Clearly the luckiest one--without knowing it--
will be the future taster
and "the rest is literature."

Storia di tutti i giorni

L'unica scienza che resti in piedi
l'escatologia
non è una scienza, è un fatto
di tutti i giorni.
Si tratta delle briciole che se ne vanno
senza essere sostituite.
Che importano le briciole va borbottando
l'aruspice,
è la torta che resta, anche sbrecciata
se qua e là un po' sgonfiata.
Tutto sta in una buona stagionatura,
cent'anni più di dieci, mille anni più di cento
ne accresceranno il sapore.
Ovviamente sarà più fortunato
l'assaggiatore futuro senza saperlo
e "il resto è letteratura".

Elogy of Our Times

There's no overdoing
the importance of the world
(ours, I mean)
probably the only one
where killing can be an art and where
art work is created to live
for the length of a morning,
even if one of milleniums or more.
No, there's no glorifying it enough.
Only now we must hurry because
the hour seems near
when too much will be inflated
according to a noted apologist, the frog.

Elogio del nostro tempo

Non si può esagerare abbastanza
l'importanza del mondo
(del nostro, intendo)
probabilmente il solo
in cui si possa uccidere
con arte e anche creare
opere d'arte destinate a vivere
lo spazio di un mattino, sia pur fatto
di millenni e anche più. No, non si può
magnificarlo a sufficienza. Solo
ci si deve affrettare perché potrebbe
non essere lontana
l'ora in cui troppo si sarà gonfiata
secondo un noto apologo la rana.

Soliloquy

The canal flows quietly
and stinks.
This is the palazzo where
"Tristan" was composed and
here's the local dive where Henry James
tasted his crêpes suzette--
there aren't any great men anymore
but just their apocryphal biographies--
no one's certainly going to write mine--
St. George's men are more important than
others, and than me, but it's not enough, not enough--
the future's got a big appetite, it's
tired of mere hors d'oeuvres, and requests
tender winged creatures roasted on the spit,
nauseating delights.
But the future may also have hardly any appetite at all:
it may just want a crust--but

a crust of the kind never seen before on any menu.
The future's also omnivorous and without regard for subtleties--
here is the house where an illustrious
pederast once lived for years before being
assassinated in another place--the future is
for him--there's nothing at all similar in my life,
nothing that satisfies the greedy jaws of
the future.

Soliloquio

Il canale scorre silenzioso
maleodorante
questo è il palazzo dove fu composto
il Tristano
ed ecco il buco dove Henry James
gustò le crêpes suzette--
non esistono più i grandi uomini
ne restano inattendibili biografie
nessuno certo scriverà la mia--
gli uomini di San Giorgio sono più importanti
di tanti altri e di me ma non basta non basta--
il futuro ha appetito non si contenta più
di hors-d'oeuvre e domanda schidionate
di volatili frolli, nauseabonde delizie--
il futuro è altresì disappetente
può volere una crosta ma che crosta
quale non fu mai vista nei menus--
il futuro è anche onnivoro e non guarda
per il sottile--Qui è la casa dove
visse più anni un pederasta illustre
assassinato altrove--Il futuro è per lui--
non è nulla di simile nella mia vita
nulla che sazi le bramose fauci
del futuro

PIER PAOLO PASOLINI

P ier Paolo Pasolini was born in Bologna in 1922 and died
in Rome (the actual circumstances remain unclear) in
1975. He graduated in 1945 in Italian literature with a
thesis on Giovanni Pascoli. He began publishing poetry
at a very young age (his first book, written in his mother's
Friulian dialect, dates from 1942). During the war he fled to
Casarsa and in 1945 published a second book of poetry (in stan-
dard Italian) dedicated to the memory of his brother Guido,
who had died in a battle between those of the Italian Under-
ground who wanted independence and those who wanted Italy
to be annexed to Yugoslavia.

Pasolini began to get more and more involved in left-wing
politics, though in 1949 he was charged with having made
homosexual advances to minors and expelled from the Italian
Communist Party, whereupon he moved to Rome. Poet,
novelist, essayist, journalist, and playwright, Pasolini first became
famous internationally for his work in film, beginning with
Accattone in 1961. (In Italy, however, he'd already created a
scandal and gained notoriety with a novel, *A Violent Life*, written
in 1959, which employed extremely crude language for the
times.) In 1968 he published his "Manifesto for a New Theater"
in *Nuovi Argomenti*, the literary magazine which he co-directed
with Alberto Moravia and others.

A constant throughout Pasolini's artistic work is his moral
critique of society and the existential "passion" he felt for
humanity, with an eye towards man's suffering and uneasiness--
though not only towards that, for Pasolini celebrated wherever
he could individuals' full, active participation in events.
Whether it was in cinema, fiction, theater, or poetry, Pasolini
tended to depict some extreme situation where, in that utterly
concrete yet expressive way of his, he managed to bring to light

the most disturbing social and human contractions of his time. The specific theme of social upheaval in Italy, moreover, was often coupled with his interest in local dialects and in popular poetry, about which he was an expert.

POETRY

Poesie a Casarsa (Poems from Casarsa) 1942
La meglio giuoventü (The Best of Youth) (Friulian dialect) 1954
Le ceneri di Gramsci (Gramsci's Ashes) 1957
L'usignolo della Chiesa Cattolica (The Nightingale of the Catholic Church) 1958
Poesia in forma di rosa (Poetry in the Form of a Rose) 1961
Trasumanar organizzar (Transhumanizing and Organizing) 1971

NOVELS

Ragazzi di Vita (Street Boys) 1955
Una vita violenta (A Violent Life) 1959
Amado mio e *Atti impuri* (Amado mio and Sinful Acts) 1982
Petrolio (Petrolium) 1992

ESSAYS AND OTHER CRITICAL WORK

Passione e ideologia (Passion and Ideology) 1960
La religione del mio tempo (Religion In My Time) 1967
Empirismo eretico (Heretical Empiricism) 1972
Scritti corsari (Pirate Writings) 1975
Poesia dialettale del Novecento (an anthology of dialect poetry of the twentieth century) 1952
Canzoniere italiano (a collection of Italian folk lyrics) 1955
La poesia popolare italiana (an anthology of Italian popular poetry) 1960

Redefining "Orthodoxy"

You, Mascolo, came and went, a half hour in all;
you smiled that smile of the severe avant-garde--
when each one rigidly at home or at the *caffé*--
a silvery light in those pitiful eyes,
that light which has a father, a husband, a man who works--
there's bound to be a carefully selected house, too, in a street
where the rain, the savage rain--
the marble on the Cathedral in Tours is all wet--
I'm here in the doorway.
Everyone can see me. And I have visions:
the shiny marble...the grey portal...
I hold out my hand that testifies to it.
The evening will carry me away, the morning
will bring me back: to vanish only to reappear.
Then one day the Cathedral
will be on its own without me; on rainy days,
or when the May light on the Loire--
I attest to the justice and stability of the Church.
I was born crippled and for this became a beggar woman,
orthodoxy is my daily bread--
and on me the Authorities rest once again their certitudes;
they point me out: here are the poor!
but I don't even look, or I don't understand.
Those who built the Church were the only ones who could
have built it. But, being part as I am, Mascolo, of the "Manifes-
to"--
since 1945 that I haven't seen
the real spirit of revolution in anyone...
They were always, like Kavafis, waiting
for the invasion of the barbarians.
Naturally there were scapegoats during the wait.
Naturally the barbarians never descended--
and so no one has ever destroyed any
Church since 1945.
We launched accusations against each other

(and the Church knows it), but no one ever had
any real disinterested love for heresy,
a heresy with no specific aim, a purely inventive force--
no, no--everyone was looking for REAL ORTHODOXY
and this at first explained each one's restlessness
and then later each one's revolt against those in power.
It was evangelical heresy, yes, it was a return
to the origins, to lost purity;
it made for an endless number of guilty people, of
the impure, of untouchables.
The analysis and condemnation of their actions were ruthless--
My last dreams before death: this
silence that the rain makes conspicuous before
it ceases, this silence yields to sunlight,
that of the new season...
I don't hold open my palm this time--it's only
one who's come to pray here inside.
There've been a few visitors, and this German boy
who's been in a trance in front of me for more
than half an hour waiting for the rain to stop--
content for having seen what his forefathers
knew how to do.
When this church empties out completely
who will I be then?
My comrades from the "Manifesto" have demonstrated
what the search for true doctrine can
amount to; as Calvinists , and "without a
body," so to speak; immaterial, ascetic;
pure reason functioning according to the rules
of true, serious science, and standing behind them,
a group of the faithful--
I don't know how to smile like you, Mascolo,
that smile of the classic avant-garde
with their fragile heroes, and nice desperate men
with those clear eyes of fathers;
and even the abnormal burdens of
civilization, with a nicely-behaved household

under a roof that the rain beats on--the barbarous rain--
Here they're building another Church, if I'm not mistaken.
Dear barbarians, my only friends,
no man of the Church has ever destroyed a Church;
the struggle is always between the old orthodoxy and the new--
This makes me despair and keeps me out of the game.

Rifacimento de "L'ortodossia"

Mascolo, venuto e partito: un quarto d'ora in tutto;
sorridevi il sorriso delle avanguardie severe,
quando, rigidamente ognuno a casa sua, o al caffé--
Un'argentea luce negli occhi pietosi
quella che ha un padre; un marito; un uomo che lavora--
ci sarà pure una casa ben scelta, in una strada
dove la pioggia, la barbara pioggia-
Il marmo del duomo di Tours è tutto bagnato--
Sono qui alla porta.
Mi si vede. E io ho delle visioni:
il marmo lucido...il portale di pietra grigia...
stendo la mia mano di testimone.
La sera mi porterà via, la mattina mi riporterà:
scomparire e riapparire. Poi un giorno
il duomo resterà senza di me, nei giorni di pioggia,
o quando la luce di maggio, sulla Loira
Io confermo la giustizia e la stabilità della Chiesa.
Nacqui storpia e per questo mendicai;
l'ortodossia è il mio pane--
È su me che le Autorità ripongono le loro certezze:
mi additano: eccoli, i poveri!
e io non guardo nemmeno, o non capisco.
Chi ha costruito questa Chiesa era il solo che poteva costruirla.
Ma essendo, Mascolo, del "Manifesto"--
dal 1945 in poi, io non vidi mai in nessuno
una vera volontà di rivolta.
Tutti attendevano come Kavafis la discesa dei barbari.

Naturalmente ci furono i capri espiatori di questa attesa.
Naturalmente i barbari non discesero;
così nessuno distrusse mai nessuna Chiesa, dal 1945 in poi.
Ci accusammo gli uni cogli altri
(lei lo sa): ma chi mai ebbe un reale e disinteressato amore
per la eresia; una eresia senza scopo; puramente inventrice--
No, no, ognuno cercava la VERA ORTODOSSIA,
in questo consisteva dapprima la sua inquietudine,
poi la sua rivolta ai poteri--
L'eresia era evangelica, sì, era un ritorno alle origini,
alla purezza perduta;
ne nacquero un'infinità di colpevoli, di impuri, di intoccabili;
l'analisi del loro comportamento e la condanna furono spietate--
I miei ultimi sogni prima di morire: questo silenzio
che la pioggia mette in evidenza, prima di cessare
e far posto al sole, che è quello della nuova stagione...
Non stendo nemmeno la mano: solo uno
è entrato per pregare, qui dentro.
Ci son stati alcuni visitatori; e questo ragazzo tedesco
che sta qui da più di mezz'ora impalato davanti a me,
aspettando che spiova--contento di aver visto
ciò che i suoi padri seppero fare.
Quando questa chiesa resterà del tutto vuota
chi sarò io?
I compagni del "Manifesto" diedero prova
di cosa può essere la ricerca della vera dottrina;
come calvinisti, e senza, si direbbe, un corpo;
immateriali, ascetici; pura ragione funzionante
secondo le regole della vera scienza, seria,
e alle spalle il gruppo dei fedeli--
Non so sorridere come lei, Mascolo,
il sorriso delle avanguardie classiche,
coi loro eroi delicati, i loro disperati
uomini gentili, dai chiari occhi di padre;
e anche gli anormali carichi di civiltà, con un ménage gentile
in una casa su cui la pioggia, la barbara pioggia--
Qui stanno costruendo un'altra Chiesa, se non mi sbaglio.

Ah barbari, unici amici miei,
nessun uomo di Chiesa ha mai distrutto una Chiesa;
la lotta è sempre stata tra l'ortodossia vecchia e la nuova--
Questo mi dispera, e mi tiene fuori dal gioco.

The Presence
What had been lost was heavenly--
and this sick, saintly soul.
Nothingness was a wind,
inexplicably changing direction but constantly
aware of its destination.
In the shifting void,
inspired in its highest realms,
and below, as capricious as a stream,
what always counted was a story.
One that somehow had been started
and so had to continue: yours.
Who had asked me to come in the first place?
Every morning the tragedy of existence began anew--
behind balconies first closed and
then open, as in a Church--a tragedy where
the heavenly winds seemed to blow for no reason,
or for only a few witnessses;
then small daily routines, sisters to the tragedy--
The sea and its wind received
our eviscerated praise...
Your *being is awareness* encountered
tremendous obstacles to overcome,
and every victory was meager,
and you had to immediately start over again
like a plant that continually needs watering.
but I am not, Maria, your brother;
I fulfill other functions, not clear to me;
not that of brotherhood,
at least not that consorting type
so close to the obedience and heroic unawareness of

men, your brothers despite everything, not mine.
And terrified by the suspicion of no longer being you
(you know even this)
you get by somehow, mothering yourself.
You let the little girl in you be queen and
open and close the windows as if this were a ritual
to be respected by guests, servants and distant observers.
Yet that little girl, that little girl
has only to be ignored for a moment
to feel lost forever.
Ah, it's not across still islands
but on the fear of no longer being you
that the wind blows,
the sacred wind
which doesn't heal
but rather sickens more and more;
and you try to stop her, the one who
wanted to go back in time;
there's not a day, an hour, an instant
when your desperate efforts can afford to let up;
your clinging to every and anything
brings on a desire to kiss you.

La presenza

Ciò ch'era perduto era celeste
e l'anima malata, santa.
Il nulla era un vento che cambiava inspiegabilmente
direzione, ma ben consapevole, sempre, delle sue mete.
Nel nulla che si muoveva
ispirato in alto
capriccioso come un ruscello in basso
ciò che importava era sempre una storia
che in qualche modo era incominciata
e doveva continuare: la tua.
Chi mi aveva chiamato lì?

Ogni mattina ricominciava la tragedia dell'essere,
dietro i balconi prima chiusi e poi aperti,
                                        [come in una Chiesa.
Che il vento divino soffiasse inutilmente
o solo per dei testimoni--
Poi le abitudini, queste sorelle della tragedia--
Il mare e il suo vento ebbero tutti i nostri sviscerati elogi--
Il tuo *"esse est percipi"* incontrava tremendi ostacoli
da superare, e ogni vittoria era una povera vittoria,
e dovevi ricominciare subito
come una pianta che ha continuamente bisogno d'acqua.
Io però, Maria, non sono un fratello;
adempio altre funzioni, che non so;
non quella della fraternità,
almeno di quella complice
così vicina all'obbedienza e all'eroica inconsapevolezza
degli uomini, tuoi fratelli malgrado tutto, non miei.
E tu, atterrita dal sospetto di non esserlo più,
sai anche questo,
e ti arrangi a farti da madre.
Concedi alla bambina di essere regina
di aprire e chiudere le finestre come in un rito
rispettato da ospiti, servitù, spettatori lontani.
Eppure lei, lei, la bambina,
basta che per un solo istante sia trascurata,
si sente perduta per sempre;
ah, non su isole immobili
ma sul terrore di non essere, il vento scorre
il vento divino
che non guarisce, anzi, ammala sempre più;
e tu cerchi di fermarla, quella che voleva tornare indietro,
non c'è un giorno, un'ora, un istante
in cui lo sforzo disperato possa cessare;
ti aggrappi a qualunque cosa
facendo venir voglia di baciarti.

MARIO LUZI

Mario Luzi was born in Florence in 1914. After obtaining his degree at the University of Siena, he returned to Florence and there became friends with Carlo Bo and Eugenio Montale, among others. In 1955 he was appointed Professor of French Literature at the University of Florence. Over the years, Mario Luzi has been involved with various important literary reviews, including *Solaria*, *Il Frontespizio* and *Il Campo di Marte*, and published collections of essays as well as poetry. His translations into Italian include works by Racine, Shakespeare, Coleridge, and selected French poets.

While Luzi's first poems, published between 1935 and 1947, are definitely Hermetic in approach, he began to move away from this movement at the start of the 1950's; that is to say, he reshaped certain of its aspects to fit his personal needs. With time his most characteristic poetic form became that which the late poet Antonio Porta called *teatro della coppia* ("couples on stage"), with ample use of dialogue. The first-person voice, moreover, represents both the character and the poet-narrator, whose self-questioning and searching emerge from the words uttered by other people.

POETRY

La barca (The Boat) 1935
Avvento notturno (Night Advent) 1940
Un brindisi (A Toast) 1946
Quaderno gotico (Gothic Notebook) 1947
Primizie del deserto (First Fruits of the Desert) 1952
Onore del vero (Honoring the Truth) 1957
Il gusto della vita: antologia (The Flavor of Life) 1960
Il magma 1963
Dal fondo delle campagne (From the Depths of the Countryside)
    1965
Su fondamenti invisibili (On Invisible Foundations) 1971
Al fuoco della controversia (In the Fire of Controversy) 1978
    (Viareggio Prize)
Tutte le poesie (Collected Works) 1979
Per il battesimo dei nostri frammenti (For the Baptism of Our
    Fragments) 1985 (Librex-Montale Prize)

THEATRE

Ipazia (Hypatia) 1972
Rosales 1984

PROSE

Biografia a Ebe (Biography for Ebe) 1943
Trame (Story Lines) 1963

ESSAYS

L'inferno e il limbo (Hell and Limbo) 1949
L'idea simbolista (Symbolist Thought) 1959
Tutto in questione (Everything in Question) 1965
Vicissitudine e forma (Vicissitudes and Form) 1974
Discorso naturale (Natural Discourse) 1984

from **In the Dark Body of Metamorphosis**

1

"Reflective life separates us from the sources of reflection.
Simple life induces mistakes and suffering from which no life
[can come."
This bounces back to me off the wall of a dream
dreamed while awake. "Impossible
to live or even think" is written on a cracked cliff,
but look closer:
a web of creases,
a Western maestro's defeated face with
nothing alive left in it except two dots--
his two eyes--and its silence.

"The word's bigger than that"--I smile
and think of my hilarity as a flock flying free
of a collapsing house.
"Lose yourself if you want to find yourself;
wanting means not having." Shooting through me is
a blinding flash. Maybe one from the innocent part of me
which like water has survived the millstone
and for this, for this, doesn't surrender.
It says: "Pray for the underwater city."
In the dirty waters of a deserted street,
a soul, out of the past or perhaps the future,
hidden inside a flashlight, comes looking for me.
"Just keep quiet," I beg, suspicious that mine may be
the one returning to that body sunk in mud.

"You've watched the city dying
and at sunset the last furious reels of its drowning;
listen now to its silence, and awake,"
says the stray soul,
perhaps no different from my own,
come searching for me in this eerie swamp.

"Awake, this is not the mental silence
of a profound metaphor--your idea of history--
but the ugly end to sound. Death. Nothing but death."
"There's no death that is not also birth. This
is all I can pray for," I say, sloshing helplessly in the mire
[while his light
blinks and fades down an alley.
The endless stretch of it has a harsh,
ambiguous reflection, one visible to the mole,
and the lynx.

4

But then an even greater sense of the inexpressible,
as when the new metal poured into history's empty molds
proves unsuitable,
and no others can be found ready to flow
during the irreversible instance of now or never.
And in this dispersion of power,
a lump that wants to be called soul--
weak-willed or drugged--
curls upon itself, skids haplessly as a clog,
and not from too little but rather too much ardor,
is worn down.
And I wonder: isn't your spirit as well
half-rubbed away from the attrition of that message--
undetectable to ear or radar--
that the world *seems* (fairly often) to send,
vibrating in its shiny vertebrae and feverish cartilage?
And in this "come to me"
shouted hoarsely by someone,
stepped out of the rain, one supposes,
with two hailballs, two white holes for eyes
on account of his time at sea,
ordering me calm and in control,
guiding me out of the whirlpool
of whipping scum--or so he tries.

While half-obsequious, half-reluctant
I lean forward yet hold myself back
in the lazy air, still night-blue, of the room.

Or when time under pressure
loses its unserviceable power
in a whirling cloud of scum,
and in some elusive part of yourself
you suffer, crave sleep--
only a restless semi-consciousness keeps you awake--
and you're not a full witness to the metamorphosis
and endless labor pains of the new-born era.

You are sickened
by your sense of the world's dissipating force,
its disunity.

"What a trifling complaint"
is the reproach the spirit sends you from
the teeming depths of childlike eyes--
the blue-charged look of creation, you think--
a beat that pierces your retina,
a laugh that drives you from the
closed space of your soul's infirmity,
calling you into the future of a growing universe.
Without allowing you to say a word.

"Didn't you know, didn't you remember?
Torment like this should only happen when the time's ripe,
when it has matured you (if not more, then less),"
murmurs a drowsiness
which is the soul or else insomnia
(the eyelids of the night tormented by the pulse of its own
[chemical colors).

"Didn't you know, didn't you remember?"
whines the wind of ruin

sniffed by proconsuls
out in disarmed provinces;
"didn't you know, didn't you remember?"
babbles Vietnamese rice fields under the hairy surface
                                        [of their waters.
"Such a memory is worth little, very little."

In this hotel,
in this hotel--they remind me--Essenin took his own life.

Da **Nel corpo oscuro della metamorfosi**

1

"La vita secondo il pensiero ci astrae dalle sorgenti
                                        [del pensiero,
la vita secondo la vita
ci induce in errori e sofferenze da cui è impossibile la vita»
mi rimanda la parete di un sogno
sognato da sveglio.
Impossibile vivere, pensare anche" reca scritto
una rupe screpolata, guarda meglio:
una ragnatela di grinze, un volto
sconfitto di maestro d'Occidente
in cui più nulla è vivo che due punti--due occhi di lui--
                                        [e il silenzio.
È più grande di così il mondo--sorrido
e penso alla mia ilarità come a uno stormo
in fuga da una casa crollante.
Perditi se vuoi ritrovarti, desidera
per non avere mi traversa
e mi snebbia la vista un lampo
forse dalla mia parte d'innocenza
che come l'acqua ha resistito alla macina
e per questo, per questo non si arrende.
"Prega," dice, "per la città sommersa"

venendomi incontro dal passato
o dal futuro un'anima nascosta
dietro un lume di pila che mi cerca
nel liquame della strada deserta.
"Taci" imploro, dubbioso sia la mia
di ritorno al suo corpo perduto nel fango.

"Tu che hai visto fino al tramonto
la morte di una città, i suoi ultimi
furiosi annaspamenti d'annegata,
ascoltane il silenzio ora. E risvegliati"
continua quell'anima randagia
che non sono ben certo sia un'altra dalla mia
alla cerca di me nella palude sinistra.
"Risvegliati, non è questo il silenzio
il silenzio mentale di una profonda metafora
come tu pensi la storia. Ma bruta
cessazione del suono morte. Morte e basta".

"Non c'è morte che non sia anche nascita.
Soltanto per questo pregherò"
le dico sciaguattando ferito nella melma
mentre il suo lume lampeggia e si eclissa in un vicolo.
E la continuità manda un riflesso
duro, ambiguo, visibile alla talpa e alla lince.

4

Ma ancora più vasto un senso inesprimibile
come quando agli stampi vuoti della storia
affluisce un metallo nuovo che poco vi si adegua
né altri se ne trovano di pronti alla colata
ora, nell'istante irreversibile, o mai.
E in quella dispersione di potenza
malato nella volontà o drogato
un grumo ancora detto anima si avvita
su di sé, sbanda in un movimento inceppato:

e non per poco ma per troppo ardore si logora.

O non è invece a limarti un messaggio impercettibile
                [ad orecchio o radar
mentre avverti, non è raro,
nelle sue vertebre lucenti,
nelle sue cartilagini febbrili vibrarne il mondo--mi chiedo.
E in quella: "vieni a me"
mi grida qualcuno con voce strappata,
uscito dalla pioggia, si direbbe, con due, "bae de tempesta"
due fori bianchi per occhi causa la consuetudine col mare,
intimandomi sangue freddo e calma,
pilotandomi fuori da un risucchio
brulicante di scorie--o almeno vorrebbe.
Mentre io tra ossequio e riluttanza
mi protendo e mi rifiuto
nell'aria pigra ancora azzurra di notte nella stanza.

Oppure quando un tempo sotto pressione
disperde la sua potenza inservibile
in una nube vorticosa di scorie
e tu stesso in una parte di te--non sai
bene quale--soffri, vorresti dormire,
ma un'inquieta
semicoscienza ti tiene sveglio,
non del tutto presente alla metamorfosi
e al lungo dolore della nascita di un'epoca.

Ne viene un senso, ti ammala,
di forza dissipata
dal mondo, dal disunito.

"Ma che piccola cosa il tuo lamento"
rimprovera dal fondo pullulante degli occhi
uno sguardo un po' bambino--lo sguardo azzurro carico
della creazione, ti sembra--
che ti buca la retina con il suo battito e ride

cacciandoti dal chiuso
dell'infermità dell'anima, chiamandoti al futuro
di un universo in crescita. E non ammette risposta.

"Non sapevi, non ricordavi
tormenti come questo di tempi
più maturi e meno di te?»
balbetta un dormiveglia
che è l'anima o piuttosto straziata nelle palpebre
del battito dei suoi colori chimici la notte stessa, l'insonnia.

"Non sapevi, non ricordavi?"
rimugina un vento di rovina
fiutato dai proconsoli
in qualche provincia in disarmo;
"non sapevi, non ricordavi?"
gorgogliano da sotto il pelo della broda le risaie del Vietnam.
"Poco, poco vale la memoria di questo>."

--In questo albergo,
in questo albergo--mi ricordano--si uccise Essenin.

from **Pieces from a Mortal Duet**

Postscriptum

As for Granata, the Siberian gulag, Ostia--
superfluous criticism? some preordained rendition?
Or rather on the endless controversy
an irrefutable lock and seal?
So she wondered, the ailing guardian
of all art and measure.
Meanwhile, the poet and the assassin
both step out of the metaphor
and head off to the bloody event,
each sure of himself, each in his role.

da **Brani di un mortale duetto**

Poscritto

A Granata, nel gulag siberiano, a Ostia--
una riprova superflua, una preordinata testimonianza
oppure sulla lunga controversia
un irrefutabile sigillo?--si chiede
lei depositaria inferma
di misura e di arte
mentre escono il poeta e l'assassino
l'uno e l'altro dalla metafora
e s'avviano al sanguinoso appuntamento
ciascuno certo di sé, ciascuno nella sua parte.

GIOVANNI RABONI

G iovanni Raboni was born in Milan in 1932 and contin-
ues to live and work there. Poet and literary critic, he
was for many years an editor for one of the largest
publishing houses in Italy and currently writes theater
criticism for *Il Corriere della Sera*. Raboni is a highly-respected
translator of numerous works of French literature(Baudelaire,
Apollinaire, Flaubert, Racine, Moliére, and, most recently,
Marcel Proust).

In Italy, Raboni's poetry is often seen as representative of
the *linea lombarda* (or "Lombard school"), for its metaphoric
allusions to of everyday objects, conversational tone, and
simplified language. While Raboni is keenly aware of poetry's
literary aspect, he seems to be working to make it shed this
characteristic as much as possible and embrace the real world
in its immediacy. It is in a certain sense ironic that the private
realm of the poet emerges thanks to his effusive sense of world
history as well as to his evident emotional involvement with
current events. The situations described or narrated often
reflect the dramatic or at times resigned feelings of malaise of
those who, like the poet, truly take the time to meditate on daily
life.

POETRY

Il catalogo é questo (This is the Catalog) 1961
L'Insalubrità dell'Aria (The Unwholesomeness of the Air) 1963
Le case della Vetra (The Houses of the Vetra) 1966
Cadenza d'inganno (Deceptive Cadence) 1975
Il più freddo anno di grazia (The Coldest Year of Grace) 1978
Nel grave sogno (In the Deep Sleep) 1982
Canzonette mortali (Deadly Ditties) 1986
A tanto caro sangue, Poesie 1953-1987 (With Such Dear Blood)
    1988
Versi guerrieri e amorosi (Warrior and Love Poems) 1990
Ogni terzo pensiero (Every Third Thought) 1994

PROSE

La fossa del cherubino (The Cherub's Grave) 1980--prose pieces
    written between 1967 and 1969

ESSAYS AND OTHER

Poesia degli anni sessanta (Poetry of the Sixties) 1976
Poesia italiana contemporanea (Contemporary Italian Poetry)
    1980
Quaderno in prosa (Prose Notebook) 1981

Hospital Interiors

for Bartolo Cattafi

1

...the thumping heart
of always when I'm about to
leave alone on a trip--it won't be,
I tell myself, very different from death,
yours for example on the splicing-screen;
courted, sat on like an egg,
discussed night after night with friends
as a battle to be lost later, with honor...

2

Flash flame, twilight patternings
and inside, all curled up and
radiant, the sick man, the sick boy
trying to dribble with death's stopper
aided by the fantastic number of minutes in a day,
of days in a life...

3

"Don't leave me alone"... And "If only
you knew how much good it's done me!"
And again, from behind the half-closed door,
while we contritely cross the white space
leading to the elevator: "Thanks, I'll be expecting you!"
Ah poor friend, what more will there be for us
to expect? I see
you groping for your glasses slowly, careful
not to unhook the oxygen tube,
avoiding bottles, medicine--and
there now, glasses on your nose, panning

the semi-darkness, adoring
the decrepit body of light,
the last threadbare glimmers in the corners...
Nothing, nothing more to expect...
yet I know (now
that you're dead I know it)
you're still a persona, an astute
labyrinth where life enters and exists,
a monument of tiny revolving mirrors, a
delicate machine, stupendous. How much life
in your just barely managing it:
in the gravel, in the thorns of your breath...

Interni clinica

1
...Il batticuore
di sempre quando aspetto
di partire solo--non sarà,
mi dico, cosa diversa dalla morte,
questa tua per esempio, alla moviola,
corteggiata, covata come un uovo,
sera dopo sera discussa con gli amici
come una battaglia da perdere tardi, con onore...

2
Vampa, vetrofanie del crepuscolo
e dentro, accartocciato,
radioso, l'uomo malato, il ragazzo malato che cerca di dribblare
lo stopper della morte
con il numero fantastico dei minuti in un giorno
dei giorni in una vita...

3

"Non lasciatemi solo..." E: "sapeste

quanto bene mi ha fatto!"
E ancora, da dietro la porta
socchiusa, mentre andiamo
contriti nel bianco verso l'ascensore:
"Grazie. Vi aspetto!"
Ah povero amico, cosa ci sarà
più da aspettare? Vedo
che cerchi gli occhiali, a tastoni, adagio, attento
a non perdere il filo dell'ossigeno,
a scansare bottiglie, medicine--e
ecco, occhiali sul naso perlustrare
la penombra, adorare
il decrepito corpo della luce,
gli ultimi, frusti bagliori degli spigoli...
Niente, più niente da aspettare...
Eppure lo so (adesso
che sei morto lo so)
è ancora una persona la tua, un astuto
labirinto dove la vita
entra e esce, un monumento
di specchietti girevoli, una macchina
delicata, stupenda... Quanta vita
nel tuo farcela appena,
nella ghiaia, nelle spine del tuo fiato...

Alibi of a Dead Man

Judas says the dead man's alibi had collapsed and
for this, the dead man endèd up in the courtyard.
But the alibi was good and the dead man was restored
                                    [to his place.
No one says Judas was wrong.

The coroner says the wounds are not
incompatible with the dynamics of a fall from on high.
The newspaper concludes then

the dead man committed suicide.

Miserable old folk, who out of kindness to themselves
should already be dead,
talk to us from mirrors; they admonish us, teach us the future;
they step out of the mirrors to kiss the dead.

The murderer was quick to badmouth the dead man.
A murderer had been heard pitying a dead man.
A murderer had been seen kissing a dead man's forehead.
See how murderers are careful not to neglect the dead.

8:30 pm   the boozer's grief
8:31 pm   the con man's reproaches
8:32 pm   the idiot's advice
8:33 pm   the hangman's last offer

The Stock Market flourishes, the Stock Market reacts
with splendid, unexpected, comforting vigor
to the news from the front, to the proclamation, to the
crystal-clear death of the Legionnaire killed by the enemy.

Wingless ravens in the
flat shadow of the balance,
trinity of hitmen
brandishing lances.

Judas says: the crowd threw stones
at my soldiers, for this they charged.
No one noticed who was present;
but the Senate decides that Judas isn't wrong.

Don't preach the dictatorship
of one class over another, that's not your job.
Don't say anything that could
provoke class hatred: others are already taking care of that.
I speak for myself but maybe also for you.

Friends, the truth:
when we feel oppressed we are happy;
it's important to be victims now, not free later on.

L'alibi del morto

Giuda dice che l'alibi del morto
era crollato: per questo il morto è sceso nel cortile.
Ma l'alibi era buono; il morto è riabilitato:
nessuno dice che Giuda aveva torto.

Il perito settore dice che le ferite
non sono incompatibili con la meccanica di
una caduta dall'alto. Il giornale conclude
che dunque il morto si è suicidato.

Miserabili vecchi che per pietà
di se stessi dovrebbero esser morti
ci parlano dagli specchi, ci ammoniscono, ci insegnano il futuro,
escono dagli specchi per baciare i morti.

L'assassino s'è affrettato a sparlare del morto.
S'era sentito un assassino compatire un morto.
S'era visto un assassino baciare la fronte di un morto.
Vedi che gli assassini non trascurano i morti.

20.30 cordoglio del beone
20.31 rampogne del furfante
20.32 consigli dell'idiota
20.33 ultimatum del boia.

La Borsa è sana, la Borsa reagisce
con splendido, inatteso, confortante vigore
alle notizie dal fronte, ai proclami, alla limpida morte
del legionario ucciso dal nemico.

Corvi senz'ali all'ombra
piatta della bilancia
trinità di sicari
brandiscono la lancia.

Giuda dice: la gente ai miei guerrieri
ha buttato dei sassi, per questo han caricato.
Di chi c'era nessuno se n'è accorto:
ma il Senato decide che Giuda non ha torto.

Non predicate la dittatura
di una classe sull'altra, non è il vostro lavoro.
Non dite niente che possa suscitare
l'odio di classe: ci pensano già loro.

Parlo per me ma forse anche per voi.
Amici, diciamo la verità:
di sentirci oppressi ci sentiamo felici;
ci importa adesso esser vittime, non esser liberi poi.

**For C., Who Died of Childbirth
at the Age of One Year and Eleven Months**

1.
It was (my love told me) my sister
who died ten years ago. I recognized her
from her blueberry eyes...
I believed her. And now we wonder
where we'll encounter you again, in
what small fish, tree, smell.

2.
Like in a book or at the opera
your death seems like a neat trick
prepared in the gestures of life
with a thousand sweet goodbyes.

3.
With you in the hamper, under the
blue-and-white linen, a flower branch,
the kind we like,
which you used to eat.

4.
Only with Elsa this morning
is it possible to talk... And as if by miracle
Elsa replies, she hasn't disappeared,
she's here to listen, she talks of pain,
of your distant young brothers;
she even laughs, she consoles...

5.
Now, tiny corpse, you rest in no place at all.
To think we don't feel bitterness
but the tepid, blood-letting
drive from paradise.

Per C., morta di parto all'età di un anno e undici mesi

1.
È (diceva il mio amore) mia sorella
morta dieci anni fa. La riconosco
dagli occhi di mirtillo...
Io le credevo. E adesso ci chiediamo
dove ti incontreremo un'altra volta,
in quale pesciolino, albero, odore.

2.
Come in un libro o all'opera
sembra un trucco squisito la tua morte
preparata nei gesti della vita
con mille dolcissimi addii.

3.
Nella cesta, con te, sotto il lenzuolo
a righe azzurre e bianche, un rametto di fiori
di quelli che ci piacciono,
che tu mangiavi.

4.
Solo con Elsa, stamattina,
si può parlare... E come per miracolo
Elsa risponde, non è più partita,
ci sta a sentire, parla del dolore
di tuoi remoti fratellini,
ride persino, ci consola...

5.
Adesso, corpicino stremato, ti riposi
in nessun posto. E noi se ci pensiamo
non sentiamo amarezza
ma la svenante, tiepida cacciata
dal paradiso.

Moon

Condition: hydroplane.
But it's not you who fly, no one
flies; home is a moon.
In the dark I grope for the laminate
and a sponge to dry the window.
I look out, a cleaner of observatories
at an altitude of 20,000 millimeters in a starry void.
I watch for the abandoned bubble of light, the
headless diving-suit. I'm a mollusk
out for my little walk in the direction of death,
observing the inside from outside my shell.
Juicy cell, sweet resinous compartment,
my life's there. It is what it is. From here,

from this projection, I can't change it. From
afar it overwhelms me, freezes me.

Luna

Condizione: idrovolante.
Ma non sei tu che voli, nessuno
vola--la casa è una luna.
Nel buio a tastoni cerco la làmina, la spugna
per asciugare la finestra. Guardo.
Io pulitore di specole
a ventimila millimetri d'altezza nel vuoto siderale
spio l'abbandonata bolla di luce, lo scafandro
svuotato della testa. Io mollusco
uscito a fare quattro passi in direzione della morte
osservo da fuori il dentro
della conchiglia. Succosa
cella, dolce scomparto resinoso,
la mia vita è lì. È quella che è. Non posso
qui, da questo aggetto, mutarla. Da lontano
mi colma, mi raggela...

Madrigal

Down at the bottom...
a trembling painful descent...
but where, come to think of it, I expected
hiccups from cocoons, anxiety from egg-whites;
there's the abundant gush of happiness
from the female guardians of warmth, damp maternal she-dogs
with pointed ears and a slow, earthy look...
There's no need, dear souls, to complain about you
or about the mud that little by little, working together,
you dig up from the depths... Nor, laughing,
disown you in a world that away from all this
simplifies, talks nonsense...

Madrigale

Giù in fondo...
Sceso tremando, con dolore...
Ma dove, a pensarci, m'aspettavo
i singulti dei bozzoli, l'ansia dell'albume
fiotta copiosa la letizia
delle custodi del caldo, materne umide cagne
dalle orecchie puntute, dallo sguardo
lento, terroso... Non bisogna,
anime care, lamentarsi
di voi, del fango che insieme, a poco a poco,
cavate dal profondo... Né ridendo
rinnegarvi nel mondo
che al fresco semplifica, sragiona...

EDOARDO SANGUINETI

E doardo Sanguineti was born in Genoa in 1930. Professor of Italian Literature at the University of Genoa, he is also a noted literary critic, essayist, playwright, and opera librettist (for composer Luciano Berio).

In keeping with his unswerving passion for experimentation and critical theory, Sanguineti is notorious for having written very dense, difficult, multi-layered poetry during the 1960s, when he was a member of the Neo-Avant-garde movement. A case in point is his first collection of poems, *Laborintus*, a descent into the inferno of his own psyche, which draws a parallel between the sort of communication problems inherent to poetry and the kind found in every society. Over time, his poetry has become more diary-like and prosy in tone, with an emphasis on daily life and on what *can* be communicated. While still highly critical of bourgeois society, his approach is less experimental and more straightforward in its caustic irony.

His stylistic ability, moreover, is such that he can make use of varied terminologies and linguistical contexts to construct a poem of impressive inner richness that yet reads close to natural speech or dialogue. "My style today is not to have any style," bluffs Sanguineti.

The poems included here were written in the period following Sanguineti's highly experimental phase. Many of the pieces are from *Reisebilder*, German for "travel journal." (Again, the idea of a "journey" infuses Sanguineti's work, though this time it is a venturing into another cultural reality rather than an exploration of self, as in *Laborintus*.)

POETRY
Laborintus 1956
Opus metricum 1961
Triperuno (Three for One) 1964
Wirwarr 1972
Post karten 1978
Stracciafoglio (Paper-Shredder) 1980
Due ballate e Alfabeto apocalittico (Two Ballads and Apocalyptic Alphabet) 1984
Quintine (Quintains) 1985
Novissimum testamentum 1986
Bisbidis 1987
Senza titolo (Untitled) 1992

FICTION
Capriccio italiano (Italian Caprice) 1963
Il gioco dell'oca (Parcheesi) 1967
Il Gioco del Satyricon: Imitazione da Petronio (The Satyricon Game: After Petronius) 1970

THEATRE
K. e altre cose (K. and Other Things) 1962
Teatro (Theatre) 1969
Storie Naturali (Natural Histories) 1971
Faust: Un travestimento (Faust: A Masquerade) 1985

SELECTED ESSAYS
Tra liberty e crepuscolarismo (Between Art Nouveau and Crespuscolarism) 1961
Interpretazione di Malebolge (An Interpretation of Malebolge) 1961
Ideologia e linguaggio (Ideology and Language) 1965
Guido Gozzano 1966
Il realismo di Dante (Realism in Dante) 1966
Giornalino: 1973-75 (Journal in Brief: '73-'75) 1976
Giornalino secondo: 1976-77 (Second Journal) 1979
La missione del critico (The Critic's Mission) 1987

from **Scartabello**

1.

The wind shoves my New Year's Day sun in my face
        [like a pie in a flickering
short by Mack Sennett) high above the sad seafront in Nervi;
        and there
I said to one of my sons that, blinded by light, I achieve my
animal bliss every time;
        (nowadays, a mystic of the body's ecstasy is
surely suspect); (but I'll keep my half-century amassed on top
        [of my hunchback,
along with all the troubles of family life);
        [and--it'll be the end-all:
a tyrannical Oedipus to interpret).

da **Scartabello**

1.

me lo schiaccia qui in faccia, il mio sole di capodanno, il vento,
        [sopra questa
mesta passeggiata di Nervi: (come una torta, in un singhiozzante
        [Mack Sennett):
        e
ho detto, lì a un mio figlio, che conseguo le mie beatitudini
        [animali, ogni volta,
così cieco di luce:
        (un mistico dell'estasi corporea, al giorno d'oggi,
è certamente sospetto): (ma mi tengo il mio mezzo secolo,
        [sopra la mia gobba,
e alquanti dispiaceri, in famiglia): (e, sarà il colmo,
        [un Edipo tiranno, da tradurre):

4.

like a disk, a trembling coin spinning on its own diameter,
                                        [I withdraw inwardly,
and with my failing sense of balance curl up
                        [in one of my classification systems
for groups, sets, unities; my things (of me and my world)
                                        [roast me over
their spit day after day;
                        today's the same: I feel how easily my concepts
fall apart (how they falsify); and I'll stick you
                        [in one of my last big clusters--
the practical-concrete--along with rubber boots,
                        [notions of psychology, and
this night ahead of us.

4.

come un disco, una moneta che turbina, tremando, intorno al
                                proprio diametro, mi chiudo,
ripiegandomi sopra il mio decrescente equilibrio, in un mio
                                sistema di classificazione
per complessi, per insiemi, per gruppi: mi schidiono le cose mie
                                (di me e del mio mondo),
un giorno dopo l'altro:
                        anche oggi, così, io li sento che si sfaldano tanto
(che si sfalsano), i miei concetti: e ti caccio
                                in un mio unico mazzo, pratico-
concreto, con gli stivali di caucciù, con la psicologia, con questa
                                notte che ci aspetta:

14.

At the offset it was calculated:
                        a planned investment in affection (ours),

in several portfolios of sweet irredeemable actions
(25-year-term),
at the average rate of one procreation every so many years,
in fact (and
futhermore negotiable and indexable, on the side);
the general terms
and actual spirit of the undersigned contract clauses
are things I
remember very vaguely, hazy as a hazy dream; (but the result is
here present, in any case, under our swollen eyes plagued
by far-sightedness);
you
are my nest egg, you (but the cost of living--my own--
increases every day);
I'm not completely at risk, my darling ingot
(and the personal capital is safe);
you're more gold to me than gold, as poets say:
(but the devaluation I've
suffered is huge).

14.

in principio era il calcolo:
fu un meditato investimento di affetti, il nostro,
in alcuni pacchetti di dolci azioni irredimibili, venticinquennali,
al tasso medio di una procreazione ogni tot anni, infatti (e poi
trattabile, e indicizzabile a parte):
il complesso delle condizioni, l'autentico
tenore delle sottoscritte clausole contrattuali, me lo ricordo
molto vagamente,
nebuloso come un sogno nebuloso: (ma il risultato è qui,
comunque, sotto
i nostri occhi gonfi, compromessi della presbiopia):
sei il mio bene di rifugio,
tu (ma il costo della vita, a me, mi cresce ogni giorno): non
sono in crisi,

lingotto mio, propriamente: (e il capitale personale è salvo): mi
sei più oro
dell'oro, come si dice in poesia:
(ma la svalutazione che ho patito è enorme):

31.

What you're reading (if you're reading me) are the effects
[of a blocked and
irritated imagination (these words are out of order;
[you must silently put
them between inverted commas), of poorly-returned desire:
they are expressions
of tenderness, desperation and lament (end of citation);
[and they are
fruit of your dream message; (if it's true that
[I persecute you like a
double sledgehammer and what I split open is my own forehead:
with this hemorrhage
of words).

31.

questi che leggi (se mi leggi) sono gli effetti di
[un'immaginazione guasta
e irritata: (queste parole stanno qui trasposte:
[tu devi mentalmente
pronunciarle come virgolettate): di un desiderio mal corrisposto:
[e sono espressioni
di tenerezza, di disperazione e di lamento (fine della citazione):
[e sono il frutto
del tuo onirico messaggio: (se è vero che ti perseguito
[con un doppio martellone
di legno, e che mi rompo invece la mia fronte:
e mi viene questa emorragia di parole):

32.

And now a few questions to end with:
                    what do you think of compassion (as an
interchangeable agreement)?; and (getting back to what
                              [I   mentioned
before) of illusion (as long as it's deliberately cultivated,
                                   [socialized,
institutionalized)?; do you know the story about Lazarus,
                              [who has forgotten
how to laugh? and the one about his book, made up entirely
                              [of bare white pages?
how do you interpret them? (expand and comment on as
                    [you wish); (I, for one,
am taking a break here today):
                    (time allowed: a normal lifespan).

32.

e adesso poche domande, per finire:
                    [che cosa pensi della compassione (come
patto scambievole)?: e (riprendendo quanto avevo
                         [già accennato) dell'illusione
(purché deliberatamente coltivata, socializzata,
                              [istituzionalizzata)?: conosci
la storia di Lazzaro che non ride più? e quella del suo libro,
                              [tutto composto
di nude pagine bianche? come le interpreti tu? (sviluppare e
                         [commentare liberamente):
(per oggi, io faccio pausa, infatti, qui):
                    [(tempo concesso: una vita normale):

from **Reisebilder**

33.

I defended Genet on the subject of terror (in London
                              [he'd concluded:
d'autres vont vous tuer) with even worse arguments (like:
                              [a policy of
fear is the surest and most honest) and met
                              [with your diffidence and
resistance; (I also said: it's obvious Genet knows human nature--
                              [that
of whites in particular); I will concede, however,
                              [that more political
action is needed;
   and that there are more substantial reasons for signing the
appeal supporting George Jackson: like his letter to Mrs. Fay
                              [in April
1970, with his definition of fascism;
                              in this sense I can even say that
there's much of the Negro in me, trapped as I find myself
                              [in the same
diabolical masquerade (though I'm clearly aware that I'm
                              [a man of
small-time cabotage, as Mao says, and that it's a fish
                              [of puny thoughts that
always sets off these horrible storms inside me).

Da **Reisebilder**

33.

ho difeso Genet, e l'argomento del terrore (a Londra
                              [concludeva: *d'autres*
vont vous tuer), con argomenti peggiori (del tipo: l'etica
della paura è la più sicura--è la più vera),

[contro la tua diffidenza--e le tue
resistenze: (ho anche detto: si vede che Genet conosce
[gli uomini--i bianchi,
in particolare): ti concedo volentieri, però, che ci vuole
[più politica:
e che ci sono
ragioni più sostanziose, per firmare per George Jackson:
[come la sua lettera
a Mrs. Fay, aprile 1970, con la sua definizione del fascismo:
in questo senso,
posso dire persino che c'è molto di negro, in me, intrappolato
come mi trovo, in un'identica mascherata diabolica
[(anche se ho chiara
consapevolezza che sono un uomo di piccolo cabotaggio,
[come direbbe Mao,
e che è un pesce di piccoli pensieri che in me scatena
[sempre queste tempeste orrende):

34.

To the mini-skirted customs official who with sibyl-dove eyes
[honed in on me
in the interminable line of travelers in transit, I told
[the entire truth,
confined within a plywood separé-confessional:
I said I have a son who
studies Russian and German and that *Bonjours les amis*,
[a four-volume French
course, was for my wife;
I was ready to concede more: that I knew it had
been Rosa Luxemburg to launch the slogan "socialism or
[barbarism," and that
I could make up an impressive madrigal on the same;
but I was sweating
as I searched my pockets in vain for the bill from the
[Operncafé; and then

suddenly you were there, even dragging in the kids,
[marvelous and marveling;
(we ordered you out with the same harsh gestures,
[my uniformed Beatrice of
democracy and myself);
but the irreparable had already been consumated for me
there at the border between the two Berlins: forty-one-year-old
[seduced
by a police officer.

34.

al funzionario doganale in minigonna, che mi ha prescelto,
[con i suoi occhi di sibilla
e di colomba, dentro una fila interminabile di viaggiatori
[in transito, ho detto
tutta la verità, confinato in un separé-confessionale di legno
compensato:
ho detto che ho un figlio che studia il russo e il tedesco:
che *Bonjour les amis*, corso di lingua francese in 4 volumi, era
per mia moglie:
ero pronto a concedere di più: sapevo che fu
[Rosa Luxemburg
a lanciare la parola d'ordine "socialismo o barbarie": e potevo
ricavarne un madrigale strepitoso:
ma sudavo, frugandomi le tasche,
cercando invano il conto dell'Operncafé: e poi,
[hai fatto irruzione
tu, trascinandoti dietro anche i bambini, meravigliosi
[e meravigliati:
(ti scacciavamo con gli stessi gesti duri, io e quella mia beatrice
democratica in divisa):
ma l'irreparabile era già consumato, lí
alla frontiera tra le due Berlino, per me:
[quarantenne sedotto da un poliziotto:

35.

I tell you it was a hard punch to my brain,
                          [the news of Jackson's
murder;
    it floored me, coming as it did almost by chance, and time
after the fact, there on the steps of the Aquarium
                          [where I stood with you
and some friends from Salerno:
                          (I saw a lot of black spots in front of
my eyes; the newspaper trembled in my hands);
                          it won't be black-panther claws
by any means, to rip through us one day:
                          [it'll be piranha teeth set in
the mouths of livid, pale faces, like that of Louis Nelson,
                          [for instance;
or the President of the United States.

35.

è stato un pugno secco dentro il mio cervello, ti dico, la notizia
dell'assassinio di Jackson:
                          mi ha steso di colpo, piombandomi addosso
in ritardo, e così quasi per caso, là sulla porta
                          [dell'Aquarium, dove
stavo con te, e con un paio di amici salernitani:
                          (mi sono visto
come tante macchie davanti agli occhi:
                          [mi tremava il giornale tra le mani):

non saranno unghie di pantere nere, davvero,
                          [a straziarci un giorno:
saranno denti da pesce piranha, in bocca a lividi visi pallidi:
come Louis Nelson, appunto:
                          o il presidente degli Stati Uniti:

48.

So it takes very little indeed: a *brasserie*
                    [with Beaujolais 1968 Reserve
and small inside terraces (as pleasant as they are impossible
                              [to find here),
with a horseshoe-shaped bar counter and fake candles
                              [winking their
wicked yellow, with servings of snails and baby goat
                    [prepared *comme il faut*;

            and we discover ourselves very cursedly latin,
no doubt about it, with other desires, other moods (and full of
good thoughts: prosperous, pulpy, and pagan);

            so it happened that yesterday, October 3rd, glancing
about me a bit and observing a Germanic sampling
                              [of chewing couples,
I discovered that all women are latin,
                    [along all parallels and meridians;

(and what warm soft winds of departure blew by then,
                              [filling the sails
of our old hearts, in the darkening port of Wittenbergplatz!)

48.

non ci vuole dunque niente, se ci basta una brasserie
                              [fornita di beaujolais
riserva '68 con terrazzette interne tanto gradevoli
                              [(e altrimenti irreperibili,
qui), con un banco di bar quasi a ferro di cavallo,
                              [e false candele
di uno scellerato giallo tremante, con porzioni
                              [di lumache e di capretto
preparate come si deve:

e ci ritroviamo molto maledettamente latini,
già, con altre voglie, altri umori:
[(e pieni di bei pensieri prosperosi,
polposi e pagani):
così avvenne che ieri 3 ottobre, guardandomi
un po' intorno, osservando un campionario germanico di coppie
[masticanti,
ho scoperto che sono tutte latine, le donne,
[per tutti i paralleli e i meridiani:
(e che aria di partenza spirò tiepida e dolce, ormai, gonfiando
le vele dei nostri vecchi cuori, nel porto ottenebrato
[di Wittenbergplatz!):

GIAMPIERO NERI

Giampiero Pontiggia uses the pen name of Giampiero Neri. He was born in Erba, to the north of Milan, in 1927. For most of his life he has lived in Milan and for many years worked in a bank.

He is regarded as the leading advocate of a certain type of prose poetry in Italy. There is much subtlety and understatement in his work, and the images produced tend to be of such a lightness and airiness as to seem ghostly and ethereal. Often things seem to be observed from a distance as regards time or space. There is nothing cold about the voice, however; Neri's even detachment makes the kind of nostalgia he expresses powerfully melancholic and at times openly metaphysical.

POETRY

L'aspetto occidentale del vestito (Western-looking Clothes) 1976
Liceo (High School) 1986
Dallo Stesso Luogo (From the Same Place)--collected works--
1990

The Inn of Angels

1.
What's become of those small black signs, image and suggestion
of enduring commitment?
In a small group they dwell,
and take on the shape of sad, lifeless symbols.
I don't remember all the details now.
                          [Having come off its imaginary
line, bad weather is near at hand and it won't be to say:
"Friends, here I am."
It's already won many return matches and comes performing its
dangerous tricks.
How will you want to receive this wind when, flipped over
on his back, he strains with impatience right by your courtyard?
Lastly, during this wait, it doesn't matter what gets talked about.
Génie littéraire hors de cause, your ants, Jean Henri,
are a closed chapter.

2.
In what strange place on earth can you find
                          [a nicely moss-covered mill,
happily rotating its paddle wheel green waters?
As to the events, only the names have been changed.
                          [The street runs
from your gate to behind the trees within a frame of dust, and
there are spots here and there, masks from another time.
Surrounded by many figures, the Greek head conserved
                          [its strange charm.
In the end, it seemed useless to continue searching or give
a different explanation.
By then it was late, and just barely possible
                          [to make out any shapes.

3.
At the theater, the gathering place was an inn with a traditional
green-lettered sign.

I remember its typical facade, the room's windows,
                              [and a curious drawing,
hung by the entrance, a sort of intuitive warning.
At the time, however, there was great interest
                              [in the performance to come;
I myself waited for it to begin--or better, I highly desired it.
So it happened that at the sound of the first words
                              [no one asked himself
where the voice was coming from.
Surrounded by an extraordinary number of shadows, we heard:
"All of you are here in my spirit."

4.

It's written that the Prince of Condé slept soundly the night
before the battle.
A detail of small importance?
I don't want to say one thing in place of another, but any friend
of the bees had best watch out, for his is dangerous love.
It isn't the first time an admirable series of causes has produced
a completely different effect.
The same goes for the Inn of Angels: the beginning
                              [was as promised and
what followed would be clear at the end.
Then, it only seemed an ambiguous sign,
                              [a small spot on the horizon.

5.

The truth is that not even a child was playing
                              [on the beach when
the storm-front broke off from its far-off line
                              [and rapidly moved in.
Skimming first over the water, it lifted two heavy wings
                              [and hid in
silence behind cloud banks; then throwing off
a sudden light, like a comet, it came at us.
It's late for putting explanations off to another day.
I see a mystic landslide of castles in the air.

L'albergo degli angeli

1.
Cosa è stato di quei piccoli segni, neri, immagine e
                                        [somiglianza
di un impegno continuo?
In una stretta compagnia dimorano, a forma di malinconici
simboli privi di vita.
Ora non ricordo tutti i particolari. Venuto via da una linea
immaginaria, il cattivo tempo è alle porte e non sarà per dire:
"Amici, eccomi".
Si è già preso molte rivincite, arriva eseguendo
                                        [i suoi pericolosi
esercizi.
Come vorrai riceverlo quando, rovesciato sul dorso, preme
con impazienza davanti al tuo cortile?
In questa attesa, infine, che il discorso si presenti a suo modo
non ha una grande importanza.
Génie littéraire hors de cause, le tue formiche, Jean Henri,
                                        [sono
un capitolo chiuso.

2.
In quale strano paese del mondo troverai un mulino, ben co-
perto di muschio, che muove allegramente le sue pale nell'ac-
qua verde?
Di quanto è accaduto soltanto i nomi sono cambiati. Dal tuo
cancello la strada corre via dietro gli alberi, in una cornice di
polvere, e sono macchie qua e là, le maschere di una volta.
Circondata da un gran numero di figure, la testa del greco
manteneva intatta la sua strana suggestione.
Infine, sembrava inutile proseguire le ricerche, dare una spie-
gazione diversa.
Era tardi ormai, si distinguevano a mala pena i contorni.

3.
Al piccolo teatro, il luogo di riunione era un albergo con la

tradizionale insegna dipinta in verde.
Ricordo bene la sua tipica fronte, le finestre della stanza e un
curioso disegno, posto di fianco all'ingresso, una specie di
sensensibile avvertimento.
Ma allora si notava un grande interesse per la recita
                                             e io stesso
aspettavo che avesse inizio, anzi lo desideravo fortemente.
Così, alle prime parole, nessuno si chiese ad esempio da dove
arrivò la voce.
Circondati da uno straordinario numero di ombre, ascoltava-
mo: "Voi tutti, che siete presenti nel mio spirito".

4.
Si narra che il Principe di Condé abbia dormito
profondamente la notte prima della battaglia.
Sembra un particolare di poca importanza?
Non voglio dire una cosa per un'altra, ma stia bene attento l'
amico delle api, perché il suo è un amore pericoloso.
Non è la prima volta che una mirabile serie di cause produce
un effetto completamente diverso.
Proprio allo stesso modo, all'Albergo degli Angeli, il principio
era come si è detto e quanto al seguito sarebbe stato
chiaro alla fine.
Allora sembrava soltanto un segno ambiguo, una piccola mac-
chia all'orizzonte.

5.
Sta di fatto che nemmeno un bambino stava giocando sulla
spiaggia quando il fronte del temporale si staccò dalla linea
più lontana e cominciò a venire avanti rapidamente.
Prima correndo sul filo dell'acqua solleva due pesanti ali e si
nasconde in silenzio dietro banchi di nuvole; e gettata all'im-
provviso una luce, come di stella cometa, ci viene incontro.
Allora è tardi per rimandare le spiegazioni a un'altra volta.
Guardo una mistica frana di castelli in aria.

A Case of the Same Name

1.
Close analysis revealed the existence of a key,
an old-fashioned latch-bolt, and countless nails.
The baroque idea seemed to demolish the castle
                              [of suppositions,
making it plummet into fantastic chaos.
It especially destroyed the lack of perspective, seeing that
through the shed window, for instance,
                              [light filters in at a slant,
absolutely inadapt.
What to say, then, of the professor reciting his part like a
                              [French actor:
"You really believe," he theorized, spinning his hat
                              [in his hands.
"You really believe that in some way I can be of help to you?"
How to cross the desert to retrieve a mirror
and a point of view?
Looking right, through the slit, the pure green river
                              [made a slow sharp bend
and disappeared behind the trees.
The idea of returning was gaining acceptance,
                              [if an intolerable
red spot had not imposed its dramatic halt.

2.
Looking to me like flowers, the light came through
                              [the windows.
In the morning, the street and houses have taken on
                              [their colors of long ago.
Long images form in my room, they've returned
with many subjects.
A similar picture will be found again, some day or another.
But did anyone notice that detail in the background?
                              [The beginning?

3.
Bad weather is upon us and caution is advised, as our
Mother Church commands.
More concretely, the storm threatened to send flying
an extraordinary number of papers.
It became more and more difficult to meet with the professor,
who was constantly occupied with correcting someone's
                                                    [homework.
And having seen him by chance:
"Doctor Livingstone, I presume," he said, while holding out
                                          [his hand and
crossing vast deserts of red bar tables and cane chairs.

4.
The tiger's owner was having breakfast. Perhaps it needs
saying that he's well-considered and respected by all?
I still remember how the interview went, true to form, and,
in the background, a portrait out-of-focus on the wall.
Signs announced other performances, the show seemed
further and further off.
Looking out from the windows of the *Caffé* was like walking
aimlessly for a long time.
Everything's bound to go as it did back then, and in the end
just some signs, a fairly simple theme, were all that was left,
                                                [afterwards.

Un caso di omonimia

1.
L'analisi approfondita rivelò l'esistenza di una chiave, un chia-
vistello dell'epoca e uno sterminato numero di chiodi.
L'idea barocca parve demolire il castello delle supposizioni,
facendolo precipitare in un fantastico caos.
Colpiva soprattutto la mancanza di prospettiva, perché ad
esempio la finestra del capanno filtrava una luce obliqua,
assolutamente inadatta.

Che dire allora del professore, recitando la sua parte come un
attore francese:
"Lei crede veramente" spiegava rigirandosi il cappello tra le
mani "Lei crede che io possa in qualche modo esserle di
aiuto?".
Come attraversare il deserto per ritrovare uno specchio
e il punto di vista?
Guardando a destra, alla feritoia, il fiume verdissimo piegava
lento a gomito e scompariva dietro agli alberi.
Si faceva strada l'idea del ritorno se una macchia rossa insop-
portabile non avesse imposto il suo drammatico alt.

2.
Dei fiori, mi sembra, una luce passava dai vetri. Nella
mattina, la strada e le case hanno ripreso i colori di una volta.
Formano lunghe immagini nella mia stanza, sono tornate con
molti argomenti.
Un quadro simile si troverà ancora, un giorno o l'altro. Ma si
notava il particolare sullo sfondo? il principio?

3.
Il cattivo tempo è alle porte e consiglia la prudenza, come co-
manda nostra madre Chiesa.
In concreto, il temporale minacciò di far volare un numero
straordinario di carte.
Risultava sempre più difficile incontrare il professore, costan-
temente impegnato nella correzione di qualche compito.
E avendolo visto per caso:
"Il dottor Livingstone, suppongo" disse, mentre gli tendeva la
mano attraversando vasti deserti di tavolini rossi e sedie impa-
gliate.

4.
Il padrone delle tigri stava facendo colazione. Si deve forse
aggiungere che gode della generale considerazione,
di una stima universale?
Ricordo ancora il colloquio come si svolse, nella sua forma

tipica e, sullo sfondo, un ritratto sfocato appeso alla parete.
Manifesti annunciavano altre rappresentazioni, lo spettacolo
si allontanava.
Guardando dai vetri del Caffé, era come camminare per
molto tempo, senza scopo.
Tutto procederà come allora e infine dei segni, un tema abba-
stanza semplice, erano quanto rimaneva, dopo.

Seasons

February, from a nook in the wall
the owl watches the movements
of the cold season.
He adapts naturally to whatever
necessity,
attentive to the sound of leaves,
to the signals of every small life.
He's fulfilled in his patient task.
Form, fate and name
which will be rewarded.

Stagioni

Febbraio, l'allocco guarda
da una cavità del muro i movimenti
della fredda stagione.
Si adatta naturalmente
alle necessità
attento al rumore delle foglie
ai segnali di ogni piccola vita.
Nel suo lavoro paziente
si riconosce.
Forma, destino e nome
che avrà la ricompensa.

Natural History

and from the red grating in the distance
we watched the wind at rest, trembling
at the palely-lit house and she
as if waiting. And the circle is clear,
nor did we tire of watching how
long would last the shy silence of the butterfly.

Storia naturale

e dalla rossa inferriata in lontananza
riposare il vento guardavamo tremando
la casa pallidamente illuminata e lei
come aspettando. E chiaro il cerchio
né ci stancammo di guardare quanto
durò il silenzio timido della farfalla.

AMELIA ROSSELLI

Amelia Rosselli was born in Paris in 1930 and died in Rome in 1996. Her mother was English and her father, Carlo Rosselli, was a famous left-wing Italian political leaders who'd been forced into exile under Mussolini (and who would be assassinated in France when Amelia Rosselli was seven). After years of living abroad in France, England, and the United States, Amelia Rosselli settled in Rome. Her formal training was in music and musical composition. Her reputation as a poet dates back to 1963 when Pier Paolo Pasolini wrote the introduction to her poems published in the literary magazine *il Menabo*. Amelia Rosselli wrote in both Italian and English.

Rosselli believed that the impulses generated by our collective unconscious can take on a shape and form in poetry--an idea closely associated with her belief that most artistic experience is translatable and therefore transmissible on a world-wide scale. "The language I write in is in truth only one, and my experience--logically, associatively and musically speaking--is certainly that of all people and so possible to find in all languages", she once said.

Rosselli the poet plays radically with the logical order and syntax of language in order to give greater stress to the power of the individual word--a lesson gleamed from the French surrealists and English Metaphysical poets. Her poetry hurls its content at the reader as if it were a fiery meteorite of intimate and private origins, which will reveal its real nature little by little throughout the poem; the clues are to be found in the poet's "psychological slips", puns, and unconcluded expressions. Rhythm and stress, as well, are of crucial importance for the emotional effect they may have on the reader.

POETRY

Variazioni belliche (Wartime Variations) 1964
Serie ospedaliera (Hospital Series) 1969
Documento: 1966-1973 (Document) 1974
Primi scritti: 1952-1963 (Early Writings) 1980
Impromptu 1981
Appunti Sparsi e Persi:1966-77 (Loose Lost Notes)1983
La libellula (Dragonfly) 1985 (written in 1958)
Antologia (anthology of collected works) 1987
Sleep (collected poems written in English from '53-'66) 1993

OTHER

Epistolario familiare (the collected letters of her father,
    which Rosselli edited) 1979

From relief to relief, the white lines, the white paper
a relief; landscape, a bike come new
with bleach that sprays the cemetery.

Relief after relief with a white jacket that looms brown
over the abyss, sideboard tatoos and telephones in a row, while,
unbuttoning, I wait for Honorable Rivulini.
                                        [From house to house

I telegraph, another bicycle plus if somehow you can push.
From relief to relief push my yellow bike, my
smoking transitives. Relief upon relief all

the paper scattered on the floor or table, smoothed down so as
to believe that the future awaits me.

That the future should await me! That waiting for me waiting
for me is a Biblical future in all its grandeur, a contorted fate
that I haven't come upon making my rounds of the
                                        [butcher shops.

Di sollievo in sollievo, le strisce bianche le carte bianche
un sollievo, di passaggio in passaggio una bicicletta nuova
con la candeggina che spruzza il cimitero.

Di sollievo in sollievo con la giacca bianca
                                [che sporge marroncino
sull'abisso, credenza tatuaggi e telefoni in fila, mentre
aspettando l'onorevole Rivulini mi sbottonavo. Di casa in casa

telegrafo, una bicicletta in più per favore se potete in qualche
modo spingere. Di sollievo in sollievo spingete la mia bicicletta
gialla, il mio fumare transitivi. Di sollievo in sollievo tutte

le carte sparse per terra o sul tavolo, liscie per credere

che il futuro m'aspetta.

Che m'aspetti il futuro! che m'aspetti che m'aspetti il futuro
biblico nella sua grandezza, una sorte contorta non l'ho trovata
facendo il giro delle macellerie.

How many fields which like a sponge
are willing to enrich your past, and even
your suffocated present.

How many small lanes, quite picturesque,
that you'd like to convert into meaning

from the essence of all this stems your suffering.

Yet in the essence of your suffering
quivers a desire for sleep or for red meat. Oh
how silent the blackbirds are. They've mistaken
your idea of peace and quiet for the sunset

which to your droopy eyes
offered only a sophisticated stealing away of
your greed for being alone, and yourself.

Quanti campi che come spugna vorrebbero
arricchire il tuo passato, anche il
tuo presente soffocato.

Quante viuzze del tutto pittoresche
che tu vorresti tramutare in significato

dell'essenza di questa tua sofferenza.

Ma geme nell'essenza della tua sofferenza
un desiderio di sonno o di carne. Oh

come i merli taciono! Hanno confuso
la tua idea della pace con il tramonto

che offrì ai tuoi occhi penduli solo
un sofisticato sequestro della tua brama
d'essere solo, e te stesso.

A sex violent as an object (whitened quarry of marble)
(moulded amphora of clay) and very well-hidden, egg-shaped,
a hailball astorm, it assaulted the solitary type in the parlor.
No connaisseur no wiseman, reptilely influenced by illustrious
examples or illustrations of candor, becoming pus for peace and
the soul. No wiseman no bonvivant but wise at trading, spurred
like a vessel against rocks, bats, a sudden fall from the heights
of discipline and dance, from the so-fa-mi-do of another day:
not wise and not worldly, masquerading as a soldier, groping
and venturing amid the pig sties, ransacking as to form, and as
object this sex did with him as it pleased.

Il sesso violento come un oggetto (cava di marmo imbiancata)
(anfora di creta ricurva) e nascostissimo in forma
d'uovo assaltava il solitario, come se fosse la grandine
a tempestare, nel salotto. Non gaudente, non sapiente
serpentinamente influenzato da esempi illustri o illustrazioni
di candore, per la pace e per l'anima purulava. Non sapiente
non gaudente, ma sapiente e mercantile speronato come
il vascello contro rocce pipistrelle, cadeva di colpo
dall'alto del rigore e della danza, dal sol fa mi do di
un'altra giornata: non sapiente e non gaudente travestito
da soldato annaspando e arrischiando tra capanne di maiale
rovistando, come forma e come oggetto, il sesso si serviva
di lui.

(poems written directly in English)

Worthless as was her itinerary to fame
she collapsed unexpectedly into a mirrored
frame which was the sordid history of
the resistance of the few of the world's
massacre. Collapsed into my brother's arms,
shiver down my faultless spine of woe! Thus
a weary maiden quivered slight into arms
softer than her brother's arms, her forces
slippery as a horse's cry, her quivered
hopes of gain collapsed suddenly into a fresh
bargain unutterable.

you might as well think one thing or another
of me; I am not a mercy's chance, nor do
I want your interpretation, having none
myself to overpower me. You withdraw into
your fevered cell, like a microscopic angel
do engage battle with my thoughts, as if
they were to my revolutionary heart, a
promiscuous bell. Hell itself is what you
want: a needle into necessity, foreseeing
I shall not do better than you want

Actions in my brain: these verbs, whose celerity
resists all pain. Tenderness itself is dangerous
when out of claim; quick birds these verbs
do claim ignorance. The black branch of thought
leaves no life to thought; it resists all
cankering with craft, spice, tiresome desires
and tries, in its black fashion that it should
not die.

Spices too dull for any brain refrain from

tinkering with the business; a solace to
warm limbs.

Negro blood flowing on his brown
or black body, grace and length enticing
looks of envy, looks of rapture
records of tolerance.

Swimming underwater he saw all
life deformed; a virgin pen wrote
his name down.

ANDREA ZANZOTTO

Andrea Zanzotto was born in Pieve di Soligo (Treviso), a small town in the Veneto region, in 1921. He began teaching school at age 16 and eventually obtained an Arts degree from the University of Padua in 1942. After World War II, he went to live for a while in France and Switzerland, then returned to his hometown and resumed teaching middle school. Without budging from there, he established contact with the intellectual circles of Venice and Rome, and lived through alternating phases of being encouraged and ignored. Now retired, he still resides near Treviso and corresponds with intellectuals from all over the world and with his numerous translators. (He himself has published translations of work by Bataille, Leiris, and Balzac). Zanzotto has also written critical essays for Italian reviews and newspapers.

As an experimentalist poet trying to stretch and even "reformulate" language, Zanzotto's particular technique is to allow the narrative line of a poem to be continually distorted--if not halted--by the voice of the unconscious. (An important note in this regard--though by no means explaining the totality of his poetry--is Zanzotto's discovery, long before it become fashionable, of the psychoanalytical theories of Jacques Lacan.) Zanzotto's poetry continually alludes to objective, historical fact, against which the poet measures not just his private life but also and especially his own cognitive processes at various ages. Because of the linguistical variety and tension, Zanzotto's poems conserve a complex profundity even when he is writing in dialect or making a description in infantile sing-song.

POETRY

Dietro il paesaggio (Behind the Landscape) 1951
Elegia e altri versi (Elegy and Other Poems) 1954
Vocativo (Vocative) 1957, revised/expanded in 1981
IX Ecloghe (IX Eclogues) 1962
La beltà (Beauty) 1968
Gli sguardi, i fatti e Senhal (Glances, Facts, and Senhal) 1969, 1990
A che valse? (What Was It Worth?--anthology of work 1938-1942) 1970
Pasque (Easters) 1973
Filò 1976
Il Galateo in bosco (Etiquette in the Woods) 1978 (Viareggio Prize)
Fosfeni (Phosphenes) 1983 (Librex-Montale Prize)
Idioma (Idiom) 1986 (Feltrinelli Prize, "l'Accademia Nazionale dei Lincei")

PROSE

Sull'altipiano (On the Plateau) 1964
Racconti e prose (Stories and Other Prose) 1990

ESSAYS

Fantasie di avvicinamento (Fantasies of Coming Close) (Vol. 1, others to follow) 1991

Subnarcosis

Birds
harsh endless chatter
on a winter tree
a harshness
maybe not real but only
the flint of the possible
childishly alien
but certainly from us who listen
        --alarmed--in the distance
        --or even soothed--in the distance
birds all of a city
saturated   unsociable
        glottic glory
        systems of insights and tricks
an unsociable me-me-meaning
not even childish but
sinister, adult in its smallness

        [dispersed species of my sleep
        that will never return].

Subnarcosi

Uccelli
crudo infinito cinguettio
su un albero invernale
qualche cosa di crudo
forse non vero ma solo
scintillio di un possibile
infantilmente aumano
ma certo da no che ascoltiamo
    --allarmati--lontano
    --o anche placati--lontano
uccelli tutta una città

pregna   chiusa
    glorie di glottidi
    acumi e vischi di dottrine
un chiuso si-si-significare
nemmeno infantile ma
adulto occulto nella sua minimità

        [disperse specie del mio sonno
        che mai ritornerà].

Existing Psychically

From this contriving flesh-land
thin whetted senses
and startlements and silences,
from this slaver of events
--suns that hit the threads of eyelashes
wheatspikes beginning to fray on hillsides--
from this long moment
swallowed by snows, swallowed by wind,
from all this that wasn't
spring not July not autumn
but just sickly opening
but just psyche,
from all this which is nothing
and which is everything that I am:
in a similar way truth moans to itself,
wants to be the apple that swells with moisture and rots.
Acid brightness that weaves
the stings of hell and atoms
with the heavy heaves
of seaweed and worms,
egg-gleam
that in the dying mucus makes words,
makes loves.

Esistere psichicamente

Da questa artificiosa terra-carne
esili acuminati sensi
e sussulti e silenzi,
da questa bava di vicende
--soli che urtarono fili di ciglia
ariste appena sfrangiate pei colli--
da questo lungo attimo
inghiottito da nevi, inghiottito dal vento,
da tutto questo che non fu
primavera non luglio non autunno
ma solo egro spiraglio
ma solo psiche,
da tutto questo che non è nulla
ed è tutto ciò che io sono:
tale la verità geme a se stessa,
si vuole pomo che gonfia e infradicia.
Chiarore acido che tessi
i bruciori d'inferno
degli atomi e il conato
torbido d'alghe e vermi,
chiarore-uovo
che nel morente muco fai parole
e amori.

Eclogue IV

Polyphemus, Phenomenological Bubble, Spring
                "Animula vagula blandula"
                --Emperor Hadrian

Personae: *a, Polyphemus*

a: "Sweet" breath stirring

shell-bursting births, comas, and the mute;
"sweet" fog of old age hanging over the
return of the settled pact;
man, vague term,
unflattering light, man I won't answer to,
he jumps and breaks his foot far above the world.

The meadows keep water, silence and violets to themselves;
lakes and snows spill from the vial.
Eye, fountainhead in the shell: I've seen
the sun wandering in the world's wandering.

World, vague word, Spring
calling me into your weak psychoid.
It seems right for me to stay with the game
a little longer, stay with the breath,
with that divine creative impulse
of emotive greenish-yellow wax,
the Spring world and me.
And I come straight or oblique,
I come humped or smooth;
like an embryo with lots of teeth
I wink, and I shuffle, and
I pull at the wools in which day
wraps its fetal chlorophylls.
I rise, I spin like a top
to a musical whip. Since here everything is "music".
Not man, I mean, but phenomenological bubble.
Ah, Sunday's always Sunday.

Phenomenological bubbles will vary with
a thousand stimuli, darken
and sparkle. Hope is just as
spherical, and so is thirst.
I abstain from the usual words.
O Spring of germs and lice
Spring of liquors, gods, suspense;

"I'd like to find new ways
to say it";
but as the petal and its fringe, or the grass
                                    [and its edge move,
so the players move with the game.
Hoards of radiant monas, corymbose bubbles
and you round in any case, arches and sole-supreme eye
of Polyphemus.

Po.: No, here one doesn't break new ground, here one
                                    [doesn't fool with the text,
here one falls back, here
in the deep socket of my eyesight
sizzles the runaway drill,
the cruel tool and highly vicious circle.
And it's precisely here on this
that I make my stand and swear:
I Polyphemus, spherical one-eyed being
drunk on the Spring wine of Ismarus,
from me life pours, a gorging and guzzling
(oh: wine of Ismarus; oh: life; oh: Spring!)

Ecloga IV

Polifemo, bolla fenomenica, Primavera

                              Animula vagula blandula
                              Imperatore Adriano
Persone: *a, Polifemo*

a--"Dolce" fiato che muovi
    le nascite dal guscio, il coma, il muto;
    "dolce" bruma che covi
    il ritorno del patto convenuto;

uomo, termine vago,
impropria luce, uomo a cui non rispondo,
salto che il piede spezza sopra il mondo.

Godono i prati acqua silenzio e viole;
da fiale laghi, nevi si versano.
Occhio, pullus nel guscio: ho veduto
nell'errare del mondo errante il sole.

Mondo, termine vago, primavera
che mi chiami nel tuo psicoide fioco.
Ancora un poco è giusto
ch'io stia al gioco, stia al fiato,
all'afflato,
di lutea possibile cera,
io, e mondo primavera.

E vengo dritto, obliquo,
vengo gibboso, liscio;
come germe che abbonda
di dente ammicco e striscio
e premo alle lane onda ammanta
il dì le sue fetali clorofille.
M'adergo, prillo, come a musicale
sferza la trottola. Poi che qui tutto è .
Non uomo, dico, ma bolla fenomenica.
Ah, domenica è sempre domenica.

Le bolle fenomeniche alle mille
stimolazioni variano s'incupano
scintillano. Sferica
è anche la speranza, anche la sete.
Abiuro dalle lettere consuete.
O primavera di cocchi e di lendini,
primavera di lìquor, dei, suspense,
"vorrei trovare parole nuove":
ma il petalo e la frangia, ma l'erba e il lembo muove,

muovono al gioco i giocatori. Monadi
radianti, folle, bolle a corimbi e tu
tondo comunque, a tutta volta, estremo
occhio di Polifemo.

Po. --No, qui non si dissoda, qui non si cambia testo,
qui si ricade, qui
frigge nel cavo fondo della vista
il renitente trapano, la trista
macchina, il giro viziosissimo.
E qui su questo,
assetandomi, giuro:
io Polifemo sferico monocolo
ebbro del vino d'Ismaro primavera,
io donde cola, crapula, la vita
(oh: vino d'Ismaro; oh: vita; oh: primavera!).

from **Prophecies or Memories or Display-Board Newspapers**

VIII

Eva, forma futuri.
But more and more now
"the beautiful and the beautiful" is easy to make restless,
to titillate and wean, up to other centers;
the beautiful aims at the sublime;
with a peck, the gardener-bird chooses
beautiful from beautiful and tosses it up,
woe is me that I'll never be able to do so,
and: discontemplate, remove from one charm
in order to pile back up haphazardly in another charm
and: origin of the sublimizing cone
the names cling together, entwine, choke, slam
names and colors jump one on another
--speaking of charm--
--attempts at hyperbole--

now no longer one but a thousand vineyards
                              [of a thousand Renzos
bubble Münchausen-blue up toward the sublime,
winter cherries fuchsias heliotropes, for example,
                              [among the first
and Augustisms and Septemberisms and more
and then enormous deposits of botanical terms
which we'll never collect--in those places,   semantic fact
hooks up badly with   phonemic fact but everything
pursues itself, darts, shoots on sight,
teaches and unteaches clamps, laces, bottonholes,
jostlings, suspense, predictableness--
ikebana prevails, the world's been ikebanized at last
ikebana, or better, small contraption of monsters-stars-ideas
up inside, forward, up on,
gone is the drought and rain, the stability and things unstable
on the lookout, flowers, leaves, stems and flower-forests
searching in nothing for nothing,
hunters and prey, murderers and game
juicy flesh, pistils, stamens and thorns
hunting deeper until you're well within the thickness
until you sink your beak into the sublime-lime
multiplied by the multiple-tiple
collapsing then as giant glowing coals Algol Vega Sol
                              [through the lens of the whole set.
Ah the explosion of meaning and expression
for the children of Mezzaselva
ah pedagogies!
and then lots of shopping among these beauties

"The colors save you"
(from the comments by an expert on a Rorschach)
(but what a figure you cut in Rosenzweig's little sketches)
Adam forma futuri.

da **Profezie o memorie o giornali murali**

VIII

Eva, forma futuri.
Ma ora il bello e il bello
si fa sempre più inquietabile,
titillare e divezzamento, su ad altri centri,
il bello punta al sublime,
l'uccello giardiniere sbeccuzza e sceglie
bello da bello e butta su,
ahi mai ci arriverò,
e: scontemplare smuovere da un fascino
per riaffastellare in un altro fascino
e: origine del cono sublimizzante
si abbarbicano si avvinghiano soffocano
picchiano i nomi
saltano uno sull'altro nomi e cromi
--a proposito del fascino--
--tentativi d'iperbole--
ora non più una mille vigne di mille Renzi bolle
                              [blu-münchausen
su verso il sublime,
alchechengi fucsie eliotropi qui ad esempio per primi
e agostismi e settembrismi e altro
e poi grandi depositi di termini botanici
che mai realizzeremo--in quei luoghi male s'aggancia
il fatto semantico al fatto fonematico ma tutto
s'insegue freccia spara a vista

insegna e disinsegna graffe laccioli asole
urti suspense prevedibilità--,
è forte l'ikebana si ikebanizza il mondo finalmente,
ikebana o meglio macchinetta di idee-mostri-astri
su dentro, avanti, su a,
via l'arsura e la pioggia la stabilità e l'instabile
a caccia fiori foglie steli e foreste

a caccia nel niente per niente
cacciatori e prede carnefici e selvaggine
polpe colme pistilli stami e spine
a caccia più dentro fino a dare nello spessore
a dar di becco nel sublime-blime molti-
plicato per il molteplice-plice
ricaduto in gran braci Algol Vega Sol nella lente d'insiemi
Ah l'esplosione del significare del comporre
per i bambini di Mezzaselva,
ah pedagogie!
e poi tanto shopping tra tutte queste belle

"I colori ti salvano"
(dal commento di un esperto a un Rorschach)
(ma che figura facevi nelle scenette di Rosenzweig...)
Adam forma futuri.

EDOARDO CACCIATORE

E doardo Cacciatore was born in Palermo in 1912. Besides poetry, he has written numerous philosophical essays. For many years he and his wife were the curators of the Shelley Museum in Rome.

Like Emilio Villa, Cacciatore has been strangely ignored by Italian and foreign critics. Like Zanzotto, Cacciatore often creates his own language from bits and pieces taken from sources ranging from newspapers to physics textbooks. The effect, however, is totally unique, and the act of reading (not to mention translating!) Cacciatore is of such a special nature that it merits description. That is, Cacciatore's work strikes the reader as an amazing rush not of individual words but of indivisible poetic snatches; indeed, the texture and structure of every poem are too rich in density for the effect to be otherwise. And if on the one hand this complicated act of reading disorients the reader, making him lose sight of a certainty as fundamental as "standard Italian", on the other hand Cacciatore makes such artful and concise use of phrasing, gender agreement, punctuation, rhythm, and sound associations as to draw the reader into his impressively allusive, original language and vision.

One feels how Cacciatore has penetrated into the mysteries of what, if alluded to in more traditional and less arduous ways, would remain totally inexpressible.

POETRY

L'identificazione intera (A Complete Identification) 1951
La restituzione (The Giving Back) 1955
Lo specchio e la trottola (The Mirror and the Top) 1960
Dal dire al fare cioé: la lezione delle cose (From The Telling To
    The Doing: The Lesson in Things) 1967
Tutti i poteri, Cinque presentimenti (Full Powers, Five Warning
    Signs) 1969
Ma chi é qui il responsabile? (But Who's in Charge Here?) 1974
La puntura dell'assillo (Bit By Torment) 1986
Graduali (Gradual Psalms) 1986
Itto 1994

from **Full Powers: Five Warning Signs**

First Warning Sign: Epiphany

III

Blast of anniversary excitement, true,
                         [but you induce in yourself
your usual yearnings--a sprinkling of paraphernalia
                                      [lit once again
by that sort of old-fashioned trembly light
                              [wrenched from reoiled fuses--
yearnings we acolutes, spartan commuters,
                                  [blow on and revive.
Descendents of a past that's slow to come among us,
its betrayed traditions hacked to pieces.
But these knickknacks are more than accessories here;
that's to say impure life should adopt them
(the bastard life of today is a necessity of circumstance).
A crowd of emotions throng around each annual return.
But in mutual dedications how much
will such an improvished touch spend? You ignore it till it's
precise happening and the breath of the run-up.
Panting is checked with a walk around, with
a walk around you have noon.

da **Tutti i poteri, Cinque presentimenti**

Presentimento primo--Il giorno dell'Epifania

III

Vento d'anniversario tira sì ma i soliti
Aneliti--parafernali sbuffi in luci
Così tremanti all'antica di nuovo fuori
Cavate da micce rimbevute - t'induci

Spoglie spole a alitarli oggi noi accoliti.
Posteri d'un passato che tra noi si attarda
Troncato in tratti di tradizione tradita
Questi ninnoli qui sono più che accessori
E li adotti perché no li adotti la vita
Spuria--l'odierna nostra è occorrenza bastarda.
Frotta d'emozioni accalca ogni annuo ritorno
Tuttavia in dediche mutue cosa sborsa
Un tal tocco da improvvisata? tu l'ignori
Fino al suo evento esatto e il soffio di rincorsa
Ansima è mozza in giro in giro hai mezzogiorno.

Second Warning Sign: the Game Heats Up

VI

Here--they've all started moving at once.
The standstill that tars the middle of the night
fuels the flashlamps and this throbbing makes headway.
Blood-sucking lizards and one heart per head is the
expired rule--for this the knarl of vehemence rewards them.
It sure is hard figuring out the cupola's piecework;
but, bolted to the centuries, the basilica
unlocks itself to the masses, and who most holds it at bay
for miles is tarnished in principle, and it seems like waverings;
the sacred is projected in sparks and the dazzlement is fine.
Hosts interpret the day ascending the scene
opposing the inclination to ruin.
There's fever in those effigies, and the narrow way continues on,
hitting and exciting them;
as the wind falls in all directions--
always opposite the Cinerama.

Presentimento secondo--Il giuoco si scatena

VI

Ecco--si sono messi in moto tutt'insieme
La stasi che a bitume notte fonda impegola
Lampeggiatori inietta e il palpitìo fa strada
Lucciole sanguisughe e un cuore a testa è regola
Perenta--perciò l'èmpito in groppo li preme.
Si tribolò sì a astrarre in cupola il cottimo
Ma la basilica imbullonata ai millenni
Si schiavarda in turba e chi più la tiene a bada
Per miglia appanna in principio e sembra tentenni
Sporto il sacro sta in scintille e il bagliore è ottimo.
Particole interpreti del giorno la scena
Vanno ascendendo avverso l'incline rovina
Febbre è in quelle effigi e per quanto il nerbo cada
In tutte le direzioni la via cammina
A cinerama in fronte--le eccita e mena.

IX

Let's try another hand, let's redo the count
of eternal cycles--whose wide-open pupils
are in the driver's seat behind the windshield
or intent on some red-tape procedure? Energy chooses and
compares for them--*crack*--their name, numbers and code.
Intercessional waves of prayer occur where once words

                                        were action;
legends that valiantly hug a cliff
used to have a port there but today
who fears anymore going off with strangers, arms outstretched,
I'm coming too, and luminous open artery is the sea.
It pulses flows pulses, the seconds wrinkle
but all the resources of serum and sediment are depleted.
He who chases and hunts has the enormous eyes of a suicide.
He's now got all the light inside him and says,

[*You're an acquaintance of mine.*
He won't have time to say, *I was wrong, cut me down.*

IX

Passiamo un'altra mano si rifà la conta
Dei cicli ininterrotti--che pupille sveglie
Dietro un parabrezza sono al posto di guida
O intente a una trafila? l'energía le sceglie
Crac il nome numeri e sigle lei raffronta.
Suffragio d'onde ha luogo ove fu il dire è il fare
Costeggiano strenuo un greppo ieri leggende
V'ebbero un porto ma oggi chi più diffida
D'andarsene tra estranei le braccia tende
Vengo anch'io e arteria a lume aperto è il mare.
Pulsa affluendo pulsa s'increspano gli attimi
Ma esauste le risorse in siero in sedimenti
Chi insegue e caccia gli occhi ha immensi del suicida
Pigliò in sé tutto il chiaro e fa *Tu mi frequenti*
Non l'avrà il tempo di dire *Ho sbagliato abbàttimi.*

Third Warning Sign: An Endless Surprise

I

There's nothing truer than fake fruit, let's say.
Its compass-perfect cheeks, its sunset season proud
against golds, drab pewter, bright china.
Unbelievably smooth is how the rain washes it;
in art or on a plate, it sits higher than on a branch.
It emits its still luster and an inspiring
pronouncement on the species--
as meanwhile the fame of others,
matured during the long wait, goes bad.
How natural--only here today it needs interpreting.
Yes there's a plot, cheating, unlawful seizure.

A gesture schemed up and carried out in aboveboard fashion.
Behind the slight sneer the usual bite that leaves its mark.
Man frees myth of the thornbush and it looks as easy
[as slipping
down to hell, but this nakedness--well, it's just fish scales
a truth to be snatched with both fists--and they call it a sham.

Presentimento terzo--La sorpresa senza fine

I

Vero talmente è un frutto ch'è finto diciamo
Guance compassa e stagione al tramonto sfoggia
Con ori e smorto peltro e ceramica accesa
Liscio incredibilmente lo lavò la pioggia
Ad arte e in un piatto sta assurto più che al ramo.
Immobile diffonde il suo lustro e con estro
Pronunzia la sua specie e intanto si fa grave
La fame altrui cresciuta durante l'attesa
Che naturalezza--oggi qui invece è a chiave
Il dramma sì c'è raggiro c'è sì sequestro.
Gesto si ordisce e perpetra non con l'inganno
Consueto dietro il ghignetto il morso che intaglia
Sprunano gli uomini il mito e sembra discesa
Agli inferi ma la nudità ecco è scaglia
Estorto in pugno il vero--posticcio lo dànno.

VII

Where do I stand and where do you? Seems like
we've lost our approximately and you don't know if
the left yields the right to the right or vice versa.
Shifts become less frequent and rounded out
and edges are not yellowish-brown as happens
with fruit--oranges, you'd say, and pears.

Friction is something else come loose from copulation.
Without an ergo of orgasm or extasy
things exhaust themselves, and form immersed in rhythm
complicates the substance, readies the dose.
The one who for someone was everything is not much.
Saturated pockets which no one will go without.
Even the one-handed can work magic and chromate passion,
concentrating into a knob the public's aspersed excitement;
but could it be that the one with the mechanical throat
inspires trust among the living?

VII

Dove sto io e dove tu? sembra d'avere
Smarrito il circa e non sai se la sinistra
Dà la destra alla destra o è viceversa
Dirada il turno e smussa e i contorni non bistra
Come ai frutti è invece e arance dicesti o pere.
L'attrito è un altro dalla copula è sciolto
Senza un ergo di orgasmo ed estasi le cose
Si spossano e la forma nel ritmo immersa
Complica la sostanza ne appronta la dose
L'uno che a qualcuno fu tutto non è molto.
Pregni interstizi e nessuno ne andrà privo
Prestidigita anche il monco e la foga croma
Perché a borchia aggranfi l'agitazione aspersa
Pubblicamente ma ha forse strozza d'automa
Chi fiducia immettendo va tra vivo e vivo?

EMILIO VILLA

E milio Villa was born near Milan in 1914. Probably the greatest of all Italian experimentalist poets (though not just an experimentalist), Villa has never received the recognition he deserves, neither in Italy nor abroad. By choice he lives today in nearly total isolation. An erudite man of vast learning, Villa devoted nearly a decade of his life to Biblical studies, semantics, and Ancient Greek, with a simply splendid translation to his credit of the *Odyssey* by Homer. From 1950 to 1970, Villa founded numerous literary magazines, both in São Paulo and in Rome. In addition to critical studies on art and literature and his works of poetry (parts of which are written directly in a range of foreign languages, including English, an example of which is included here), Villa is also an abstract artist: in May 1994 a retrospective exhibition was held in Milan of his drawings, paintings, and collages.

Villa's work in poetry has been so varied and prodigious that without the work of the critic Aldo Tagliaferri much of it might already have been lost. A seminal figure in the European avant-gardes, Villa has written many volumes of verse, concrete poetry and other experimental writing, all of which push the Italian language to its verbal and semantic limits. The problems of translating Villa's work are never-ending, for Italian in his hands becomes another language, with frequent "spillovers" into Latin, Greek, French, German, English, or Portuguese. At times, Villa even finds it necessary to use an invented language similar to Provençal.

On one of its many levels his poetry is an endless flow of sounds and vibrations destined to influence to reader in myste-rious ways. But it is really "the listener", rather than "the reader", that Villa wants to address, for his work--like that of Cacciatore's--must be read aloud to be appreciated; often the test itself resembles a musical score. If today in Italy there is much preoccupation with the "musicality" in poetry, contemporary poets owe this to Emilio Villa.

POETRY

Oramai (Now-Never) 1947
Heurarium 1959
Traité de pédérastie céleste (Treatise on Divine Pederasty) 1970
L'Homme qui descend quelque (The Man Who Descended Some) 1974
Hisse-toi re d'amour de mourire 1975
Opere, Volume 1 (Collected Works--Vol. I) 1989 (second volume to follow)

CRITICAL ESSAYS ON ARTISTS

Fontana 1947
Pollock 1950
Burri 1951
Wols 1952
Capogrossi e Rothko 1953
Piero Manzoni 1960
Attributi dell'arte odierna (collection of aforementioned essays) 1970

Natus de muliere, brevi vivens

Without doubt man in nature
was invented like a close-up
shout: hate,

ire, apparel; multiplying
in appearance or universal fever: born to hear
laws and faith, born of woman

so as to eat the leaf, to measure it
long, to measure it short,
swallow as much as he can

saliva; born of woman so as to eat the leaf, talk and want
manners of every sort,
the dry leather of shoe soles

makes teeth grind; he acts
chemical actions, things that are
lawful or unlawful, a free choice,

honest ones that make for a good impression, or
dishonor; commercial ones, generous, which
rook others and consume the desires and

freshness on a face;
which lead to nothing, cold ones that
bring on chills; servile ones that humiliate the

served and the servers;
public ones, which are strains not at all on the
light side, which take a long bit of work, and no heart

at last!; born of woman
he swears and goes about his business,
cunning or not, clean or immortal; he gets by,

he reads inside hearts, eyes,
inside stones and newspapers,
and as soon as he can, dies; he eats,

constructs conglomerated feelings
from phone books, slaps tiles
one on top of each other,

red tiles that use up a lot of mortar
and keep draughts off
joints and limbs,

and all right
but they can't talk
neither like flowers nor like a set of teeth:

making a man nothing but
a way like another
to get off the hook easy:

man, no one ever grants him that he's right
neither right nor wrong
and neither law nor faith;

and so he competes: actions
that he can neither know or want,
he measures, sells, believes, pulls out all stops

and obtains nothing: he will be
food for the latest disease, bait
for the darkest bacteria: why

because a dead body is narrow: the wind blows
hard and along with it the soul flees,
skiddish, vile, strong,

overtaken by the national passion:

and maybe it's

that maybe everyone here should
get away for a change: a bit of advice,
a decisive argument.

Natus de muliere, brevi vivens

L'uomo in natura senza dubbio
fu inventato come un grido
a bruciapelo: odio,

ira, indumenti; propagato
nell'apparenza, o febbre
universale: nato a sentire

legge e fede, nato di donna
per mangiar la foglia, per contarla
lunga, per contarla corta,

manda giù quanto più può
saliva: nato di donna
per mangiar la foglia, parla e vuole

maniere d'ogni sorta,
secco il corame delle suole,
fa digrignare i denti; agisce

azioni chimiche, cose
che son lecite o non sono, a voglia,
oneste che fan gran figura, o diso-

nore: commerciali, generose,
che fregano il prossimo, e consumano
i desideri e la freschezza al viso;

che non arrivano a niente, fredde
che mettono i brividi; servili
che umiliano serviti e servitori;

pubbliche, che son strapazzi
mica tanto lievi, che molta
opera chiedono, e non cuore,

finalmente! nato di donna,
sacramenta e fa i suoi fatti, scaltro
o no, igienici o immortali; s'arrangia,

legge nei cuori, negli occhi,
nelle pietre, nei giornali,
e, appena può, muore; mangia,

costruisce sentimentali agglomerati
sugli elenchi telefonici, sbatte
quadrelli uno in pigna all'altro,

i quadrelli rossi, che mangiano
calcina, difendono gli arti
e le giunture dai colpi d'aria,

e va bene
ma non possono parlare
come né i fiori, come né i denti:

fare l'uomo non è che una
maniera come un'altra
per scamparla bella:

uomo, nessuno gli dà mai ragione,
e né la ragione né il torto,
e né la legge né la fede;

e allora gareggia: azioni

che non può sapere né volere,
misura, vende, crede, tribola

e non ottiene: sarà cibo
al morbus novus, esca
ai batteri più scuri: perché

perché la salma è stretta; l'aria tira
forte, e via con essa l'alma
sfugge, temeraria, vile,

forte presa dal piacere
nazionale: e forse è

che forse qui bisogna cambiar aria
tutti quanti: è un consiglio,
un argomento decisivo.

excerpts from **Words**

An ugly season of putrifying buzzards,
sneaking away from wives for lack of foodspreads
                    [of scandals of orgasms
and of new affairs, it'll mean forgetting with indifference, and
with heart-felt expression, the fields picked over by
                    [one's close friends,
lands fenced, green trapezoids under afternoon lightening,
behind the embankments the tepid disagreements
                    [of a nationswide spring,
and the fountains of occult knowledge grain to grain
                    [the similarities of flowers
of winds of those breathless in unmarked places,
                    [and weeks that in
chiasmal overlaps the unanimous-inanimous flesh arises
                    [in the chiasmal overlaps

and it'll mean massacring the well-dressed cock
                    in the patchwork hamlets of Lombardy,
the gesture that robs the night of fresh blood, the trees
and the high altitudes of vain stars
and the North Star that crosses the paths
of horizontal coordinates, and it'll mean pushing again,
                                        [precisely like that,

candid ghosts against drastic horizons shattered by drums
and tearing off, like leaves, orthogonal directions and in empty
                                        [spheres sniffing
the ironwork among the panic roses and
the scent of dew from opposing farms and the crude reasoning
of the thousand anglings eradicated in the trouts' leap,
the sound spirals of shrapnell and the bare sky

the slow of the azaleas
true, you looked with your eyes into the liqueur of the Atlantic

1.

lend me a battle of unavoidable suggestions,
of mosquitoes of gaieties of classical manners
        [or impetuous ones, decisive, neither timid nor tender,
and typical contact with all which the accumulated
                                [foreboding of the future
will accumulate of the relatively extraordinary and of
the unusual power to be found in order, so to speak,
stemming from fear, hypothesis,
earthly boredom

more hot conjectures unimaginably large
roughly measured in the orbit of frenzies as if
one were looking straight down the plank used by divers:
                                        [as if to say,
more or less, cross-eyed, or something like that, on a diagonal,
                                        [and so on

well, blow me apparent speculations already tried out
                                    [in a chiasma
of cuts and links   the total rightness of the distant
married to the omnipresent

please, let me have that lightening-fast consultancy
                                    [which goes unhonored by
bold symbol give me your solemn pauses
(increased, if anything!)   and sing to me on an abacus
                    the magnificent matter
                    of parabolas without matter
                    of glances without meaning
                    of vacations
                    of small, infernal acts of carelessness

sing to me of ascertainable directions that meet up
                                    [with each other
in the spectral safe-and-sound of intensity   the rip
in the sides of the shroud, the temple curtain
prex (orphic) pex (perspective)

the algebraic dimension of things shattered intensifies the forms
most genteel most cunning most exhalted most general of the
finalizing gesture, Dies Irae

and concentrates the last bits of human intellect
in an inaccessible hollow of curses   as if in
a palm of a hand or in a lake of reasoned air
or music-scored air while they screech

on the record of horizontal divinity, scissor, awl,
knife, leather-punch, pitch and string

2.

trees were moving
rocks were gods

the sea possessed a body and head

all images were of polluted
silence, all figures were the pulp
of the invisible, all lips
strong as shoulder blades and jaws.

the wind was seed
the voice a process of hydrogenization
language was the seasons--
extreme, not eliminated

smells were frost and night,
and time was that--such that--
the soul: "distance for equality",
and numbers madness, the purest madness

music was a knot, was
a mat, and effort
was a shadow constantly contemplated
in inconceivable multiplications
crossing attritions juxtapositions

force for form was the wedge
and the soul of the future was the soul of an undivided soul
and so we read together
enuma eliš theogonistical rancors
and the inescapable silly stuff in Kierkegaard
and the curses of the
Old Testament.

4. (NB: Villa wrote this part in English)

it is world of the back hune wone it is
it is world of the horse half heart head
it is world of the workwork it is is

it is father of the snakewife
it is world of the tree and tree and
and it other is father of the other
and of the all all all all other.

what is it? native. what and why?
why, christ, why, we tell. alien.
I tell: yes. I. native and alien. Signe
vivant. I. signe signe signe. with mien
with deep mien and dark drag.

what is it and what other? what
between it-rock-ruin and other (water,
fire, air)? between I and me
is water, fire, air and all streaming chaos?

it is work of work and it
is world of the world of the horse
upon trees and fragrant breath

as pleasure. revolves and dies. I
see, now and plus tard. plus
tard de la lune

word wind wife blowing
espace tombé d'après nature:
what is it? christ! what is time?
I felt what. I felt what
all kingdom is workwork
of the snake-abyss, as native
olives and all alien things.

e givme a tickling spring, christ,
with wings and with
hushed rumbles and exquisite resemblances.

and talk me and tell dark hours

dark oblivions dark tree dark
leaves dark darkness and
whitering water. it is
a world in intimo semine

da **Le parole**

Una stagionaccia di tumescenti avvoltoi,
svignate le mogli per mancanza di cibarie di scandali di orgasmi
e d'altre storie, toccherà dimenticare con indifferenza,
[e con sentita
espressione, i campi spremuti degli amici intimi, i terreni
recinti, i verdi trapezi con i lampi pomeridiani, i tiepidi
screzi della primavera nazionale dietro i terrapieni, e le fontane
occulte del sapere grano a grano le similitudini dei fiori
dei venti dei trafeli nei luoghi non segnati, e le settimane
che nei chiasmi risorge la carne unanime-inanime nei chiasmi

e massacrare il gallo forbito tra i brughi lombardi
il gesto che trafughi alla notte il sangue fresco gli alberi e le alte
quote degli astri vanitosi, e la polare che valica i sentieri
delle ascisse, e risospingere proprio così

contro i drastici orizzonti frantumati dai tamburi
[i candidi fantasmi
e sfogliare le direzioni ortogonali e nelle vuote
sfere annusare le ferraglie tra le rose paniche e il sentore
di rugiada dai poderi avversi e il crudo
raziocinio delle millesime angolature divelte
[nel guizzo delle trote,
le cuspidi sonore degli shrapnell e il cielo nudo

lento delle azalee,
vero che tu vedevi nel liquore dell'atlantico con gli occhi

1.

imprestami una battaglia di suggestioni tassative, di zanzare di
allegrie di classiche maniere o impetuose, decise, non timide
[né tenere

e caratteristici contatti con tutto quello che il presentimento
accumulato nel futuro accumula di relativamente straordinario
[e di
inconsueta potenza nell'ordine, diciamo così, per paura,
[per ipotesi,
per noia terrestre

calde congetture in più e di grandezza inimmaginabile
liberamente misurata nell'orbita delle frenesie   come
se uno guarda dritto sull'asse dei capofitti: come a dire,
press'a poco, strabico, sguercio, o simili, di sbieco, e via

beh, spirami speculazioni apparenti e sperimentate nel chiasmo
dei tagli e delle congiunture   la piena ragione del distante
coniugato con l'ubiquo

cedimi, prego, la fulminea consulenza prestata dal simbolo
temerario   cedimi le tue pause solenni
(aumentate, magari!) e cantami sul pallottoliere
            la materia magnifica
            delle parabole senza materia
            delle occhiate senza ragione
            delle vacanze
            delle sbadataggini infernali

cantami i disastri accertabili che s'incontrano di solito
nell'incolume spettrale della intensità   lo squarcio
sui fianchi del sudario, velum templi

prex (orphica) pex (perspectiva)
intensifica la dimensione algebrica del lacero   le forme

più gentili più scaltre più esaltate più generali del gesto
finalizio, dies irae

e concentra gli ultimi frammenti di umano intelletto
in un cavo inaccessibile di improperi   come in un
palmo di mano o in un lago d'aria ragionata
o musicata aria mentre stridono
sul disco della divinità orizzontale forbice e lesina
coltello punteruolo pece e spago

2.

gli alberi si sposavano
le pietre erano gli dèi
il mare possedeva corpo e capo.

le immagini erano il silenzio
inquinato. le figure erano la polpa
dell'invisibile. e le labbra
forti come le scapole e le mascelle.

seme era il vento.
la voce un processo di idrogenazioni.
il linguaggio erano le stagioni
estreme, non eliminate.

gli odori erano gelo e notte,
e il tempo che, tale che.
l'anima era lontananza per uguaglianza,
e il numero follia purissima follia.

la musica era il nodo era
la stuoia. e lo sforzo
era l'ombra fissamente considerata
in inconcepibili moltipliche
incroci attriti giustapposizioni

forza per forma era il cuneo
e l'anima futura era l'anima
dell'anima senza divisione.

e così leggemmo insieme
l'enuma eliš i rancori
teogonistici e le sciocchezze
senza scampo di Kierkegaard
e le maledizioni dell'antico
testamento.

GIULIA NICCOLAI

G iulia Niccolai was born in Milan in 1934 of an American mother and an Italian father. By training she is a photo-journalist. For many years she co-directed with the late poet Adriano Spatola the experimental literary magazine *Tam Tam*. She has frequently participated in exhibition-performances-readings of concrete poetry, and *poesia sonora* ("sound poetry" incorporating music or musical principles). A polyglot by background and choice, she has translated and-or written poetry in French and English. Her Italian translations from English and American literature include Gertrude Stein's *Geographical History of America*.

Niccolai's longest and perhaps most characteristic work of poetry, *Frisbees*, shares with that flying plastic disc of collegiate fame the misleadingly simple shape that surprises on account of its strange and sudden evolutions. The 'frisbees' included here are of two types: anecdotal prose paragraphs connected and yet seemingly unconnected with each other; and extremely rapid, ironic poems that expand on brief or innocent situations in a comic or even grotesque style which leaves its surrealistic mark upon the reader.

On the surface, word play is what Niccolai's relationship with language is all about. (She calls language "a garden to cultivate".) But on a more profound level, language for Giulia Niccolai is also nostalgia: a return to a place, a condition, a person. Links which can be read in new ways, fused together in an everlasting present; links that poetry reveals to us at the same time as it itself names the conditions whereby the revelation can continue.

POETRY

Poema e oggetto (Poem and Object) 1974
Harry's Bar e altre poesie (1969-1980) (Harry's Bar and Other
   Poems) 1981
Singsong for a New Year's Adam and Eve (published in English)
   1982
Lettera aperta (Open Letter) 1983
Frisbees in facoltà (Frisbees by Right) 1984
Frisbees (poesie da lanciare) (Frisbees--poems to toss) 1994

Fiction

Il grande angolo (Wide Angle) 1966
Escursioni sulla via Emilia (Excursions Along the Via Emilia)
   1986

from **Frisbees**

Careful that these *Frisbees*
may become nauseating.
The order they follow each other in is important.

Certainly there may be something
as yet elusive
in all this
whether for me or for you!
I'm becoming a committed poetess.
I'm becoming a committed poetess?

To be able to fathom
the morning after,
serenely,
by the light of day,
that even my own presumption
and stupidity
are bottomless,
are limitless...
is a most beautiful thing...

Bach is beautiful to have in the blood.
The organist and harpsichordist
who plays Johann Sebastian
is named Janos Sebestyen.
What else could he do?

I gave myself a clay-mask
facial with the "Orchestral Toccata"
(in E major BWV 566)
by Bach.

The way I walk
has always made me wear down

the outside edge of the heels of my shoes.
Playing *Frisbees*
I'd like to begin wearing down a little
the inside one as well.
For equilibrium.
I'd also like the *Frisbees*
to help me
make my mind work
a new way.
Do I ask too much?
For this purpose
it might do good
to start calling them
Frisbeezen or *Zen-frisbees*.

So what's this?
A *Frisbee* of head or legs?

And why didn't I write
a *Frisbee* of legs or head?

(The first steps
are always a little problematic)...

IS asks passing through Piazza Sempione:
"So is this called
Arch of Peace or
Arch of Triumph?"
"Triumph in Paris, Peace in Milan".

When I wrote yesterday
that I gave myself
a clay-mask facial
with the "Orchestral Toccata"
I meant to say
that the "Orchestral Toccata"--
while being toccata and played--

dissolved on my face,
smoothed away
the lumps of anxiety and fear.

One of the reasons why
as a girl I was a photographer
was that I could
always study behind the camera,
never in front.
(In fact, who photographs
is almost never photographed).
Not in the mirror
but in the photos that caught me
I made out the fear on my face.

Anna glances
at the first page of *Frisbees*
and asks me:
"Are they all about food?"
"Minestrone, minestrone," I tell her.

G. G. F. fired one of his editors
with a gun in his hand.
Evidently G. G. F.
was thinking in English
while he was doing it...

Cultivating language like a vegetable patch
Cultivating the vegetable patch like language.
Picking peahs and string beans
reminds me of correcting proof.
How you never are able to
spot all the mistakes.
Through oversight a couple always remain on the plant.

Evidently
but unknown to me,

I am beginning to practise
surrealist automatic writing
or surrealist automatic writing is beginning to practise me.
See the *Frisbees* about the facial mask
that follows the one on Janos.
Janus. Two-faced Janus.

Affectionately I would call my father "Rhinoceros",
"old yellow Rhinoceros".
Years after his death
I dreamt of a rhinoceros
sniffing with his long horn
at a poppy in the field.
And he got furious.
He got beastly
and pissed off
because with his horn (stopped up)
he couldn't smell the scent.
(In the dream I knew that
poppies have no smell
but I didn't dare get too close to the rhinoceros
to tell him).
In the distance the rhinoceros
stomped and fumed.
Then in anger, with contempt,
he pissed on the poppy.
POPPY
POP PEE
Ciao, Sigmund!

Food for thought.
We do not teach
And we are not taught.
And we are not taut...

Roman Polanski.

And we have a Roman Polanski Pope.
It was Paul Vangelisti
from Los Angeles
who made me realize
that Poles and Italians resemble each other.
Petrus, where are you?
I missed you at the *Pasticceria*.
They make an excellent Paradise Pie.
Ça va sans dire...

Seen the other night
in the wings
at San Maurizio
after the Bach concert:
a cello case
used as a hanger
for a man's jacket.
Dear Man Ray, was that your jacket draped on the case as
on a dummy? Did you put it there while playing
                              ["Le Violon d'Ingres"?

That *Frisbee* written
I feel the urge to consult
Man Ray Photographer (Idea Books)
and as soon as I open it
my eye lights on the name
Manrico Nicolai
commissioner of Pietrasanta
author of the brief introduction.

I think magic
brushes against us continually.
It's our fault
if we don't recognize it.
If we don't understand it...

Dear Giorgio,

Dear Dioloch,
could a *Freeze*
be
frozen words in space
which want to fly?
Or a *bee* looking for honey?
Or an Hamletic *be*?...

In *Auto da Fè*
written in 1935
Elias Canetti
created Fischerle
a dwarf
chess player
who dreams of going to America,
beating Capablanca,
and calling himself Fischer.
Tiens tiens: Bobby Fischer!

Elias Canetti
in the photo for the Nobel
has white hair.
Tiens tiens: Capablanca!...

These last *Frisbees*
I've recopied
from the marble top
of the kitchen table.
Written in pencil
like the sums
of the butcher d'antan.

I tell the cashier at the *"Scimmie"*
I want to pay for two reds
"Wine?" he asked me.
(He must be very politicized).

Soon after at the bar
I see Pavese's double
and Sanguineti's double.
Can these possibly be
the cashier's two reds?...

Corrado tells me
he keeps a house full
of *full* honey jars.
Not to eat.
Just to look at.

(But look!
Sex!
What liberties it takes!
What transformations!)...

To explain to her woman friends
American and English
how little she knew Italian
my mother would always say:
"I give *tu* to strangers
and *lei* my husband".

I have never understood
whether she realized what she was saying.
But perhaps my playing with words
comes from having understood
the double meaning of that *lei*.

I was born 12-21-34.
12 and 21 are anagrammatic
and so we have 1,2,3,4.
It would be elegant
to die at 56
to be able to make 1,2,3,4,5,6.
I'll be 56 in '90.

1991 would be better though.
It would make pair with 12-21.
In this case I'd favor
a stone planned this way:
Born 12-21-1934
Died 3-4-1991.
But Giulia,
we can't have everything in life!

When I'll want to embrace you
and you'll happen not to be around...
I'll start washing
your heavy, large, English woollen cardigan.
I'll get into the tub with it...

Perhaps even Geppetto
knew English.
Anyhow,
it can be read like this:
the wood is the would...

We could throw Frisbees eternally
and they would make haloes
        haloes
          haloes...

Da **Frisbees**

Attenta che i *Frisbees*
possono diventare nauseanti.
È importante l'ordine in cui si susseguono.

Certo che può esserci qualcosa
che ancora sfugge
sia a me che a voi
in tutto questo!

Sto diventando una poetessa impegnata
Sto diventando una poetessa impegnata?

Poter constatare
la mattina dopo,
serenamente,
alla luce del giorno
che anche la propria presunzione
e stupidità
non hanno fondo
non hanno limite
...
è una cosa bellissima...

Bach è bello averlo nel sangue.
L'organista e clavicembalista
che suona Johann Sebastian
si chiama Janos Sebastyen.
cos'altro poteva fare?

Mi sono fatta
una maschera facciale
con la *Toccata concertata*
(in mi maggiore BWV 566)
di Bach.

Il modo in cui cammino
mi ha sempre fatto consumare
il lato esterno dei tacchi delle scarpe.
Giocando a *Frisbee*
vorrei cominciare a consumare un po'
anche quello interno.
Per equilibrare.
Vorrei anche che i *Frisbees*
mi aiutassero
a far funzionare il cervello
in modo nuovo.

Chiedo troppo?
A questo scopo
potrebbe essere utile
cominciare a chiamarli
Frisbeezen o *Zen-frisbees*.

E questo cos'è?
Un *Frisbee* di testa o di gambe?

E perché non ho scritto
un *Frisbee* di gambe o di testa?

(I primi passi
sono sempre un po' problematici)

Chiede IS passando per Piazza Sempione:
"Ma questo si chiama
Arco della Pace o
Arco di Trionfo?"
"Trionfo a Parigi, Pace a Milano".

Quando ieri ho scritto
che mi sono fatta
una maschera facciale
con la *Toccata concertata*
intendevo dire
che la *Toccata concertata*
--mentre veniva toccata e concertata--
mi scioglieva sul volto,
mi spianava
i grumi di ansia e di paura.

Una delle ragioni per cui
da ragazza ho fatto la fotografa
è anche quella
di essere sempre dietro la macchina fotografica
e mai davanti.

(Infatti, chi fotografa
non viene quasi mai fotografato).
Non allo specchio
ma nelle fotografie che mi ritraevano
distinguevo la paura sul mio volto.

Anna dà un'occhiata
alla prima cartella di *Frisbees*
e mi chiede
"Sono tutti sul cibo?"
"Minestrone, minestrone". le rispondo.

G. G. F. fired one of his editors
with a gun in his hand.
Evidently G. G. F.
was thinking in English
while he was doing it...

Ho due portacenere
a forma di cuore.
Lo so che fumo troppo.
Mi farò cremare.

Coltivare il linguaggio come l'orto.
Coltivare l'orto come il linguaggio.
Raccogliere i pistelli e le taccole
mi ricorda la correzione delle bozze.
Come gli errori
non si riesce mai a individuarli tutti.
Per svista ne rimangono un paio sulla pianta.

Evidentemente
ma
a mia insaputa,
sto cominciando a praticare
la scrittura automatica surrealista
oppure

la scrittura automatica surrealista
sta cominciando a praticare me.
Vedi il *Frisbee* della maschera facciale
che segue quello su Janos.
Giano. Giano Bifronte.
Chiamavo mio padre affettuosamente "Rinoceronte",
"Rinoceronte ingiallito".
Anni dopo la sua morte
ho sognato un rinoceronte
che, con il lungo corno,
annusava un papavero in un campo.
E si infuriava,
si imbestialiva
e si incazzava
perché con il corno (otturato)
non era in grado di sentirne il profumo.
(Io, nel sogno sapevo
che i papaveri non hanno odore
ma non osavo avvicinarmi al rinoceronte
per dirglielo).
Il rinoceronte da lontano
si dimenava e scalciava.
Poi, per rabbia, per spregio,
pisciò sul papavero.
Ci fece sopra una lunga, poderosa pisciata.
PAPAVERO.
PAPA' VERO.
Ciao, Sigmund!

Food for thought.
We do not teach
And we are not taught.
And we are not taut.

Roman Polanski.
E abbiamo un Papa Roman Polanski.
È stato Paul Vangelisti

di Los Angeles
a farmi capire
che polacchi e italiani si assomigliano.
Petrus, dove sei?
Mi sei mancato alla *Pasticceria*.
Fanno un'ottima Torta Paradiso,
ça va sans dire...

Vista l'altra sera
dietro le quinte
a San Maurizio
dopo un concerto di Bach:
la custodia di un violoncello
usata come gruccia
per una giacca da uomo.
Caro Man Ray, era tua la giacca drappeggiata
                              [sulla custodia come
su un manichino? L'avevi messa lì mentre suonavi
                              [il Violon d'Ingres?

Scritto il *Frisbee*
mi prende la voglia di consultare
Man Ray Fotografo (Idea Books)
e appena lo apro
l'occhio mi cade sul nome di
Manrico Nicolai
assessore di Pietrasanta
che firma una breve introduzione al libro.

Credo che la magia
ci sfiori in continuazione.
È colpa nostra
se non la riconosciamo.
Se non l'apprezziamo...

Caro Giorgio,
Caro Diòloch,

could a *Freeze*
be
frozen words in space
which want to fly?
Or a *bee* looking for honey?
O un'amletica *be*?...

In *Auto da fé*
scritto nel '35
Elias Canetti
crea Fischerle
un nano
giocatore di scacchi
che sogna di andare in America
battere Capablanca
e chiamarsi Fischer.
Tiens, tiens: Bobby Fischer!

Elias Canetti
nelle foto del Nobel
ha i capelli bianchi.
Tiens, tiens, Capablanca!...

Questi ultimi (Frisbees)
li ho ricopiati
al piano di marmo
dal tavolo in cucina.
Scritti a matita
come i conti
dei macellai d'antan.

Chiedo di pagare due rossi
al cassiere delle *Scimmie*.
"Vino?" mi chiede lui
(Deve essere molto politicizzato).

Dopo poco al bar

vedo il sosia di Pavese
e il sosia di Sanguineti.
Saranno mica questi allora
i due rossi del cassiere?...

Corrado mi dice
di avere la casa piena
di vasetti di miele *pieni*.
Non da mangiare.
Solo da guardare.

(Ma tu guarda!
Il sesso!
Che razza di libertà si prende!
Che trasformismi!)...
Per spiegare alle sue amiche
americane e inglesi
quanto poco sapesse l'italiano,
mia madre era solita dire:
"I give *tu* to strangers
and *lei* my husband".

Non ho mai capito
se capisse quello che diceva.
Ma forse risale al fatto di aver capito
il doppio senso di quel *lei*
il mio giocare con la parola.

Sono nata il 21-12-'34
21 e 12 sono anagrammati
e poi abbiamo anche 1,2,3,4.
Potrebbe essere elegante morire a 56 anni
per poter fare 1,2,3,4,5,6.
Avrò 56 nel '90.
Il 1991 però andrebbe meglio.
Farebbe da pendant al 21-12.
In questo caso sarei favorevole

a una lapide così concepita:
Nata il 21-12-1934
Morta il 3-4-1991.
Difficile scegliere tra i 56 anni
e il 1991.
Ma Giulia,
non si può avere tutto dalla vita!

When I'll want to embrace you
and you'll happen not to be around...
I'll start washing
your heavy, large, English woollen cardigan.
I'll get into the tub with it...

Forse anche Geppetto
sapeva l'inglese.
Comunque,
lo si può leggere
anche così:
the wood is the would.
Si potrebbero lanciare Frisbees per l'eternità
e si farebbero aureole
                aureole
                        aureole...

from **Frisbees '88**

(...)
    "What's that?" the boy asks his mother, pointing to the flag
over the entrance to the nursery school she's taken him to. "It's
the Italian flag," she tells him in a neutral voice, with just a
slight hint of wanting to teach him something. "*Red, white and
blue*".

    At nine sharp the phone wakes me up and a woman's voice
with a strong Southern accent asks me to hold for a moment.

Rock music blares from the receiver for over a minute. Then the woman's voice returns to say: "If you know the title of this song I'll give you a million lires."

I apologize for not knowing it and try to justify myself by saying I haven't listened to this sort of music in years. I mean to say that I tried to respond with polite reasonable words, since in no way did the woman's voice lead me to think this was a joke.

I thought rather it was a case of visual illiteracy. The T.V. series "Backwards Astern" had ended about a week before and my suspicion was that the woman was incapable of fathoming the irony.

I imagined a monsterous sort of solitude.

A desert.

Passing by the flower-stand in Piazza Aquileia I hear the florist explain to a lady: "The rosebuds are sold in bunches of ten each; otherwise, one all alone wouldn't say much to anyone."

I continue on silently. That's exactly what I want, one that's quiet.

G. E., a teacher just back from a trip to Paris with her students, tells me that what she liked most this time was the Eiffel Tower. It looked to her like a giraffe.

In the waiting room of the eye clinic at "San Raffaele" Hospital, I hear a girl say to the doctor that her brother is much better now. Still, ever since the day those few drops of bleach accidentally got into his eyes, he continues to see colors a bit faded.

On the walls of Milan appear a huge pair of flying lips in close-up heavily smeared with lipstick. Underneath there's a car and the message: *Polo. Kissed by success.*

I think of poor Man Ray. Then after a moment I have fun thinking of this ad as the image of myself "before treatment", that's to say of my narcissistic ego avid for success. Well, if not exactly success (I wasn't so naive as to believe that success comes from writing poetry nowadays), then at least it was a matter of my ego looking for a bit of recognition, this without doubt. 'What a prison that was,' I admit myself after passing by the billboard. It's only now (three years later) that time and distance allow me to see the trap I didn't ended up in.

But having spit this all out, it's only right to make another, subtler observation.

The recognition my ego was after *didn't* concern me as a whole person, me as the woman in front of you, Giulia Niccolai, 53 years of age.

Only a part of me deep down and in silence desired this type of compensation, nostalgic for the devotion and gratitude I had felt for certain poets and writers when I was young. For the quality and the wholeness of that esteem which made me strong and invulnerable and which now has been lost to all.

I honestly don't believe there's anyone young who can feel such things about a writer today. The world's changed and less ingenious.

I have the suspicion--continuing suspicion--that it's touching on an important truth to say that revolution is nostalgia. And I'm positive that writing is, too...

Though the following may make me unpopular , though it may pass for an instance of masochism or worse, and though the Devil is very good in loading the dice I'll say it anyway: pain is light.   (I'm bound to know something about this, for the anagram of the name 'Giulia Niccolai' is *joy, lights, throws.*

Pain is light because it forces us to see what we do everything to avoid, namely pain...

Ever so often certain expressions that I heard as a child and that aren't said anymore come back to mind. When I think, say, of "and that's the end to the bucket!", I begin to smile and imagine the scene. A man or a woman hauls a full bucket of water up from the depths of a well. Suddenly the cord chain breaks, or else someone makes the bucket drop back down after it's been set on the edge.

Being full, the bucket doesn't float but sinks and ends up at the very bottom of the well where it's always dark as night and where no one can find it again.

It's great thinking that the moon's reflection shines down there in the well too.

I put all these *frisbees* together cutting and snipping here and there from the jottings in my datebook for this past year. Going backwards into the past in homage to or in conformity with the brief passage on revolution, writing and nostalgia.

Should anyone desire to, therefore, he can actually start reading them here, starting from *nostalgia*, and ending with *"What's that?"*.

Da Frisbees '88

Che cos'è?, chiede il bimbo alla mamma, indicando la bandiera sopra il portone della scuola materna dove lei lo sta accompagnando. È la bandiera italiana, gli risponde la madre in tono neutro, appena un po' didattico: bianca, rossa e blu.

Vengo svegliata alle 9 in punto dal telefono e dalla voce di una donna che con forte accento meridionale mi chiede di attendere un attimo. Dal ricevitore comincia a diffondersi una musica rock che dura più di un minuto. Torna poi la voce della donna che dice: se sa il titolo della canzone le regalo un milione.
Mi scuso perché non la conosco e cerco di giustificarmi dicendo che non seguo più da anni questo tipo di musica.
Ho tentato insomma di rispondere con delle parole educate, ragionevoli, perché dal tono di voce della donna non poteva essermi venuto in mente che si trattasse di uno scherzo.
Ho pensato piuttosto a un caso di analfabetismo visivo. Le puntate di *Indietro tutta* sono terminate da poco più di una

settimana e il mio sospetto era che la donna non avesse potuto capirne l'ironia. Ho pensato a una solitudine mostruosa. Al deserto.

Passando davanti al chiosco di Piazza Aquileia, sento la fioraia che spiega a una signora: le roselline si vendono a mazzetti da dieci altrimenti da sole non dicono niente. Proseguo ripetendomi in silenzio: appunto, ne vorrei una che stesse zitta.

L'insegnante G. E. che è appena tornata da una gita a Parigi con i suoi alunni, mi dice che questa volta la cosa che le è piaciuta di più è stata la Torre Eiffel. Le è sembrata una giraffa.

Nella sala d'attesa del reparto oculistico dell'ospedale S. Raffaele, sento una ragazza che dice al medico che ora suo fratello sta meglio. Tuttavia, dopo l'incidente in cui gli erano entrate delle gocce di candeggina nell'occhio, continua a vedere i colori un po' sbiaditi.

Appaiono sui muri di Milano labbroni in volo, scontornati e fortemente imburrati di rossetto con sotto un'automobilina e la scritta: *Polo. Baciata dal successo.*
Penso al povero Man Ray. Poi però mi diverte attribuire la pubblicità al mio Ego di prima-della-cura, al mio Ego narcisistico desideroso di successo. Beh, non proprio di successo (non ero così illusa da credere che ai giorni nostri esistesse il successo in poesia), ma certo il mio Ego cercava un po' di riconoscimento, questo sì e non ci sono dubbi. Che galera è stata quella, mi confesso dopo aver superato il manifesto, ora che il distacco e il tempo (sono passati 3 anni), mi permettono di vedere la trappola nella quale mi ero andata a cacciare.
Ma, sputato il rospo, è giusto che aggiunga qua un'altra osservazione, più sottile.

Il riconoscimento che il mio Ego desiderava, non riguardava me in toto, non l'immagine di me che appare, non Giulia Niccolai poetessa di 53 anni.

Solo una parte di me, nel profondo e in silenzio, esigeva questo tipo di risarcimento per nostalgia della devozione e della gratitudine che avevo provato adolescente verso certi poeti e scrittori. Per la qualità, la pienezza di quella stima che mi rendevano forte, invulnerabile e che sono andate perdute per tutti.

Non credo infatti che alcun giovane le possa più provare oggi per un letterato. Il mondo è meno ingenuo ed è così cambiato.

Ho il sospetto, il continuo sospetto di sfiorare una verità importante quando mi dico che la rivoluzione è nostalgia. E ho la certezza che anche la scrittura lo sia...

Per quanto questa asserzione possa rendermi impopolare, per quanto possa venire presa per masochismo o altro, per quanto Lucifero sia abile nel cambiare le carte in tavola, lo dico lo stesso: il dolore è luce. (Ne so qualcosa perché anagrammando il nome Giulia Niccolai si ottiene: gioia luci lanci).

Il dolore è luce perché ci costringe a vedere ciò che facciamo di tutto per evitare: il dolore...

Ogni tanto mi tornano alla mente certe espressioni che udivo bambina e che ormai sono cadute in disuso. Quando penso a: *e buonanotte al secchio!* mi viene da sorridere e mi figuro la scena. Un uomo o una donna tirano su dal pozzo un secchio pieno d'acqua. La catena o la corda si spezza o inavvertitamente qualcuno fa cadere il secchio dopo che è stato issato sul bordo.

Essendo pieno, il secchio non galleggia, affonda, finisce sul fondo del pozzo dove è sempre buio, dove è notte e dove nessuno potrà più ripescarlo.

Bello è pensare che la luna si riflette anche nel pozzo.

Ho messo insieme questi *frisbees* spulciano a ritroso tra gli appunti dell'agenda di quest'anno. A ritroso, in omaggio o in conformità al breve testo sulla rivoluzione, la scrittura e la nostalgia.

Volendo si potrebbe dunque cominciare a leggerli da qui, da *nostalgia*, per finire a *che Che cos'è?*.

SECOND GENERATION:
Poets born between 1935 and 1945

CESARE GREPPI

Cesare Greppi was born in 1936 in Pezzana, a small village near Vercelli. In 1961 he obtained his degree in Italian Literature, soon after which he moved to Milan and began teaching secondary school. During the sixties he and friends founded several small (and in a certain sense 'fringe') magazines, *Ant-ed* and *Pianura*, where they bluntly expressed all their uneasiness with the phenomenon of the Neo-Avant-garde.

From 1974 to 1981 Greppi lived and worked as a cultural attaché for the Italian Embassies in Madrid, Spain and Bordeaux, France. Upon his return to Milan he reassumed teaching Italian at the *liceo* level until his retirement in 1994. Besides poetry, Greppi has done numerous book-length translations of such authors as Gòngora, Cortàzar, Ronsard, and Bonnefoy for leading Italian publishing houses.

Greppi uses words sparingly and the terms he does choose are extremely precise; yet because language always contains in it the riddle of its own uncontrollable allusions and nuances, Greppi is in reality playing with its unavoidable ambiguity: a poem seems to be traveling along one route that unforseeably becomes another. The tone is soft, and the familar sort of vocabulary, as well as the adjectival diminutives, create a sort of hush, preparing the reader for the delicate maneuvering that is to follow.

POETRY

L'opposta persuasione (The Opposite Persuasion) 1963
Descrizioni della poesia (Poetry Descriptions) 1970
Stratagemmi (Stratagems) 1979
Saeptus septies 1987
Supplementi alle ore del giorno e della notte (Supplements to the Hours of Night and Day) 1989
Corona (Crown) 1991
Omaggio (Homage) 1993 (published in the magazine *Idra* 7)

FICTION

I testimoni (The Witnesses) 1982 (a novella)

If you dropped me on the table,
on a board, on glass,
in a place where rustling
and trembling like a leaf or mouse
would be an excessive reaction.
Or if a message would fall
from the branch above;
it sits in the grass like a piece of fruit,
swaying it between what's more and what's less,
but definitely slanted towards you.

Mi lasciassi cadere su tavola,
su assicella, su vetro,
in un punto che stormire
e trepidare come foglia e topo
fosse risposta smodata.
Oppure se cadesse dal ramo
più alto un biglietto:
sta nell'erba come un frutto,
dondola fra più e meno,
e verso il tuo pendio.

What words must rush in
and then here get
sleepy.

(Like a little girl rising
and seeing how the night will be.)

The hidden splendour
of this contract:
shut them off, please, and
list them as soft sentinels.

Quali parole debbono
precipitosamente
venire e qui avere
il sonno.

(Così si alza una bambina
e vede come sarà
la notte.)

Lo splendore clandestino
di un contratto
per chiuderle nel tempo
freddo e sotto il nome
di dolci sentinelle.

A subtle erratic vocation
musical musical
that doesn't mix with anything:
no season renders it
not even this temperate one
the color of vertical milk,
the most natural white
affirmed live
between erasings.

la sottile vocazione intermittente
musicale musicale
non si combina con niente:
non c'è stagione che renda
e nemmeno questa continente
color di latte verticale
il più naturale bianco
vivo affermativo
fra tutte le cancellature

Those quiet little feet in the reflected room
remain with me:
one step two steps from the faint myriad;
over the flame of names
silently simmers the ideal, marking time,
awaiting final evaporation
(forget the rest)
things experiencing "that lucky touch"
slow adjustments.

sono ancora con me
i quieti piedini della stanza riflessa
su su dal fioco visibilio:
al caldo dei nomi si crogiola
il quieto modello, o ritardante,
fino alle sue ultime esalazioni
(dimenticato il resto)
"cose toccate con mano felice"
aggiustamenti lenti

A rain of hollow malice
(and you laugh and cry) as if high above
baby buzzards   roosters   silences
(He's got a hunger and thirst all his own;
and look what legs he walks on!)
Between solid symmetrical cases,
between wetting and not wetting,
between reflecting and not reflecting,
a rain of white malice
(nothing!) and bristled fur.

una pioggia di cava malizia
(e ridi e piangi) come in alto
grifoncini galli silenzi

(ha la sua fame e la sua sete
e su quali gambe cammina!)
fra solidi simmetrici casi
fra bagna e non bagna
fra specchia e non specchia
una pioggia di bianca malizia
(nulla!) e d'arricciato pelo

Like a handful of leaves,
sinking, adhering to the bottom--
no better put together than that--
he called out:
"Stop it, eat the right things."
Even the water--
rapid muscles, brownish guardian--
turned on its tail.
Not in the thick of the
woods, no,
but in the garden,
in the land of stutters.

Come una manciata
di foglie, immersa, non meglio
compiuta, chiamò,
stampo del fondo:
"chiudi, mangia cose buone".
Anche l'acqua, rapidi
muscoli, bruna custode,
rivoltò la sua coda.
Questo nel folto
del bosco no,
ma nel giardino, nel regno
del balbuziente.

If it had been possible
to live for the most part acknowledged,
you would have been
that shiny ardor among houses,
that river of special days.

Nudity, dear sir, is serpentine,
cold on our tongue's saliva.

If everything's watching us,
as from a rustling ditch
we emerge, white in the face...

Se fosse stato possibile vivere
largamente accolti, saresti
fra le case quel lucido ardore,
quel fiume di giorni
particolari.

La nudità, signore, serpentina,
fredda sulla saliva
della nostra lingua.

Che tutto ci guardi
come da un fosso frusciante
usciti, impalliditi...

The Boy's Afraid of the Live Tiger

1

The gold armchair is witness to his calm.
He shakes himself, now he dries himself,

                         [now he exposes himself:
assenting to very few inflexible things,

combs made of moon rock!

From the cottage a huge tongue
follows me to a final rehearsal.
Now, vacation, tell me about the
quality of this twisting issue!

They're not ghosts and they can't fly,
soft filaments compensate for blindness.

2

And then there are seven doors
a key turns in the first
a voice comes from the second
headlights hit the third
there's the fourth
(three doors to go)
the fifth is half-open
the sixth hides a theatre
the seventh is mine.

3

The other is lodged in
yellow red violet,
hammered in with his own strength.
Someone takes his place;
with voices as musical
as a tree
(straight on without a turn);
someone attributes an almost-necessity
to him, the same of
certain rocks and bushes
scattered familiarly about
the field into which he plunges.

4

One look tells you he's an old martyr,
one looks tells you that nothing
can compare to the splendor he radiates;
the wound mends then burns
fits in with the centuries-old background harmonies
but I can't use this in poetry,
so quick to make its frontal attacks;
full of echoes and curves
is the fellow's singleness.

5

And then who's going to toss
a small crown of flowers letters echoes--
immunity oscurity everything that
the enormous pocket in the meantime inflated? And
everything that trembled with yearning?
(by nature
there are intolerable interruptions)
inside
a sumptuous fingernail plays the game
of circling and centering:
A   Tears welling up
B   Rarefication

6

How he abstracts it and stirs it up,
how he stirs it up and molds it;
He who makes these tricky maneuvers on
his walk between five and six o'clock.

How he diverts it and disclaims it:

the fear is of a low awkward
noise, completely real,
objectively underfoot.

7

How to point out, halfway-up there,
new proof curled up on itself.

A young inexhaustible seal,
always a good guide.

Where what's silent and what's arid
circulate, and are in part reassorbed.
A polar contrast, an elbow in the ribs
because finally

8

The water in its oblong motion
must be more patient than patient.
Whoever's underneath has
hidden emerald scales and can see the future,
the changeable shape of this place,
mournful sweet tight

Il bambino ha paura della tigre viva

1

Lo scranno d'oro assiste alla sua flemma,
ora si scuote ora si asciuga ora si espone:
concedere poche cose inflessibili,
pettini di pietra di luna!

Tutto lingua dal cottage mi segue

fino alla prova generale:
ora dica la qualità di questa
tortuosa emissione, vacanza!

Non sono lemuri e non possono volare,
dolci filamenti compensano la cecità.

2

E poi sono sette porte
nella prima gira una chiave
dalla seconda esce una voce
alla terza sbattono i fanali
c'è la quarta
(ancora tre porte)
la quinta è socchiusa
la sesta nasconde un teatro
la settima è la mia.

3

l'altro alloggia
nel giallo rosso viola
conficcato dalla sua forza,
qualcuno lo sostituisce
con voci compiutamente
musicali come albero
(quando va senza voltarsi)
qualcuno gli attribuisce
una quasi-necessità la stessa
di certe pietre e cespugli
disseminati familiarmente
nel campo dove precipita.

4

Questo è un vecchio martire, si veda:

allo splendore che emana da lui
nulla si può comparare e si veda:
la piaga che si scioglie e brucia
propizia all'intonazione secolare
del fondale,
ma non posso usarla in poesia
così pronta all'attacco frontale
piena di echi e di ululati
la singolarità del tipo.

5

Intanto chi pensa a lanciare
coroncine di fiori di lettere echi
immunità oscurità ciò che
l'enorme tasca intanto
gonfiava? ciò che spasimava?
(per natura
ci sono interruzioni intollerabili)
dentro
un'unghia sontuosa gioca il gioco
del cerchio e del centro:
A   lacrimazione
B   rarefazione

6

Come la sottrae e la solleva
come la solleva e la fonde
uno che cammina con insidiosa
manovra tra le cinque e le sei

Come la deriva e la declina:
la paura è del rumore maldestro
basso, del tutto reale,
oggettivamente fra i piedi.

7

Come indicare una nuova evidenza
a mezz'altezza, raggomitolata

una giovane foca inesauribile,
eternamente buona conduttrice,

dove circola e un po' si riassorbe
tutta la silenziosa l'arida,

una polare antitesi, un dare
di gomito perché finalmente

8

Nel movimento l'acqua oblunga
deve pazientare e pazientare,
chi sta sotto gli nascono squame
smeraldo, può guardare il futuro,
la mutevole forma del posto,
la funebre la dolce la stretta

GREGORIO SCALISE

G regorio Scalise was born in Catanzaro in 1939 and lived in Udine and Trento before moving definitely to Bologna. He has worked at the City Gallery of Modern Art in Bologna and written for various newspapers and literary reviews as well as for television and radio. Since the beginning of the 1980s he has channeled most of his energy into writing for the theatre.

Scalise's poems are descriptive "looks" not at objective reality but at overlapping images deposited in his memory; this he does with neutral and even commonplace language that has the surprising and unexpected merit of giving expression to an evocative poetic vision with numerous metaphysical twists to it. Certain of his poems give the impression of being imaginary, surrealistic apologies, where the work or author mentioned in the title (Kafka, for example, or--as regards the poems included here--the "Dora Markus" of Montale) serves only as a pretext, a starting point for something impossible to describe--and so the poet will talk of other.

POETRY

A capo (Back to the Beginning) 1968
L'erba al suo erbario (An Herb For Each Herbarium) 1969
Sette poesie (Seven Poems) 1974
Poemetti (Short Poems) (included with work by other poets in
   Quaderni della Fenice No. 26) 1977
La resistenza dell'aria (Air Resistence) 1982
Gli artisti (Artists) 1986
Danny Rose 1989

ESSAYS

Bruciapensieri (Flaming Thoughts\ Fired-off Reflections) 1983
Ma cosa c'è da ridere?: un pamphlet contro la comicità (But
   What's There to Laugh About?) 1993
Il diabolico in Italia (The Diabolical in Italy) 1995

THEATRE

Grazie vivissime per il ricordo (Many Thanks for the Memory)
   1978
Il pupazzo azzurro (The Blue Puppet) 1979
Vita di Carrol (Carrol's Life) 1979
Ultima lettera allo scenografo (Last Letter to the Screenwriter)
   1981
Io e Manhattan (Manhattan And Me) 1983
Secreteria telefonica (Answering Machine) 1983
La Donna allo specchio (The Woman in Front of the Mirror)
   1985
Dove sei Willy Loman? (Where Are You, Willy Loman?) 1986
Milena risponde a Kafka (Milena's Reply to Kafka) 1986
Merylin 1988
Case piene di ricordi in affitto (Houses Full of Rented
   Memories) 1991
Racconto d'autunno (Autumn Tale) 1991
Servi di scena (Servants Onstage) 1992

Amitié Amoureuse

The man with wrinkly lips
has the aura of an heir;
better to admit disappointment from the start:
a romantic adventure would ruin his past.
The images of the center in motion
lurk in a doorway; the wind plays
constantly between the lines of those years,
the half-moon in the sky records
the unconscious performance;
a strange bird carries a piece of straw
in its beak: exercising the prerogative of speech,
these early ideas will declare themselves
a decade later.

I shall pass in review the light of these constructions,
the main point being that
no one can change them. In this place
memory sings, and the sky
of the coldest depths waits for
it to become clearer.
Making impersonal sounds, these constructions
come and go between the structures of words,
and the wind blasts the metaphor
invented for fun.

Immersed in the most exhausting aspects
of his profession
an actor who is rarely introspective
leads a pretty happy existence.
We look forward to the days of his appearance
with their costly finale.
The syllables uttered give shape to its contours.

The travelers in a crowd
knock destiny off its track,

and all of a sudden Ophelia appears--
though she doesn't want a thing.
From the top of this table
trees look insignificant
and ideas bounce back into the corners:
in the end it's enough to have a body
while one works.

For most of the night
the rain fell;
the emperor had no desire
to review the troups;
the others were not to realize how old he was;
he thought it useless to reveal his intelligence.
He wasn't aware that on his nose
a transparent bead had appeared.

His house is an agency
glittering with light and dust.
He writes his letters
on unfamiliar terrain
where fog wets the stones
and a coat of paint covers the stars.
On the first day his language
made the sky, and on the second,
thanks to the volumes, the mountains,
just by going round them,
were overturned.

Amitié amoureuse

L'uomo con una piega sulle labbra
ha il fascino di un erede:
è meglio essere subito delusi,
una escursione romantica guasterebbe
il suo passato: nel movimento

di quel centro le immagini
si nascondono in un portone:
dileguano i giochi del vento
fra le righe di quegli anni,
una mezzaluna registra nel cielo
quella recita involontaria,
e un uccello sconosciuto
porta nel becco un filo di paglia;
con la prerogativa di un discorso
quelle idee iniziali
le ritroveremo un decennio più tardi.

Scorrerò la luce di queste costruzioni:
la tesi fondamentale
è che nessuno può mutarle: in questo luogo
si canta la memoria e il cielo
nel fondo del freddo attende
che diventi più chiara.
Con impersonale rumore
vanno e vengono fra le strutture delle parole,
l'aria colpisce a fondo
quella metafora inventata per gioco.

Immerso nei più faticosi particolari
di questa professione
un attore raramente introspettivo
conduce una vita quasi ridente.
I giorni di questa apparenza
ci attendono con un finale di lusso.
Le sillabe ne delineano i contorni.

I viaggiatori fra la folla
scompongono il destino
e Ofelia appare all'improvviso
senza desiderare nulla.
Dall'alto di un tavolo
gli alberi appaiono insignificanti

le idee si ribattono negli angoli;
alla fine basta un corpo
mentre si lavora.

Per buona parte della notte
è caduta la pioggia:
l'imperatore non aveva voglia
di passare in rassegna la fila:
gli altri non dovevano accorgersi
della sua vecchiezza, pensava che era
inutile mostrarsi intelligente,
non si accorgeva che al suo naso
era apparsa una goccia trasparente.

La sua casa è una agenzia
dove luccicano polvere e luce.
Scrive le sue lettere
fra terra incerta dove la nebbia bagna sassi
e un intonaco copre le stelle.
Il suo linguaggio nel primo giorno
fece il cielo, nel secondo,
attraverso i volumi, i monti
furono girandole capovolte.

Testing out the door-posts
means taking steps of old-fashioned patience,
guides urged along by the movement of the lips.
The light shows shattered
symbols in a room,
a kingdom without a king.
The street reveals--in a jotted-down note--
some private affair, like a cloud or a travel bag.
The children, disguised as the truth,
shine like something in a skid.

Per saggiare gli stipiti delle porte,
annotano passi di una antica pazienza:
guide pressate dal movimento delle labbra,
la luce illumina simboli
frantumanti in una stanza
o un regno senza re:
quella strada mostra, fra note di lavoro,
una storia personale,
come una nube o una borsa da viaggio:
i bambini, travestiti da verità,
brillano come qualcosa di sbandato.

A passion circles round our body
and a singular selfishness
allows an instant hit on the surface;
but with children it's necessary
to stick to the obvious, and the
follow-up to the story is the
noise of grass blades blown through
the teeth. The half-moon's painted face
has fuller days; it knows about
the immense scattering of
leaves off peach trees or about
overlapping times
clotting atoms of hope.

Una passione ruota attorno al corpo
e per un singolare egoismo
la superficie lo coglie in un atto immediato:
ma con i bambini bisogna
parlare dell'ovvio, e il seguito
di questa storia è di suoni d'erba
fischiati tra i denti: il viso dipinto
da una mezzaluna conosce
giorni più densi, la grande dispersione

delle foglie dei peschi,
oppure l'incrocio dei tempi
che raggruma atomi di speranza.

There have never been men crazier than these.
The rays stand for excess, and the
investigation shapes up as
an amalgamation of elements.
The man listening wants to complicate
it further:

he enjoys stressing his sense of
inertia; like a branch, his tremors
are serious; he exits from the wind
like an emptied wound, and the daughter
of a foggy autumn reigns in new anarchy.
Ruffled by the gathering light,
she isolates herself in her truth:
the elegy of dreams is like the cadence of this rhythm.

Non si sono mai visti uomini così pazzi,
il senso di quei raggi
è l'eccedenza: l'inchiesta si presenta
come un amalgama di elementi,
l'uomo ascolta e vorrebbe complicare
tutto questo:
si compiace di sottolineare il senso
dell'inerzia; come un ramo i suoi brividi
sono seri, esce dall'aria
come una vuota ferita e la figlia
di un nebbioso autunno
guadagna nuova anarchia.
Increspata nella luce raccolta
si isola nella sua verità: l'elegia
del sogno è come la cadenza di quel ritmo.

The days pass on that face
like a curious déjà-vu;
they write their dispatches
in a house where the children
are known for some intellectual habit;
a distorted photograph
dominates over all and offers its
misery like a magician of words
at the sound of women.

I giorni passano su quel viso
come un antefatto curioso,
scrivono i loro dispacci
nella casa dove i bambini
si distinguono per una abitudine
intellettuale: domina una fotografia
scomposta, e offre la sua miseria
come il mago delle parole
che sente il rumore delle donne.

Dora Markus and Her Actors

Many winters have gone by
with a general sensation that
the devils in biographies
can be glimpsed between clothes lines in courtyards.
Their sick laughter grazes the grey hairs
on one's head; on this bare day, Dora Markus plays
the piano with existential subtlety.

The youth of Vienna lived along
flowery embankments and proceeded towards
their delicate ruin in opera hats and silk shoes;
a skater glides through this rubbish
waving his belongings.

The mind hunts for images at random;
I hope they won't give out their
own description.

All afternoon we sailed along
in a European ritual; the wind
hit the deserted area and
gave to the outlines of all figures
a metaphysical and slightly-intoxicated
light.

The cobbler at the theatre
says that life uses us for its own end.
He applauds the troubadour poets,
having brought them to us after
delicately roundabout allusions.
To ensure the survival of the species,
the roses have neither beginning nor end.
A saxophone goes wild in a town
where art is never explainable.
When they talk people are careful not to
make the alphabet creak.
His hair is a cliché,
it burns at the earth's center.
He's had to face much tougher enemies.
Even the outline of a cloud
skims along the asphalt;
between nostalgia and experience
a woman in a *caffé* becomes a simple idea;
with yellowed hair
she lights her Christmas candles:
the avant-garde used to meet at her place
but then a claque for some winter's tale
brought out the precise measure of her violence.

Her face used to appear
on tall buildings;

now she looks at the clothes on the chairs.
There are lean days, like storms
that leave nothing intact.
The story of her life might
fade with one special name,
and thanks to eye magic,
the sequence of a syllogism
is reflected in the shadows of windows.

Amidst a stretch of green branches
Elizabethan poets sing.
This is a return to the origins of light,
the errors of the wind push along
a religious conscience, and roots
grow like tongues wearing
their best clothes.
Flowers are actors
meditating a difficult role and
growing thanks to strange visions;
between spaces of light
life becomes a sign of cunningness;
they reach the doorways of a laboratory
where the moon has become a favorite sign.

The wind shelters the emigrants and their
thin detachment from their homeland.
If writing is the sign they had imagined in their minds,
no one can ask poetry to be that sign.
A mirror clouds over,
reflects at false angles,
then reasons through to a conclusion
found horrible or mad.
Actors use new citations when they give their lines,
the doors to the stairways creak,
and in the wells it's bright midday.

Dora Markus e i suoi attori

Molti inverni sono trascorsi
con una sensazione generale:
nelle biografie si vedono i diavoli
stesi fra i fili del cortile:
la loro insana allegria sfiora
i capelli grigi: Dora Markus
in un giorno disadorno
suonava il piano con sottigliezza esistenziale.

Vivevano lungo argini fioriti
e delicate disfatte i ragazzi viennesi
col gibus e scarpe di seta:
un pattinatore scivola fra quelle cianfrusaglie
agitando gli oggetti di sua proprietà.
La mente cerca immagini a caso:
non vorrei che facessero
la loro descrizione.

Per tutto il pomeriggio abbiamo navigato
in un rito europeo: l'aria colpisce
una zona deserta e traccia attorno
alle figure una luce
metafisica e un po' brilla.

Il ciabattino del teatro
risponde che siamo usati per vivere:
batte le mani ai poeti provenzali,
li ha condotti fin qui fra delicate perifrasi.
Per la continuità della specie
le rose non hanno né inizio né fine:
brucia un sassofono nel paese
dove nessuna opera è spiegabile:
si parla badando a non far scricchiolare l'alfabeto:
i suoi capelli sono un cliché,
ardono al centro della terra.

Ha dovuto affrontare nemici ben più forti.
Anche lo schema di una nuvola
sfiora il selciato: fra nostalgia e vissuto
una donna al caffé è una semplice idea:
con i capelli ingialliti
accende le candele di Natale:
la sua casa conosceva l'avanguardia
ma la claque di un racconto d'inverno
ha reso esatta la sua violenza.

Il suo volto era apparso
fra grandi palazzi:
ora guarda i vestiti sulle sedie,
vi sono giorni scarni come tempeste
che non lasciano niente d'intatto:
forse la biografia
sbiadisce con un nome particolare,
e con la magia degli occhi
la sequenza di un sillogismo
si riflette nell'ombra dei vetri.

Fra una distesa di rami verdi
cantano i poeti elisabettiani:
siamo alle origini della luce,
l'errore del vento sospinge una coscienza
religiosa, le radici crescono
come lingue che abbiano indossato
i vestiti migliori.
I fiori sono gli attori
che meditano una parte difficile
crescono per strane visioni
e fra spazi leggeri la vita
diventa segno di malizia:
giungono alle soglie di un laboratorio
dove la luna presta il segno preferito.

Con lo scarno distacco dalla parte

il vento alloggia gli emigranti.
Se scrivere è il segno che avevano pensato
nessuno può chiedere alla poesia
di essere simile a quel segno.
Uno specchio si appanna
riflette angoli falsi,
prima di fare un ragionamento
si crede orribile o folle.

Gli attori recitano con nuove citazioni,
cigolano le porte delle scale
e nelle pozzanghere risplende mezzogiorno.

Man comes last: he's got to
complete his surveying, become
an alibi in a future design;
in any snatch of countryside
impossible objects collect
together on the road.
On account of the quality at ground level
he lives with a mix of language;
without those guidelines it would
be impossible to find the bad
part of the moon.
The herb doctor circles
in a humpbacked room,
his heart won't perceive the news
for which living becomes absurd;
the syllogism rises again from
solid species to hardened constellations;
only at sunset do the terms
meet up, for the game
needs some rules. There are
paths, along which
no one has noticed the
fusion called serious play.

Ultimo viene l'uomo: deve compiere
quel sopralluogo, diventare alibi
di un futuro disegno:
in un buco qualsiasi di provincia
la strada accosta
impossibili oggetti;
per la qualità verso il suolo
vive in un impasto di lingua:
senza quelle linee
sarebbe impossibile trovare
la parte peggiore della luna:
l'erborista gravita
in una stanza gobba,
il cuore non vedrà la notizia
per cui vivere è assurdo:
il sillogismo risale da specie solide
verso costellazioni indurite:
solo al tramonto i termini
si riconoscono, perché il gioco ha bisogno
di regole: vi sono sentieri dove nessuno
ha osservato la fusione
fra serietà e gioco.

SILVANA COLONNA

S ilvana Colonna was born in Belluno in 1942 but grew up in Bologna and moved to Milan as a young married woman. While her degree is in law, she has preferred teaching Italian literature and history in a private secondary school. She has contributed poetry reviews to the newspaper, *Unità*, and to the monthly magazine, *Poesia*. An able translator (she and her husband have lived in such countries as England, France, Spain, and Holland), she has translated works by E. A. Poe, P. Quignard, and F. Arrabal, and has received national recognition for her translation of Marguerite Yourcénar. For puppet theatre and shadow-puppet theatre, Colonna has adapted numerous works by Italo Calvino and others. Her poetry has appeared in magazines and anthologies in Italy as well as in Spain, Russia, and England.

Colonna's poems contain fragmented, reinvented thoughts, whose order is calculated to suggest a new chain of invisible events. The poetic voice is outstanding for its mix of reserved intimacy and yet light airiness, and even the choice of vocabulary reflects an interest in things aethereally or elusively spiritual; for example, Colonna will often use abstract nouns in a context that progressively renders the concepts implicit to them more and more subtle and metaphysical in meaning.

POETRY

L'orientamento lontano (Orientation From Afar) (appearing with
the work of others in the mini-anthology, *Poesia Uno*,
published by Guanda) 1980
L'orientamento lontano (with different poems from the
aforementioned text) 1984 (Biella Prize)

PUPPET THEATRE

La Barba del Conte (The Count's Beard)--adapted from Italo
Calvino--1983
O che merlotti o che follia (Oh What Simpletons, Oh What
Madness) 1983
Il Palazzo delle Scimmie (The Monkey House) -adapted from
Calvino- 1983
Re Tuono (King Thunder)--adapted from L. Capuana--for
puppet theatre 1985

So it tries to reach her inside her mind,
and even inside the mind of others,
where it presses on ignorantly,
with hasty silent glimpses,
accustomed to gently pushing her life a
bit from behind.
Very slightly--while she's already on the
edge of distraction,
it falsifies her memory,
and changes her dreams as she sleeps.

allora cerca di raggiungerla dentro la mente
fin dentro la mente degli altri
lì dove preme senza conoscenza
adocchia in silenzio di sfuggita
abituato a spingere di spalle
delicatamente un poco la sua vita
dentro di lei che già sta per distrarsi
e falsifica d'un niente la memoria
e si modifica i sogni quando dorme

Orientation From Afar

1
How hard to control the route,
follow distinguishing marks;
the bewilderment of the wings.
But what dimension, what color, the sea;
regulating oneself by the direction of the light,
the duration of time perhaps,
the infinite vibrations of fear.

2
She comes lightly forward, motions
to make her presence known,

as if it were possible
to perceive things in a dance,
which she describes as fast, with arching circles
and constant changes in direction.
I ask myself why I don't understand
the fear in tensed glands
the hardened, protruding bladders,
at the same time that she staggers off in a daze
while strangely dancing in your ear;

these signs are very incomplete
and don't reveal the place they were found;
their subject isn't defined,
yet they begin to fly about,
unaided by any scouting bee.

3
But the walk ramp is polarized;
the smell of the nest extends in one direction,
that of honey in the other;
the larvae are carried off by that smell of nest.

L'orientamento lontano

1
così difficile controllarne l'itinerario
seguire il contrassegno
lo smarrimento delle ali
ma quale dimensione quale colore il mare
guidarsi per la direzione della luce
la durata del tempo forse
le infinite vibrazioni da paura

2
viene incontro leggera e si muove
per farsi riconoscere

come fosse possibile
avverte per una specie di danza
che descrive rapida con archi di cerchio
spesso cambiando direzione
io mi chiedo perché non capisco
la paura delle ghiandole in tensione
le vesciche indurite che sporgono
e lei che stordita trascina
curiosamente ballandoti nell'orecchio:

questi segni sono molto incompleti
non indicano il luogo della raccolta
l'oggetto non viene precisato
comunque si mettono in moto
senza che la bottinatrice accompagni

3
ma la passerella è polarizzata
l'odore del nido cresce in un senso
quello del miele dell'altro
le larve trasportate dallo stesso odore del nido

Disconnections

1
You go--it seems to me--with a hint
(we all know how to stand on ceremony here)
of a smile, what with the door as it shuts
and that desire I can't stop for
"the beautiful life",
there's no way this guy doesn't understand.

She, too, I believe, imagined herself to herself.
She put together her ideas as we would
and arranged them in a similar fashion;
how taut this paper is that you've placed on top to conclude.

She fixes in place the contours, the disconnections
(clean, unnoticeable ones are preferred here);
even for her dreams, too, floated out of the
side of the brain that doesn't talk,
and she created colors in amazement, in fright.

2
The rising of waters perhaps
which separate and melt and continue to
seal in the cold of your smell;
your head stretching forward again to signal your presence,
which hardly grants you a right to live;
the burning thirst that neither your competence nor
modesty, they say, enables you to foresee.

3
But a secret life enters from somewhere
in mysterious lines of pain,
these shift the boundary lines you
pulled forward for a while then crossed--
the recognition of a nickname now,
the precise moment when the game ends.

Sconnessioni

1
te ne vai accennando mi pare
(qui tutti conosciamo il cerimoniale)
a un sorriso tra la porta che si chiude
e il desiderio che non so fermare
della vita bella
in nessuno modo l'amico non capisce

anche lei credo s'immaginasse
come noi componesse le sue figure
se le fosse composte allo stesso modo

ben teso questo foglio che hai messo sopra per finire
ferma i profili le sconnessioni
(qui piacciono puliti non invadenti) i sogni
anche in lei galleggiavano
dalla parte del cervello che non parla
e formava con stupore i colori con paura

2
l'aumentare di un'acqua forse
che si divide e si scioglie di continuo sigilla
il freddo dei tuoi odori
la testa che si allunga ancora a mostrare
la presenza che così poco ti autorizza a vivere
l'arsura che per competenza e con pudore
dicono non hai capacità di prevedere

3
ma la vita segreta entra da un'altra parte
in righe misteriose di dolore
mentre spostano i confini
che trascinando hai lasciato
poi il riconoscimento del soprannome
il momento preciso in cui il gioco finisce

But what an idea she'd gotten into her head:
a failure was something awful; a defeated woman was
a horror; none of this was called for.
Quiet men of few words hover now,
don't enslave yourself
in this alert mind that does no shouting;
and in so far as loving and falling in love begin
anew each time in water,
she still sees a disfigured shadow
that never wavers.

che idea però che s'era fatta
d'una disfatta come d'un orrore
di tutto questo invece niente
era richiesto
taciturni ragazzi adesso oscillano
non schivati
in questa mente accorta che non grida
e per quanto amare innamorare
ricominci ogni volta nell'acqua
sfigurata vede ancora quell'ombra
che non trema

Without muscles without slipping,
seeing who can dream most,
leaning the shoulders against something,
the cells having decided to be rid of it,
now comes his light whistle,
the soft flute.

senza muscoli senza scivolare
a gara nel sognare
appoggiando le spalle da qualche parte
le cellule che decidono di disfarsi
adesso il suo fischiare leggero
il flauto dolce

But your imagining was wrong
if they move--and young people move together--
(ever since I started to second-guess someone
and someone lazily started to second-guess me;
and he enchants or enchants himself--
indifferently--and torments),
paralyzing me slowly slowly
in the spot where we learned tenderness.

ma il tuo immaginare è sbagliato
se muovono e si muovono ragazzi insieme
(da quando un altro ne indovino e un altro
pigramente m'indovina e incanta
o s'incanta indifferente e strazia)
e mi paralizza lento lento
lì dove questa tenerezza abbiamo appreso

He spins about (laughing) then shows
one face two faces three faces,
bleached hair and hermaphrodite wrists;
--finally--
of the same dark liquid as books
demented hooting madman,
rising on
small hollow elbows.

ruotando su se stesso (e ride) poi
mostra una faccia due facce tre facce
capelli decolorati e polsi ermafroditi
--finalmente--
di liquido scuro dai libri
sballata schizoide che fischia
alzando su
piccoli gomiti vuoti.

NANNI CAGNONE

Nanni Cagnone was born in Ponente (Liguria) in 1939 and lived for many years both in Rome and Milan, before moving to Conturbia, a small village in the countryside around Novara. He has held many jobs over the years and presently works as the art director of an advertising firm, in addition to serving as a Public Relations consultant to companies. He founded--and headed until its folding--the important small literary press, *Coliseum*. Another of Cagnone's initiatives has been the creation and promotion of the "Communication Arts and Methods Group" in Milan. The organizer of many a literary event, Cagnone has also written articles and reviews for such Italian newspapers as *Il Giornale* and *Il Messaggero* as well as for the magazine *Leggere*. A collection of his critical essays is in the process of being published.

Cagnone's poetry is calm, elegantly paced, and reflective. At certain moments, his language may take on overtly prophetic or proverbial overtones (all the more so in his poems inspired by myth, though this is a feature of his style in general), only then to become mysteriously open-ended (an effect re-enforced by anacolutha or ambiguous shifts in referents). While mythical references are present in much of Italian poetry from the eighties onwards, Cagnone stands out as one of the few to focus on myth already in his experimental work of the sixties. Furthermore, while many of his contemporaries have tried to reintroduce a mythological dimension into ordinary life, Cagnone has done if anything the opposite, shedding references to everyday existence and evoking the mythical as a purer dimension in which we would willingly abide had it not been cursedly lost to us.

POETRY

What's Hecuba (published in New York) 1975
Andatura (The Pace) 1979
Vaticinio (Prophecy) 1984
Armi senza insegne (Emblems Without Insignia) 1988
Anima del vuoto (Spirit of Emptiness) 1994
Avvento (Advent) 1995

FICTION

Comuni smarrimenti (Common Forms of Bewilderment) 1990

ESSAYS

L'Arto fantasma (The Missing Limb) 1979 (essays by others
    edited by Cagnone)
G.M. Hopkins--translated with an introduction by Cagnone)
    1988

It isn't any of this
but it's offered as
a hard nest for the stars,
as a sunset here and a
dawn in the West, or the
decisive death of whoever
in this century has dreamed
wedding upon wedding. Still,
things that seemed finished
now kindly open themselves, and
their hems, buttonholes, edges
slowly ease--unable to say
why the sand is solid
and resurrection, or culmination,
a resolute yielding
of minutes to minutes.

Tutto questo non è,
pure si pone
come aspro nido delle stelle
come tramonto qui e aurora
in Occidente o decisiva morte
di chiunque abbia sognato
in questo secolo, nozze
su nozze. Ma gentilmente
aprono sé stesse tutte cose
che apparvero finite,
cedono orlo asola sponda
non sanno dire
perché sia solida la sabbia
e resurrezione, o culmine,
il fermo cedimento
di minuti a minuti.

General names, no other

sort of servitude, and mind that
you don't take pleasure in objects;
my dying friend's set on what he knows nothing about.
For a short while your shadow's deep,
then it dissolves; the room
that your detachment remains tied to
out of fright, like a boat, solitary,
which the water tries to lead into the current.
All pretenses dissolve. You're constant now.

I nomi generali, nessun'altra
servitù, e non prendi da una cosa
il tuo diletto, mio morente amico
deciso a ciò che ignori--profonda
l'ombra tua per poco tempo
poi diradata, stanza ove rimane
legato da timore il tuo distacco
come una sola barca, sola,
che acqua vuole indurre
alla corrente. Sciolta
ogni parvenza,
diventi costante.

It lies--when urged to, it lies--
like a despairing glance
on a wandering boundary,
or a gleamed bulk on a dark edge, the
protection that eyelids offer.
The darkened glance, like
a night-time orchard
emerging curved and bent,
no resplendent wings.

Giace, se consigliato giace

come sguardo che dispera
all'errabondo confine
o racimola grandezza all'orlo scuro
riparo delle palpebre,
sguardo annerito come
frutteto notturno
che curvo spicca,
non splendenti le ali.

No place is extreme
that can always fold its own return
over itself--extreme is that
which draws to no conclusion,
carries everywhere with it,
wears a collar but isn't tame;
it squeezes in on me now like
you, horrible
envied feared resemblance.

Estremo non sarà un luogo,
che sempre può piegare su sé stesso
il suo ritorno--estremo è che non giunge
a compimento, porta ovunque con sé,
tiene collare senza domatura,
mi stringe adesso come
te orribile
invidiata temuta somiglianza.

from **Vaticinio**

Book Three: On Preparation

What desire lurks
behind the shield,

so afraid of similar blood?
What unpassed sieve from the past
covers him with the whiteness of
the women of Thebes
and the anonymous bliss
of disobedience.
The reaching is too far off,
been left unattended
yet unravels in all directions,
and the unsheathed way appears.
How profound.

You all see, he weakens.
Persistent shadows, feeding
a wound in the darkness, and
the path's been seen to,
now it's clear.
He sees the earth rise
suddenly, and the outline of a head of hair--
nightmare seizes the earth, trembling advance,
shouted reawakening.

He comes
dragging his feet, weak
now for being so near,
unable to move the
mirror off this eternity,
knowing that the shield only
protects head-on.
His advance is so profound
that where a smudge of blood remains--
if his disenchantment is sincere,
the rain won't wash it away--
he'll advance up to the
edge of the continuous rustling.
Who has been a witness
no longer can remember,

and at the same time fears that he'll undo his own farewell.

A strange figure
follows him at a distance now,
a demon of himself
or a revealed sphinx
whom he can hear ask wordlessly:

"He who has been promised to himself
cannot rule. Rather, he would be wise to let himself go limp,
carefully and deliberately, then go back
somewhere else without being irritated."

Servant to the ear,
tongue-tied, empty
as a breathless emptiness;
he no longer blows on the fire
but feels the ropes extremely tight
and everything around him lifeless
(a new well covered over with earth).

You'll be fed by hostile people
and hoisted up on shields too late.
Countless waves don't make for a sea storm
but just surf--a multiple coming undone--
and your assigned role rolls about
inside the secret of all forefathers.

Every demon is protective--
provided he who fears him
has not made himself inaccessible;
otherwise, the hungrying demon won't
be able to keep away,
he'll nab him at various times while
he is assuming the obscurest of forms,
in small withered gardens,
vials as bitter as a wooden fruits,

the resina of Adonis.

Da **Vaticinio**

Libro Terzo. Della Preparazione

Quale desiderio sarà
dietro lo scudo, che s'impaurisce
del sangue uguale. Quel vaglio
non passato anticamente
fa cadere su lui il pallore
delle donne di Tebe
e la benedizione ignota
della disubbidienza.
Giungere sarà troppo lontano,
il luogo è incustodito
tranne che si sparge in direzioni
e senza fodero è la via,
come profonda.

Vedete, egli indebolisce
ombre perseveranti, alimentando
nel buio una ferita, e riguardato
ora si apre il cammino.
Questo vede: la terra alzarsi
di colpo, e il contorno di una
acconciatura--incubo preme
la terra, tremendo avanzo
fa gridare il risveglio.

Strisciando i piedi, adesso
indebolito dalla vicinanza
né potendo distogliere lo specchio
da questa eternità, egli viene
sapendo che lo scudo
regge solo davanti.

Così profondamente avanza
deve è rimasta una patina
di sangue, se il disinganno
non è tanto volubile
che su lui possa la pioggia--
avanza fino all'orlo
del ripetuto fruscìo.
Chi ha veduto non sa
più ricordare, e insieme
quest'addio teme di togliere.
Ora una figura dissimile
lo accompagna a distanza,
dèmone presso di sé
o rivelata sfinge
da cui senza una voce
ascolta domandare:

"Chi fu promesso a sé
non può regnare.
A lui conviene
abbandonarsi immobile, con cura,
e tornare altrove
senza irritazione."

Servitore dell'orecchio,
lingua cucita, vuoto
come un vuoto ansimante:
più non soffia sul fuoco
sente molto tese le corde
e disanimato intorno tutto quanto,
coperto dalla terra
un pozzo inaugurato.

Verrai nutrito da gente ostile
e issato sugli scudi troppo tardi;
molte onde non fanno mareggiare
ma risacca--disfatta moltitudine--

e la parte assegnata è rotolante
nel segreto dei padri.

Ogni dèmone è salvaguardante
purché non si renda inaccessibile
colui che lo teme; altrimenti
insaziato non potrà trattenersi
da lui, prendendolo più volte
in forme oscure, in piccoli
appassiti giardini, fiale
amare come il frutto del legno,
la resina di Àdonis.

Fifth Book: On Limitation

Pólis, place defended
by its limits, fence
without cracks, without openings.
Its substance not found
in a root but in the strange
assembly that won't hold together
under a mere glaze of peace.
Pólis, tired grandeur:
undone, calculated
place on earth.

The door where
the enemy gets stuck
in his own blood
is called by another name: a name
that alienates
like the stranger who steps
into the hall;
hostile, unharmed,
fallen in among people who
don't want to accomodate

him in their language--
because the secure being, once at rest
on the bottom, has now
been bewildered.

In confused warehouses
where idols ferment
and where things upon things
mix their sweat,
a wind prevails on certain nights.
It tops the walls, passing as look-alike
to all Wanderers,
those who without footing
in the emptiness of the past
set out their mat
and have neither a temple
nor money for a temple,
yet are grateful for
unequipped sites.

Wanderers, immature people
who sow fire and who fear
only the tumults of the earth.
It's said that they collect
the energy of dust
and attack without warning,
without song;
desert-red face powder
on far-too-young ink
and a market of insomnia
in the last rooms within bodies
mushrooming in size, short-lived, decked out in poverty.

To love backwards and forwards
earthern surfaces, and
like oaks or lindens
those rows of columns

that hold the sky up,
sand this roof which the god hinders.
Oh injunction of melancholy, hiss
trouble, a scraping of minds
like one going hoarse, and
bodies tire themselves out
at an unnameable price
till finally,
bandaged and bent in two,
down on their deepest level,
they fix on fate like arrows.
A holy place is where
between the bones of the earth
one prays to the existing void
and asks it to appear;
the sacred
has no navel nor
does it turn on hinges;
it pays back harshly with prodigies;
infected place,
pregnant with the weight
of all the dead, which
amber and honey protect during
the motionless, growthless voyage
of one and only one distance.
If any labyrinth
is a play on words,
a long tracing of curves that when they halt
go completely straight,
where the needle on the scales
wavered dazed
in a spot in the darkness
between seed and fruit.
When he who has won
pulls free from the comb that
separates and retains
all victims, he finds himself up over an abyss,

unfulfilled, like one who, unrecognized by his peers,
vanishes.

Libro Quinto. Della Limitazione

Pólis, luogo difeso
dal suo limite, recinto
senza fessura senza vano.
La sua sostanza non è
in una radice, ma nella strana
adunanza che non tiene
nell'unico smalto di una pace.
Pólis, stanca statura,
luogo della terra
disfatto, calcolato.

Altro nome ha la porta,
dove s'impiglia nel suo sangue
il nemico: nome di lontananza,
come straniero che metta piede
nel vestibolo, ostile
e illeso cadendo tra una gente
che non deve ospitarlo
nella lingua, poiché
l'essere sicuro che dormiva
sul fondo ora si è smarrito.

Negli intricati depositi
dove idoli fermentano
e cose su cose
si scambiano il sudore,
certe notti prevale il vento.
Supera l'orlo delle mura
questo vento, sosia
degli Erranti, di coloro
che senza fondamenta

nel vuoto del passato
dispongono una stuoia
e non hanno denaro per il tempio
né tempio, ma riconoscenti
luoghi non preparati.
Gli Erranti, gente incompleta
che semina fuochi e teme
solo i tumulti della terra.
Si dice che raccolgano
la forza della polvere
e vadano all'assalto
senza esordio senza canti,
cipria di deserto
su inchiostri immaturi
e spaccio d'insonnia
nelle ultime stanze dei corpi
ingranditi e caduchi
ornati d'indigenza.

Amare avanti e indietro
quei luoghi di terra battuta,
e come quercia e tiglio
quegli ordini di colonne
che sostengono il cielo,
e il tetto che questo cielo
impedisce, e il cielo
che impedisce il dio.
O ingiunzione
di malinconia, di malattia
del sibilo, rasura dei venti
come si sgola e senza prezzo
si stancano quei corpi
finché in bende, piegati,
nel più profondo suolo
fissano il destino come frecce.
Luogo sacro è dove
tra le ossa della terra

si prega il vuoto esistente
di apparire; il sacro
è senza ombelico, né gira
su cardini--ripaga duramente
con prodigi, luogo infetto
gravido di tutto il cumulo
dei morti che ambra e miele
riparano nel viaggio
senza moto senza crescita,
di una sola distanza.
Mentre gioco di parole
è il labirinto, cammino
di linee più curve
che si fermarono dritte
dove l'ago della bilancia
si è stordito
in un punto delle tenebre
tra seme e frutto.
Uno che ha vinto, quando
esce dal pettine che divide
e tiene indietro le vittime,
si trova elevato su un abisso
e incompiuto, come uno
non riconosciuto dai suoi
perde sembiante.

PATRIZIA VICINELLI

P atrizia Vicinelli was born in Bologna in 1943 and died in Bologna in 1991, after having lived a very difficult life for years. She was involved in experimental theatre (along with Emilio Villa) and contemporary music productions. She participated in numerous underground films, such as A. Grifi's *Virulentia* and G. Castagnoli's *Notte e giorno*. She performed her "sound poetry" and presented her concrete poetry in exhibitions in Italy, France, and the United States.

Vicinelli's poetry can be compared to a musical continuum of images, for, like music, its development may overwhelm or, to the contrary, still the mind. Musical, too, is the pacing, with those sudden accelerations and stops, with that desired effect of rhythmic dissonance. Each phrase becomes the voicing of a desire and dream images abound. What is important about love for this poet is its irreversibility through time, which in Vicinelli is immediately to be associated with images of death-- death, however, viewed not as tragedy but rather as a sweet loss, whereby love may continue to live.

POETRY

a, à. A. 1967
Apology of schizoid woman 1979
Opere (Collected Works) 1994

When time--irreversible--begins to doze,
I return with the courage to talk like
Virgil. But I don't know
how many blue crypts will appear to me, for
there's an absence of hieroglyphics and
too much cleopatra, too much;
there's been a postponement somewhere, a strike;
through the shutters I see myself in
the window glass and note to myself   the
space that will remain still for me if I
really want, if I really
want, so come on, patrizia, fall--
you must surely have wanted a bit of
this blushing life ,
but when it laughs at you
the trumpet is sacred.

ritorno è assopito il tempo irreversibile
quindi mi oso di parlare virgilio non so bene
quante cripte blu mi si presenteranno c'è un vuoto
di geroglifici e troppo di cleopatra molto
c'è stato un rinvio uno sciopero
alle imposte mi vedo nel vetro e mi rimando
lo spazio che mi resta fermo se proprio voglio se
proprio voglio allora patrizia vieni càdi
un poco di questa vita di rossori - avrei voluto -
ma è sacra la tromba quando ti ride

I Met The Thieving Miss Magpie

I met the thieving miss magpie, number 123
in the small trees
in the deep garden of summer;
after her blind nosedive,
she then flew way up high.

For some obscure reason she took
a fancy to my ankle and brushed against it with
her chin;
a lady merchant with black inventive eyes,
I thought her a beauty,
truly outstanding in her impossible humanity.
Like Saint Francis of Assisi, we had ourselves a
nice chat, exchanged a load of secrets, her in
her black and blue dress, me in
my usual Moschino jeans.

L'ho conosciuta la gazza ladra

L'ho conosciuta la gazza ladra, la numero 123
degli arboricoli
nel profondo giardino d'estate
in picchiata scorrazzante, in seguito volò alta.
Per qualche oscuro motivo le piacque
la mia caviglia col suo mento la struscia
un mercante dagli occhi neri e fantasiosi,
la trovai una bellezza
tanto eccellente nella sua umanità impossibile.
Come San Francesco ci siamo fatte delle belle
chiacchierate, un sacco di confidenze,
lei col suo abito nero e azzurro, io con i miei
soliti pantaloni blu di Moschino.

from **The Foundations of Being**

4. *Crossing the River*

Like a seesaw, like a rainbow, the colored
penetration of the high and the low, he tries to
repeat the motion. The abyss--internalized--
is a structure of being. Typically, he torments

himself during immersion as well as in practice.
Taking the outcome of his destiny into his own hands,
incorporating it, becoming the eager self of dreams;
the moon, shining directly over the mind,
never stops influencing it. Unleashed diseases
spread anguish and it's an iron-hold,
though in comparison there's no forgetting the
beginning, nor the fight, nor the surrender, nor
the incessant course
of this flow of this life of this cosmos.
During its opening and its closing, there's a line of
near-sighted seekers, who dive into dark wells and
shoot upwards, as if vacuumed, towards the stars,
after a tiredness already like death.
Time for all had stopped flowing forever
when a light appeared;
it wasn't like any feeling
nor like any familiar form,
not even one as captured in a snapshot
of a horse halting in the moonlight.
He said that poetry, too, should be read aloud in
a different way, so that it might make for
other formations, so that it might become
an active journey of no return
every time desire took on form and gained the upper hand.
Immersed in womb-like darkness, he knew that
it was his choice and no longer his condition;
he'd let himself be cornered again without fear,
like a child who increasingly craves not sweets but sense.
He's seen the clouds fall, precipitating
into what was finally a static universe;
he watches for hours whatever he feels like,
inventing patterns like a wizard with his wand.
He has to sleep, and in his sleep creates his paradise,
giving it details and consistency,
and he remembers that it was like weaving,
this making destiny and life into one and the same thing.

He's had good teachers in the spiritual realm,
and all his past worry and procrastinating were due to
a sort of uncontainable desire, always the same, one
termed passion--the body diving into it,
then doing its awful duty, meanwhile
enriching the mind in its
best and possible way.
The infirmity accumulated in the hundreths of
waiting time seemed irreversible,
and only after an invincible sacrifice
did he allow himself any enjoyment,
overcoming, that is, what was left of himself,
remains which then re-emerged as new energy.
That calm is an inner structure. From there
it was possible to dictate orders to the mind and
re-enforce the seals on his unity of self.
In this way strength makes its own melody
similar to that of a man who has stopped hoping
and started dominating, now that
his soul has visited all opposites.
Creatures that wander about like madmen
almost never reach the shore, almost never
shatter the mirror, and rarely hitch themselves
to their own destiny,
because they never set their mind at rest,
or else they never stop.
Meanwhile, Orpheus takes his
fiery faith over there beyond the stones and wonders why
this enormous fear will once again disappear
from the world if you accept this immense
lake of solitude--the condition, the condition.
Still-standing oaks sway at such moments,
though there's no mind; their breathing beats
on other minds in harmony.
The outcome is never clear,
the great collapsed recess of desire, the
broken dam on the immense river,

a place where these words are utterly useless;
Orpheus stood upright in the company of
his refound soul, cell after cell, an erect androgyne
full of horror and resentment;
he haplessly traveled beyond his own existence
having reached the surface of the well; but, yes,
under that calm, under the stars up above,
"peace," he said, he hoped, and the sudden air of
quiet evening.
Trembling like him are those who are
as yet inside their aging bodies; crying,
they stick the famous star on their foreheads;
like him they travel slowly onwards,
no longer afraid.
Naturally there was the sound of uselessness,
and the desire to laugh softly at all those
discussions of beauty,
and how full he felt he was of it, like a shepherd,
describing "what has happened" and "what is mine",
the coincidence of being, and how full a sense of this
he had while he was headed towards a
distant stillness and giving up all hope.
This coincidence was there in the center of
the red-hot heart of dawn, nothing
to stop it, an inevitable
risk, the journey already finished;
it was from a distance then
that he saw the other shore
and all that stood in between.

Da I fondamenti dell'essere

4. Attraversare il fiume

Come un'altalena, come un arcobaleno, il penetrare
in alto e in basso, colorato, a croce lui

ripete l'andamento. Interiorizzato l'abisso
è una struttura dell'essere, egli si strazia nell'immerso
come nella sua pratica, il solito.
Prendere in mano la sorte del suo destino e integrarlo
e diventare l'agognato essere dei sogni,
a picco la luna sulla mente
non smette di influenzare. Morbi
scattanti angustiano, ed è una morsa di ferro
ma il principio non è dimenticato,
neppure la lotta, neppure la resa, neppure
l'incessantemente corso
di questo fluire di questa vita di questo cosmo,
a paragone.
Nella chiusura e nell'apertura, si schierano i miopi
cercatori, s'immergono nei pozzi oscuri e scattano
come risucchiati verso le stelle, dopo
una stanchezza che pareva già morte.
Sempre il tempo per ognuno ha finito di scorrere,
quando giunge la luce
non somigliò a nessun sentimento
o a quelle forme conosciute
di cui si ammantava piuttosto un'istantanea
mentre un cavallo si era fermato sotto la luna.
Disse che anche la poesia andava detta
in un altro modo, perché servisse ad altre schiere,
e perché diventasse movimento attivo
senza ritorno, ogni volta che il desiderio
avesse preso una forma e il dominio.
Immerso in una oscurità da utero, seppe
che era una scelta e non più una condizione e
se ne stette rincantucciato senza temere,
come un bambino sempre più goloso, ma di senso.
Vide le nuvole cadere precipitando
in quell'universo finalmente statico, guarda
per ore tutto ciò che vuole, inventando schemi
come un mago con la sua bacchetta.
Dove dormire, nel sonno crea il suo paradiso,

lo fornisce di dettagli e consistenza,
ricorda che era come tessere,
fare tutt'uno del destino con la vita.
Ebbe buoni maestri, nel campo dello spirito.
Tutto l'assillo e il procrastinare furono dovuti
a una sorta di concupiscenza, sempre quella,
e nominarla passione, dove il corpo può immergersi
fa il suo tremendo mestiere il corpo arricchisce
la mente nel suo modo possibile e migliore.
L'infermità accumulata nei centesimi del tempo
di attendere sembrò irreversibile
e solo dopo l'invincibile rinuncia
se lo permise di godere
scavalcando così i suoi resti
riemergenti allora in nuova energia.
Quella calma è una struttura interiore, da lì
fu possibile dettare ordini alla mente e rinforzare
i sigilli della propria unità.
Così la forza forma la sua melodia come di un uomo
che ha finito di sperare
e che ha iniziato a dominare, poiché
la sua anima ha visitato gli opposti.
Le creature così vaganti da impazzite, quasi mai
raggiungono la riva, quasi mai infrangono lo specchio,
raramente congiungono a sé la propria sorte,
perché non si danno pace, oppure non si fermano.
Intanto Orfeo conduce al di là dei sassi
la sua fede rovente e si chiede perché,
questa paura smisurata ancora una volta abbandona
il mondo tu se lo accetti questo lago immenso
della solitudine, la condizione, la condizione.
Querce immobili in quei momenti fremono senza vento
batte il loro alito su altre menti in consonanza.
Mai diviene certo cosa risulti,
la grande ansa del desiderio abbattuta la diga
dell'immenso fiume abbattuta,
luogo in cui queste parole sono proprio inutili,

tenendosi dritto Orfeo in compagnia della sua
ritrovata anima, cellula per cellula eretto
un androgino pieno d'orrore e di risentimento,
si lasciò percorrere al di là della sua storia
avendo raggiunto la superficie del pozzo, ma sì,
sotto quella calma, sotto quelle stelle in alto,
pace disse sperava, e un'aria improvvisa di sera tranquilla.
Tremanti quelli come lui ancora dentro quei loro corpi
al lungo vissuti, essi sempre piangenti si cacciano
la stella famosa in fronte, come lui proseguirono
piano, finalmente senza più temere.
Sì il timbro dell'inutile veniva da ridere sommessamente
a tutte quelle rincorse sul bello
e quanto si trovò colmo di esso come un pastore
dicendo come è passato e come è mio, la coincidenza
dell'essere, e quanto si trovò colmo del senso,
mentre se ne andava in un lontano fermo
e rinunciando alle sue speranze.
Essa stava lì nel centro cuore bollente aurora,
da non fermarla, ecco il rischio inevitabile,
il cammino già dato.
Così da lontano vedeva la sponda, anche
tutto quello che c'era nel mezzo.

ANTONIO PORTA

Antonio Porta was the pseudonym used by Leo Paolazzi, who was born in 1935 in Vicenza, graduated from university and resided in Milan, and died of a heart-attack during a brief trip to Rome in 1989. His vast experience in the literary and publishing worlds began in his undergraduate years when he was part of the editorial board of the avant-garde literary review, *il verri*, headed by Prof. Luciano Anceschi, at the same time as he was acquiring practical experience working for the national magazines owned by the publisher Rusconi and Paolazzi. As of the publication of the anthology, *I Novissimi*, Porta was an integral part of **Gruppo 63**. From the late sixties till the start of the eighties he also held important positions for Bompiani and Feltrinelli, and founded and headed such prominient magazines as *Alfabeta* and *La Gola*. Off and on during the eighties, he contributed articles to *Corriere della Sera* and *L'Europeo* and taught Italian Literature as visiting professor at the Universities of Chieti, Rome, and Pavia, as well as at Yale. In addition to his works of poetry, Porta wrote for the theatre and published translations of Spanish-American poets (in anthology), Paul Léautaud, Jacques Roubaud, Ted Hughes and Edgar Lee Masters (among others); curiously enough, he also translated into Italian the book of poems that his fellow poet, Amelia Rosselli, wrote originally in English (entitled *Sleep*).

Porta's early experimentation led him in the direction of concrete poetry--of text divided up into geometrical formations (triangles, circles, etc.), though with no connection between form and content; it also spurred him towards the sort of hypnotic repetitions (of words or entire lines) that his friend Nanni Balestrini advocated. The only link with his later lyrical work (represented here) lies perhaps in his choice of titles

(*Rapporti*, or instance, or *Quanto ho da dirvi*), in that his concerns would continue to be precisely that: relations and relationships on the one hand, and a need to communicate clearly with his reader on the other. The brevity and tone of Porta's last poems bring to mind Japanese haiku or Ancient Greek lyrics, at the same time as they obsessively free from all enigmatic obscurity.

POETRY

Quanto ho da dirvi, raccolta di poesie 1958- 1975 (All the
   Things I Have to Tell You--collected works 1958- 1975)
   1977
Passi passaggi (Steps and Passages) 1980
L'aria della fine (Winds of Ending) 1982
Emilio (a poem for children) 1982
Invasioni (Invasions) 1984
Nel fare poesia, antologia con scritti sul proprio lavoro (On
   Making Poetry--selected poems accompanied by short essays
   about their creation) 1985
Melusina, una ballata e diario (Melusina, a ballad and diary)
   1987
Il giardiniere contro il becchino (The Gardener vs. the Grave-
   digger) 1988

FICTION

Partita (Game) 1967
Il re del magazzino (The King of the Warehouse) 1978
Se fosse un tradimento (If It Were Betrayal) 1981

THEATRE

La presa di potere di Ivan lo sciocco (The Rise to Power of Ivan
   the Idiot) 1974
La stangata persiana (The Persian Thrashing) 1985

La festa del cavallo (A Party for The Horse) 1986

OTHER

Poesia italiana degli anni settanta: un'antologia (an anthology of Italian Poetry of the Seventies, edited by Porta, with his introduction) 1979

Dialogue with Herz

"Becoming a hare terrified me
until I accepted and got the hang of it."
"If that were true, I'd consider suicide."
"What is a hare's fate?"   "A simple death."
"I was overcome by a disgusting fear and
yelped at night as I nibbled at cabbage and
tobacco leaves. Winters, I ate up my supplies."

"I don't want to be a hare but a bird, and
get caught in the thorns."   "A hare dies from the cold,
hunger, old age, gunshots. For a bird a strong
night wind is often enough, *tramontana* over frozen ducks."
"Herz," he said on the terrace, "we'll be
sucked down by a gutter pipe some rainy day, emblem of
all violence."

"For a long time I'd had the urge to move from
tree to tree as a bird, and in the summer foilage
find an underground passage and reach the foundation."
"Touch the roots and lick nourishing substances."
"The old woman's barking," you said, "and the fool
with the wheel ran into the wall. Vexed, he picked up
his mask off the stones and has relapsed into the
uncertainty of a universe in furious evolution."

"I slip while swimming among dangerous algae.
I descend into thick vegetation, am covered by
ants and leaves. I chew on feathers,
and almost achieve awareness;
with the light of day between the
cracks, and dust that rises in a swarm
of protection and salvation."

The wind grabs us by the hair, it's true,
a shining sky comes to a halt behind a cloud:

in its tarnished shadow he hears Herz's voice.
That evening, on the terrace, they'd continued
happily: "Will there ever be an end to the
arbitrary nature of night and day?"

Dialogo con Herz

"Fui preso dal terrore divenendo lepre
e accettare, poi, entrò nelle abitudini".
"Fosse vero potrei uccidermi". "Quale è
il destino delle lepri?" "La morte semplice".
"Mi possedeva una paura rivoltante, squittivo,
di notte, e brucavo le foglie, di cavolo
e di tabacco. D'inverno consumai le riserve".

"Non voglio divenire lepre, ma uccello
e impigliarmi tra le spine". "La lepre muore
di freddo, di fame, di vecchiaia o fucilata.
Basta agli uccelli, spesso, un forte
vento notturno, tramontana tra le anitre
congelate". "Herz", disse sulla terrazza,
"verremo risiucchiati da una grondaia in un giorno
di pioggia, emblema di violenze".

"Desideravo da tempo muovermi
tra gli alberi: divenire uccello e nel
fogliame estivo scoprire il cunicolo,
giungere al fondamento". "Toccare le radici
e leccare sostanze nutritive". "La vecchia
abbaia", hai detto, "e lo scemo ha urtato
il muro, con la ruota. Stizzito solleva
la maschera dalle pietre e ricade nell'incertezza
di un universo in furioso divenire".

"Scivolo nuotando tra alghe pericolose.
Affondo in fitte vegetazioni, ricoperto

di formiche e di foglie. Mastico piume,
è quasi la conoscenza: con la luce
del giorno tra le fessure e la polvere
che si alza in un formicolìo di protezione
e di salvezza".

Per i capelli ci afferra il vento, è vero,
dietro la nuvola si arresta un cielo specchiante:
nell'ombra maculata lo raggiunge la voce di Herz.
La sera, in terrazza, continuarono, felici:
"Avrà mai fine l'arbitrio del giorno e della notte?"

Traveler

1.

When he reaches for a photo of old times
(a curved man in the middle of a curved room)
the egg doesn't explode against the window glass but contracts,
the way out is obscured by a million precautions;
his feet take shriveled, mincing steps,
he understands that changes and movements happen in the air,
he greets the birds, lifts his wig, sets off.

4.

Here's where a tree seems a breadfruit tree
tied to the mast of an anchored ship;
beyond the suspended valley there's a much larger hole,
birds and leaves fall as if there were wind;
between the traveler and the stream, the broken walking stick.

The busy bees have lost their way,
it was the dog to bite his hands,
where once there was a house only a rafter remains,
between the traveler and the woods, a burned field.

5.

A fox must have passed this way;
crow's feet and a stiff magpie--
the traveler rests on the feathers;
he eyes a white pheasant forgotten in a cage,
if he started digging he'd find tiny bones, he thinks
he must have very sharp teeth
the fired caretaker
and those of the main house, soaking wet with water, the table;
if someone sets the mind on fire
lines superimposed on lines
oaks on oaks
roots on roots
the need to write it down immediately
so that a clear sign remains of this moment.

6.

He falls asleep in manure where it's warm.
When the starry night settles on the tongue
he follows with his mind's eye the hopes a dog has,
nothing to separate the air and the world,
there's no way back to the beginning nor to what remains;
he walks quickly through air that feels purer.

7.   *for Mario*

Night with its black holes
forgotten funeral rites
shrubs giving off their inseparable mix of smells
the rain's stopped;
shell-less animals on the loose dart about underground,
breathing nostrils generate pleasure and refusal,
trees at night are fondled by a steady gaze,
inside the dark halo the universe of leaves begins to shake,

later a bird in the bushes makes its necessary sounds,
the starry sky expands with serenity,
and so a man reproduces himself, mute with his own ignorance,
servile shining gaze,
eyelids nearly closed
(as if the traveler could hoist him up)
he goes a distance with him
every thought is quiet.

10.

Lying in a small boat
a meter at most from somewhere
he holds out an arm and doesn't see his hand,
the image across the wall is body,
there aren't any smells but a screeching noise,
a tree immersed in water approaches,
tiny wings flap all about,
summer umbrellas cross in the light,
a mouth swallows its lips:
he rests his hand,
sits down in the shade and says: more.

Passeggero

1.

se allunga la mano sulla foto di un'età
curvato al centro di una stanza curva
invece di esplodere sul vetro l'uovo si restringe
di molte precauzioni circondata è l'uscita
zampette raggrinziti muove i suoi passetti
capisce che accadono spostamenti mutazioni nell'aria
saluta gli uccelli alzando la parrucca s'incammina

4.

ecco dove l'albero sembra l'albero del pane
sta legato all'albero di una nave all'ancora
oltre la valletta sospesa è un buco più vasto
cadono uccelli e foglie come da vento
tra il passeggero e il ruscello un bastone spezzato

le api al lavoro si sono perse
le mani le ha morse il cane
di una casa è rimasta una trave
tra il passeggero e il bosco un campo bruciato

5.

dev'esserci passata la volpe
zampe di gallina e una gazza stecchita
il passeggero riposa sulle piume
guarda un fagiano bianco dimenticato in gabbia
se cominciasse lo scavo scoprirebbe ossicini crede
deve averci i denti molto aguzzi
il guardiano licenziato
i padroni bagnati di vino addormentati sotto la tavola
qualcuno se appiccasse il fuoco nella mente
le righe si sovrappongono alle righe
le querce alle querce
radici sulle radici
bisogna subito scriverlo
che un segno chiaro rimanga del momento

6.

si addormenta nel letame dove si trova caldo
quando la notte stellata si adagia sulla lingua
insegue con la mente le speranze del cane
tra l'aere e il mondo niente che li distingue

non c'è via che conduce né al principio né al saldo
cammina veloce nell'aria che sente più pura

7.   *per Mario*

la notte con i suoi buchi neri
i riti funebri tutti dimenticati
arbusti emanano odori non separabili è spiovuto
animali sgusciati guizzano nel sottosuolo
le narici in aspirazione producono piacere e ripulsa
alberi notturni toccati da uno sguardo fermo
dentro l'alone oscuro l'universo di foglie si agita
più tardi un uccello da cespugli emette suoni obbligati
la volta stellata lievita nella serenità
così un uomo riproduce se stesso muto d'ignoranza
supino sguardo luccicante
palpebre quasi abbassate
come potesse sollevarlo il passeggero
lo accompagna lontano
muto ogni pensiero

10.

disteso in una piccola barca
un metro al limite da una meta
allunga un braccio la mano non trova
l'immagine distesa sul muro è corpo
non ci sono odori e un suono stridente
un albero immerso nell'acqua si fa vicino
ali minuscole sbattono all'intorno
ombrelle estive attraversano la luce
bocca che inghiotte le sue labbra
appoggia una mano all'ombra si mette
seduto e dice: ancora

from **Essences**

1.

nearby creatures of the air
I'm now behind that far-off window glass
but when I draw closer
my weight disappears in the air
and the window opens to the mind
which undoes the tightest ties;
from inside, one passes to entering outside
(it lasts not even a minute,
that's what we've learned)

   it moves with rough force
   it moves with a colored breast
   with its beak it tastes
   with its warble it sings
   the gift of food.

2.

To become a tree:
unearth the small sprouts under the moss,
and give them the softer,
more conservative soil they require,
poison-free.
To do this, my friend,
listen and remember these words,
signals showing where
and how the rippling rain
frees us of encrusting death.
Meaning for me is one thing only:
it has the shape of a shapeless tree,
an apple tree, a very dark orange.
I'm a girl with a shiny bark,
with leaves that sniff the

seed I drink.
I have no beginning nor end that
I can see or feel;
you can sniff me, smell,
disappear.

5.

White bars from the window
on lowered eyelids,
the only light black signals impress,
I wonder with my head bowed and
my neck almost outstretched: "Am I ready?"
But the light shifts
and I am left suspended between
the hour, the here-and-now, and the
never; I'm in bliss,
I'm free and I'm back on my feet;
my voice in my throat--interlaced with thirst--
rises, yes, my voice
in a round glass
jingles and polishes to a shine.

Da **Essenze**

1.

creature dell'aria vicine
io dietro quel vetro lontano
ma quando divento vicino
scompare il mio peso nell'aria
il vetro si apre al pensiero
che scioglie i legami più stretti
si passa dal dentro e si entra nel fuori
(non dura neppure un minuto
è quello che abbiamo saputo)

si muove con forza selvaggia
si sposta col petto a colori
col becco l'assaggia
con l'ugola canta
il dono del cibo

2.

Per diventare albero
fa uscire le gemme dal muschio
occorre un terreno più morbido e cauto
e senza veleni. Per questo,
compagno che ascolti, conserva
queste parole, segnali del dove
del come dalla morte che incrosta
ci libera la pioggia che increspa.
È solo il senso che affermo:
ha forma di un albero informe,
un melo, un arancio più scuro.
Io sono una ragazza di lucida scorza
di foglie che annusano il seme
che bevo.
Non ho né principio né fine
ch'io possa vedere o palpare,
mi puoi annusare, odorare,
svanire.

5.

Sbarre bianche dalla finestra
sulle palpebre basse
unica luce imprimono
neri segnali, e mi domando, a capo chino
quasi porgendo il collo, "sono pronto?".
Ma quella si allontana
e rimango in sospeso, tra l'ora
e il qui, e il mai, mi imparadiso

e snodo, e risalgo, dalla gola
s'intreccia alla sete, e si alza
la voce sì, la voce
in un bicchiere tondo
tintinna, e lucida a specchio.

ANGELO LUMELLI

Angelo Lumelli was born in Momperone, a town in the hills near Tortona, in 1944. Shortly after university he went to live and work in Germany for several years. After living in Milan for a time, he moved back to his small Piedmont town at the beginning of the eighties. He has been a middle school teacher, mayor of Momperone, and president of the agricultural cooperative that sells the produce, wine, and beef of the region. Besides poetry, Lumelli has published a much-discussed translation of the German poet Novalis.

Instead of talking of themes per se, it would be more exact to talk about the magnetic currents on which Lumelli's poetry rides. This sort of poetic language creates links as it flies along, spanning even the sudden gaps (which seem to serve as a medium for communication rather than its opposite). Sentences fall one after another like seeds of thought that will, a moment later, spring to life, generating still different thoughts in an impressive sort of automatic writing. One's impression is of rapidity and speed, which in theory should make all reflection impossible but which in fact instills profundity precisely in those points where the transitions seem the most mysterious, the most difficult to explain.

POETRY

Cosa bella cosa (Thing Pretty Thing) 1978 (Viareggio Prize)
Trattatello incostante (Short Erratic Treatise) 1980
Bambina teoria (Little Girl Theory) 1990

there are no pacts
(the trams seldom pass at this hour)
(the sink in the apartment overhead) (such a dense city)
it means they have something
to do with each other or maybe
here's the fact that intercedes
(the mole that moves
like the sky) a prayer
more violent (unnecessary,
their being born all the same)
tell him please in protest
(it's the worst of all pacts) (the least-binding)
tell it to him anyway.

non ci sono patti
(i tram passano rari a quest'ora)
(il lavandino al piano di sopra) (così fitta città)
vuole dire che c'entrano
l'uno con l'altro oppure
ecco il fatto che intercede
(la talpa che si muove
quanto cielo) una preghiera
più violenta (non necessari
essendo nati ugualmente)
digli che per favore per protesta
(è il peggiore dei patti) (il più mite)
diglielo lo stesso.

they could be reservoirs for water
or actions suspended (from afar)
they are shifts between things
the present is invisible
everything is equally very very long
each name each object
for this, neither on your knees nor on your feet

everything happens in place
the bandages are in the sun
the cracks will dry
We are obedient obedient obedient
protests bleach out
the light is too bright
faced with the sunflower we have our doubts
        (even lying--whatever!
          it engrosses us I tell you).

saranno cisterne per l'acqua
o azioni che pendono (da lontano)
sono spostamenti tra le cose
il presente è invisibile
tutto è uguale lunghissimo
ogni nome ogni cosa
per cui né in ginocchio né in piedi
tutto avviene al suo posto
le bende sono al sole
le crepe asciugheranno.
Siamo ubbidienti ubbidienti ubbidienti
le proteste si sbiancano
la luce è troppo forte
di fronte al girasole siamo in dubbio
        (anche mentire--qualunque cosa!
          ci assorbe ti dico).

you first, shift your attention (that is, if you withdraw)
you and those who are connected
(everything was multiplied by you
then another then another
multiplied by two by three
it was a lot of things
it was the exchange counter)

even further off the others (if they withdraw)
(they were moved further off as a precaution
this kept the game slimmed-down
we'd say: our place is that one there
and from here we can look at our place, multiplied)

then (if they withdraw)
we are motionless to the bone
(the thing is sweet the thing is harsh
the thing is nice the thing what thing)
there are no tricks we won't run off
we aren't being multiplied we aren't being held
we are good we are who knows.

prima togli tu l'attenzione (cioè se ti ritiri)
tu e quelli che sono legati
(ogni cosa era moltiplicata da te
poi l'altro poi l'altro
moltiplicata per due per tre
era tante cose
era il luogo degli scambi)

più distanti anche gli altri (se si ritirano)
(erano dislocati più distanti per prudenza
era meglio per la snellezza del gioco
dicevamo: il nostro luogo è quello là
e da qui guardiamo il nostro luogo, moltiplicato)

allora (se si ritirano)
fino all'osso siamo fermi
(la cosa è dolce la cosa è severa
la cosa è bella la cosa cos'è)
non ci sono trucchi non scappiamo
non siamo moltiplicati non siamo tenuti
siamo buoni siamo chissà.

Candid Camera

Reappearing like bindweed
soggy tender time
or treasure in dim light
but you--don't return.
A language which reappears
with a hundred remedies
floats,
fantastic knowledge
this sound is water
its motion enchantment
but breaking open
with a crowbar
and placing you or me
among all the names for beans
a thousand vain species, disjointedness
enumerating takes time:
things that coil round
things that love water
unfindables still unfound;
don't compete with he who may last
it's not true that all's begun
we absolutely need to start
or convert into currency
but wriggle and dart
or find another bed in town
crest of saffron
it's one's necessary anger that thwarts
tight curl of all neuroses
but a thing desired
merits praise;
irate time-waster
the same for the geraniums that
one hears about,
the rose arbors...
but what offer to diminish are the

fresh spurts in the night sky of spring,
like tracks in the sky, like sudden
feathery movements, they don't make you budge;
other small soft pendulums that lift
huge sky that empties,
moonlit night;
but this lowering is sweet dizziness
if we want to finish off a thing
among desirous people
desiring essential guests,
or imitating a disappearance
under the leaves, throughout the rooms,
dew on you, my hairy one, pearls.

But neither a good sloping
nor a long rustling
just pure disparity
the only distance, the only game
if I lie in wait for you
or you for me
where what's hidden ends
how you want to wear me out
lucky two the closing
but the third comes of itself
the King card
just as the cawing magpie
staggers about with his dazzled throat
his fight against the sun.
Oh wonderous, arid love
your long train of abandonments
neither embroidered mantle
nor coverlet with figures
complaints about belonging too much
as if forever consecrated
but so desolate
like the honor of every thing.

But a quick
budding inclination
how one pales at setbacks
time an immense foilage
this rustling of light inside the eye
perhaps they're your silk stockings.
But nights continue to pile up even now,
and watering cans too, and huge dahlias;
lasting is whatever wants to last,
to head toward a sense is tiresome,
an apple appears
and it doesn't mean your lover,
the solitude of water is greater;
from somewhere during sleep
it's a reminder
evenly round pearl beads
the lions don't rest now
everything, an eternity, sweet majesty,
a description always smacks of Sunday
everything that's equal
that's similar
even calling out many times
it's not easy to fall into something else.

It means you haven't been broken down enough to know,
broken down to pollen, to communal water,
or diminished to the clarity of slow flour;
hide even your name, razor-thin.

Or like listening at night to the changes inside us
such empty, driven sails, such gulfs
a driven wind in the whiteness
our nudity of years ago
suspended at night in its well
and if it doesn't become as soon as possible
either a tree or a hare.

Let's wish ourselves all good luck at varying.

Wood pigeons or other birds
fly up to the right frequency
as when one tilts
or rumbles into the next minute.

There are other difficulties in our state:
understanding how exteriors are formed
kitchens visible from windows
and inside it all a technique
between heavy curtains
each place separated off in its enjoyment.

But how to conduct a search or get rich when
even the moon in the fullness of nights among the vine tendrils
quantity quantity blackest curls
she's exhausted, richer in the shadows, thankful;
in such fullness don't give your error any time,
describe the languages galore of all sectors, and the divisions;
but these collisions, nervous matchsticks, cheery flames of
brushwood, mane-like tongues, anyway it's done,
so much more than a burning bush, but you
silent nest
remorse
just barely worth keeping, old tin can
desire that muddles
dawn arising, tail end to the rhythm;
on valleys the rain of motion of gentle change
rain of all gardens, ceaseless time
that brings or leaves it leaves it.

Candid Camera

Ciò che convolvolo ritorna
fradicio tenero tempo

o come tesoro nei barlumi
ma tu non tornare
lingua che ritorna
con cento rimedi galleggia
favoloso sapere
questo rumore è l'acqua
che incanta il suo andare
ma con che piede di porco
scassinare
insinuare me o te
tra tutti i nomi dei fagioli   ·
le mille speci vane sconnessioni
ci vuole tempo per enumerare
ciò che si attorciglia
ciò che ama l'acqua
introvabili tuttora introvati
non competere con chi può durare
non è vero che tutto è iniziato
ci serve assolutamente iniziare
o tradurre in moneta
ma guizzare
o trovare un'altra stanza in città
cresta di zafferano
è l'ira necessaria che avversa
ricciolo di tutti i nervosi
ma ciò che è voluto
sia lodato
iroso mangiatempo
così anche i gerani
di cui si sente parlare
i pergolati di rose.

ma ciò che si offre al declinare
freschi zampilli nel cielo notturna primavera
come orme nel cielo o come apparsi
movimenti di piume non muovono te

più dolci pendolini che sollevano
grande cielo che si svuota
sera lunata
ma discendere dolce capogiro
se vogliamo finire una cosa
tra volitivi volendo
ospiti essenziali
o imitare la scomparsa
sotto le foglie, nelle stanze
rugiada in te, pelosa, come perle.

ma né felice pendenza
né a lungo stormire
ma puro diseguale
unico lontano unico gioco
se mi metto appostato per te
o apposta tu me
dove finisce il nascosto
come mi vuoi consumare
beato due la chiusura
ma il tre che vien da sé
la carta del re
così la gazza che fischia
traballa per la gola abbagliata
la sua rissa contro il sole
oh beata, arida amata,
il tuo lungo corteggio di abbandoni
né manto trapunto
né coltre di figure
lamenti del tanto appartenere
come per sempre dedicata
ma come desolata
così l'onore di ogni cosa.

tuttavia veloce
nascente inclinazione
come si sbianca per rovesci

immenso fogliame il tempo
questo fruscio della luce dentro l'occhio
forse sono le tue calze di seta
ma ancora si depongono sere
e innaffiatoi, grandissime dalie
il durevole ciò che vuole durare
verso il senso come ci si stanca
appare una mela
e non significa l'amata
più grande è la solitudine dell'acqua
da qualche parte nel sonno
è un promemoria
esattamente rotondi chicchi di perla
ora non stanno accovacciati leoni
le cose, tempo venerato, dolce maestà,
sempre domenicale è la descrizione
tra ciò che si uguaglia
ciò che rassomiglia
anche chiamando molte volte
non si cade facilmente in altra cosa.

allora tu non sei disfatto abbastanza per sapere
disfatto fino al polline all'acqua comune
o diminuire fino al chiarore la lenta farina
nascondere anche il nome assottigliare

o come di notte in noi l'ascolto del mutare
così vuote vele sospinte così golfi
un'aria sospinta nel biancore
o antica nudità
sospesa di notte nel suo pozzo
ma se ciò non diventa al più presto
o albero o leprotto

auguriamoci fortuna nel variare

colombacci o altri uccelli

spiccheranno a una giusta frequenza
così quando si inclina
o rumoreggia nell'altro minuto

ci sono altre difficoltà nel nostro stato:
capire come si formano gli esterni
da finestre si vedono cucine
più all'interno di tutto una tecnica
tra spesse cortine ogni luogo
separato nel suo godimento

ma come perlustrare arricchire che anche
le lune nel pieno di notti tra tanti viticci
quantità quantità più neri riccioli
sfiancata è più ricca in penombra ringrazia
non dare tempo all'errore nel tutto pieno descrivi
a bizzeffe tutte le lingue settoriali i reparti
ma queste collisioni cerini nervosi le fiamme
rallegranti sterpaglie crinite lingue uno stile
qualunque più rovo ma tu
silenzioso nido
rimorso
malapena vecchia tolla
volontà che ingarbuglia
l'alba sorgente la breve strisciolina del ritmo
su valli, pioggia del movimento, del dolce mutare
pioggia di tutti i giardini, tempo incessante
che porta o lasciare lasciare.

TIZIANO ROSSI

Tiziano Rossi was born in Milan in 1935. As a boy he lived through numerous bombings of Milan during World War II before his family sought refuge in a tiny village in the hills near Bergamo. He holds a degree in Italian Literature from the University of Milan, where he wrote his graduating thesis on early Italian Romanticism. For many years he worked as an editor for such publishing houses as Feltrinelli and Garzanti. Since 1989 he has been a freelance consultant in Milan for the scolastic textbook division of Einaudi. He has written for numerous newspapers and reviews, and is especially known for his column on aspects of the Italian language, which appeared regularly in *Unità* during the sixties.

Rossi's poetry is a meditated reflection on the past, be it the war era and its effects on his family or the experiences of his life since then. This filtering of the past is done with such control over language that any harsh aspects are finely mitigated, emerging, where they must, in the form of questions left unanswered or in clipped aphorisms. The tone is that of an amiable tête-à-tête, the author presenting himself to the reader as a friend worth listening to. Rossi's recent poems have extended to such subjects as the solar system; here, he has developed a personal pocket-sized cosmogony, as it were, giving new expression to the theme of mankind's forcible acceptance of the unpleasant side to existence.

POETRY

Il cominciamondo (The World Beginning) 1963
La talpa imperfetta (The Less than Perfect Mole) 1968
Dallo sdrucciolare al rialzarsi (Slip-Sliding Then On Your Feet
    Again) 1976
Quasi costellazione (Almost a Constellation) 1982
Miele e no (Not Always Honey) 1988
Il movimento dell'adagio (The Motions of a Slow Proceeding)
    1993

OTHER

a critical edition-anthology of Foscolo (1965)

Insomnia

Insomnia thinks and pronounces syllables.

What the devil does our highly adventuresome
enterprise consist in?
"You should know, dear Rossi, that in..."
then the good part of the intellect clouds over
and other, more genuine, wounded figures
put a line through the helpless time everyone lives.

Red and sticky the jam at tea time,
so many insects bouncing in the doorway,
and up in some attic a nice roll in the hay;
say something to the lady, tell her, "*ciao, ciao*"; and
what wonderful balance pedaling down
the exact middle of the wide road,
making even the bus slow its speed.

Oh faces of shaved sand, you rise halfway
in the air, along with us on our pilgrimage,
only then you go your separate way!
A detour to dig nails into the night,
pregnant lady who has lain with all.

Insonnia

L'insonnia pensa e dice le sillabe.

In cosa diavolo consisterà
la nostra alta ventura impresa?
"Deve sapere, caro Rossi, che nel..."
poi s'è appannato il ben dell'intelletto ed altre
più vere trafitte figure
rigano il tempo di tutti, indifeso

Rossa si appiccica la marmellata
della merenda, quanti insetti
ballonzolano dove è la soglia, in quale
soffitta si abbracciano le paglie,
saluta la Signora, falle ciao ciao, e con
che splendido equilibrio si pedala nel
centro esatto di quello stradone
mentre rallentava perfino la corriera

Oh, facce di sabbia rada, a mezz'aria
sollevate, insieme a noi pellegrinanti, e dopo
per proprio conto divaricate!
di là a striare la notte, compagna
incinta rimasta di tutti.

Pot

Your house like the upper deck of a ship,
or better, on the order of a large pot,
presently on route to a confusing island,
and you--the three of you--
getting all exercised there by the lamp,

with bubbles of words which in a trail begin to burn,
which display undeciphered qualities
capable of giving you a slap, say,
though of affection.

It's simply beyond comparison
the way, loving each other,
you wear each other down within
your narrow bounds of territory;
for that world, that world that will never be,
though the dripping sound of your loss
is hardly noticeable.

All honor to you, therefore, and honor
to the floor, to the chairs, to the hot radiator,
and to other numerous companion gadgets.

(End of your daily episode.)

Pentola

La vostra casa come alta tolda di nave
o, meglio, somigliante a una gran pentola
ancora in rotta verso un'isola confusa
e voi che in tre
vi agitate in vicinanza della lampada

con bolle di parole, brucianti in una scia,
e sfoggiando qualità non decifrate,
magari per darvi uno schiaffo, ma d'affetto,

ah, come incomparabilmente
amandovi vi sciupate
in questa ristretta competenza territoriale
per quel mondo, quel mondo che mai sarà,
ma quasi nemmeno si nota
lo stillicidio del vostro perdere.

Onore quindi a voi, ed anche all'impiantito,
alle seggiole, al caldo termosifone
e agli altri numerosi ammennicoli compagni.

(Fine della vostra puntata giornaliera)

Possibility

You who smile from the disarmed
edge of this house and send your thousand

cheerful best wishes spinning into the void:
I hope you're still faithful to yourselves.

I hope that you maintain sovereign control over
your few but charming things (down to the ways
in which you make your polite withdrawals or
compassionate silences) and that
your feelings still dart out to surprise!

Then--although no one has said what in
dark times counts most--
the becalmed room turns on its side;
the napkins, the erect glasses, the brown
beer bottle remain sitting on the table;
and sailing over us the most
wonderful thing: possibility.

(You too--go and get a bit of rest now.)

Possibilità

Voi che sorridete sulla riva
disarmata di questa casa, nel vuoto roteando
i vostri cento auguri spiritosi:
spero che voi siate ancora con voi!

e che restiate sovrani di poche
cose, ma garbate (perfino coltivando le
forme della ritrosia beneducata,
del riguardoso tacere) e che ancora
guizzino inattesi i vostri affetti!

Poi--benché non si sia detto
ciò che nel tempo grave più conta--
la stanza placata s'è girata su di un fianco,
sul tavolo rimangono seduti i tovaglioli,

gli impettiti bicchieri, la bottiglia
marroncina della birra; e sopra
ci veleggia la cosa più bella:
la possibilità.

(E vada a riposare un po' anche Lei, adesso)

Beach

No oasis anymore; and beauty
here has stopped counting.
So just what are we chasing after in this sand
that isn't a beach but a misery, as
now, wedged in between relic-old driftwood and
the too many legacies of our predecessors (a repeated sowing
every summer), we strain towards a dirty but
beloved sea?
While an invincible transistor radio
broadcasts along blood-red backs and through
a sum total of sweats, and over the wheeze of an asthma
it's SUMMER VACATION,
the VACATION that we pursue in this form because
being stuck together means remaining together.
But will proximity help us?

So much violent rubbish whirling about the temples
that we can't hear each other anymore. Never mind,
we are still free to do our huddling together, be
monuments of strange value, and
from so little and so bad at least
obtain some austere juice.
(Even from looked-for troubles something good!)
My son's frown disappears once
he unearths from under this foulness,
and waves heroically,
a tattered toy English flag.

Spiaggia

Non oasi da nessuna parte più; e non conta
oramai qui la bellezza.
Cosa quindi rincorriamo in questa sabbia
che non è spiaggia ma la miseria, adesso noi
già un po' incollati in mezzo ai
reliquati pezzetti di legno e i troppi làsciti
dei predecessori (ad ogni estate
qui si ripete un seminare), protendendoci al
mare sporcato che si ama?
Mentre la radiolina invincibile trasmette
lungo le schiene quasi cruente, in
una somma di sudori e sopra
il soffio di un'asma, è LA VACANZA
LA VACANZA che inseguiamo così fatta
perché congiunti più insieme si rimanga.
Ma vicinanza ci aiuterà?

Tanti detriti violenti vorticano alle tempie
da più non sentirci, però ancora ci resta
l'abbracciarci tra noi, monumenti
di strano valore
che da così poco e male almeno un succo
austero caveremo. Ed anche
(da quali rovistate disgrazie il pregio!)
la smorfia di mio figlio ha fine
quando, riemersa da sudicia terra,
in mano eroicamente gli risventola questa
lacerata bandierina d'Inghilterra.

Leaving

The unraveling wins out: I leave my home--
a place grown estranged to me.
And though I lack that daring battlefield quality,

I'm going to pierce a hole through another
onion skin of life and drink down the
dying light, make my change;
after worlds of excuses and the profoundest pretexts,
I'm stealing away on nobody's orders
(dark courtyard, defensive line of doors,
old youthful discipline,
vows, other small pieces of years lived:
how the thought I carried inside me
gets turned inside out!).
My son knows everything but doesn't turn around.
He's found his balance of precocious wisdom,
he cuts out paper soldiers, he'll cut me out too,
make me win for a bit, then perish in the end.

Slowly, with a voice that wavers and a head that betrays,
I march off, example of ineptitude. I follow certain
unexpected arabesques of love but leave behind me
neither shining trace nor spittle.
Elbows and eyes remain stubbornly in place
but the sky expands, why delay?
Stories broken, reknit, broken.

Partenza

Lo sgomitolo vince, mi tolgo da casa mia
maturata per me a foresteria
ed anche se sono povero di quella
ardita virtù delle battaglie, forerò
un'altra buccia della vita cipolla
per inghiottire le penultime luci, fare svolta:
dopo mondi di scuse e pretesti profondi
mi trafugherò su comando di nessuno
(buio cortile, difendersi di porte,
antico rigore giovanile
e giuramenti ed altri pezzetti di età,

come il pensiero che portavo è stravoltato!).
Mio figlio sa tutto e non si gira, s'è
calibrato precoce una saggezza,
ritaglia i soldatini, ritaglierà anche me,
mi farà vincere un po', e nell'ultimo perire.

Così inseguendo certi impreveduti
ghirigori di amori
ma non lasciando dietro le spalle
né fulgida traccia né bava,
io voce che svaria, testa che tradisce
lento mi defilo, esempio di inettitudine:
qui gomiti ed occhi si impuntano ancora, ma
il cielo si allarga, perché ritardare?
Trame rotte, annodate, rotte.

System

And then as regards the great wave
of liquid structures, overturned in
all its floating mass during the evolution
of the Earth's rotations,
immense whirlpools can be seen that

sometimes become tidal waves
uprooting tree trunks, or else it's possible to see
lightning in the making and its
incalculable energy which varies
with creative effort.

So the Sun as a planet is neither hot nor cold,
for it is nothing less than a fruit
incarnating what has been generated by the bodies
in its system; bodies that in far-off millenniums
strained under the weight of
its enormous purpose.

Sistema

Quando poi pensi alla grande marea
delle strutture liquide, che vengono capovolte
con tutto il suo carico galleggiante
nelle evoluzioni dei giri della Terra,
si vedono le estensioni di risucchio che in certi

casi prendono forma di trombe d'aria sradicando
fusti di albero, oppure come si crea
il fulmine e la sua incalcolabile potenza
a seconda del suo sforzo creato.

Dunque il Sole non è un pianeta né caldo né freddo,
perché è nientemeno che il frutto dove termina
l'incarnazione causata da tutti i corpi
del suo sistema
che nei millenni remoti si sono trovati a portare
il suo enorme intendimento.

Law

No planet revolves around the Sun
but rather, each one in place submits to a
whirling, even along its external seams, on the
basis of the extent of its formative influences.
For this reason the Earth's weight has never really
been zero and in its small way can
manifest itself in the universe,
allowing us to assume that tiny lizards
can crawl over it without falling off.

And so if we think of the sequence repeated
under the laws of rotations and the
weight obtained, we start to back off
and we are left covered by a blanketing layer,

that's to say atmosphere,
which follows us about as a
figure that pirouettes and as
the relative phases of the seasons.

We're living through hard times,
for even close relatives are cold to each other
and very few merit love.
Best wishes.

Legge

Nessun pianeta gira attorno al Sole
ma bensì ognuno nel proprio punto
a seconda dell'ampiezza del suo influsso formativo
e anche in giro alla saldatura esterna
ne viene a subire il ruotare.
Per questo il peso della Terra in realtà non è
mai stato zero e nel suo piccolo
può farsi il suo materiamento nella sfera universale,
che supponiamo delle lucertoline
potrebbero camminarci sopra
senza mai più staccarsi da esso.

E allora se pensiamo alle susseguenze a ripetizione
sotto la legge circolatoria e il peso raggiunto,
s'incomincia a prendere il largo
e siamo circondati da uno strato di coltre,
cioè atmosfera,
che ci segue in figura di avvitamenti e
relative fasi stagionali.

Viviamo tempi difficili, che c'è
freddezza anche tra i parenti
e ci son pochi da volergli bene.
Cari saluti.

THIRD
GENERATION:
Poets Born After 1945

DARIO VILLA

Dario Villa was born in Milan in 1953 and died in 1996. He was a professional translator of French and English fiction and poetry (he translated much by English poets Basil Bunting and Tom Raworth), and published his own poetry and essays in various literary reviews both in Italy and abroad. He served as overseas editor for *Address* (New York), and recently co-directed *Arte Nanetta, a portable museum to pocket the last decade of the millenium,* as well as *Biancaneve*, a polyglot journal of poetry and the arts.

Villa's poetry reserves continual surprises for the reader, of the sort that only a solid understanding of the "tricks" inherent to language make possible. A slight grammatical anomaly may unleash a vortex of meanings that seem to have appeared out of nowhere when in truth they've been lurking in the background all along. Content-wise, his poems read somewhat like special instruction manuals, or rules for living, and yet there is no manifest intent to teach or preach. If anything, it is the reader who feels eager, as he would with an oracle, to gleam something of his destiny from Villa's monologue.

POETRY

AA.VV. Architettura, pittura, fotografia (Architecture, Painting, and Photography) (work by various poets) 1980

Lapsus in Fabula 1984 (Mondello Prize)

Proemi in posa (Posed Preludes) 1985

Tra le ciglia (a dual language edition, English translation, *Between the Eyebrows*, by British poet Tom Raworth) 1993

La bambola gonfiabile e altre signore (The Inflatable Doll and Other Ladies) 1994

Abiti insolubili (Insoluble Habits) 1995

Venere strapazzata dai lunatici (Venus Mistreated by Lunatics) 1995

it is
(the shadow that remains on its feet when I fall)
more like me than me.
                I'm so much more human
so detached from myself
my hand plunged between two riverbanks of thirst
where nothing flows but an idea of time
gushing from someone else but swallowed by all

today this house has the order of the windows
the inclination of the roof
the argument of the rooms
the internalised door
the question put by the bed and the famous clocks

life has sinuous rhythms
like the languors of a woman
tatooed by the grooves in this or that
meaning overturning
                as the wave splatters
and where the fish elaborated by the abyss
flounders, full
of spiny hopes
  where if there is no water if nothing else pushes
        depth surface
politics lie beyond the interests of the dead
a pity I would have been a good ghost

a stunned tantalus at the edge of the pool

è più simile a me
l'ombra che resta in piedi quando cado
di quanto non sia io
                tanto più umano

così staccato da me

con la mano tuffata tra due rive di sete
dove non scorre che un'idea del tempo
scaturita da un altro e bevuta da tutti

oggi la casa ha l'ordine delle finestre
l'inclinazione del tetto
la teoria delle stanze
la porta interiorizzata
la domanda del letto e gli orologi famosi

la vita ha ritmi sinuosi
come i languori di una donna
tatuata dal solco in questo o un altro
senso che si rovescia
                        dove piove l'onda
dove naufraga pieno
di spinose speranze
il pesce elaborato dall'abisso
            dove   se non c'è acqua   se nient'altro preme
                    profondità superficie
la politica esula dall'interesse dei morti
peccato sarei stato un buon fantasma

un tantalo intontito sull'orlo della vasca

...then if I think about it,
I've lived once already.
I've already drunk,
already downed the subtle liqueur
of the seasons.
With you or others,
I've already been inebriated with this hour,
with a wine of shadows, with a deed undone...

...poi, se ci penso, sono
già esistito in passato,
ho già bevuto,
ho già bevuto il liquore
sottile delle stagioni,
con te o con altri mi sono
già inebriato di quest'ora,
di un vino d'ombre, di un atto mancato...

...in the end,
        positions
                (time stood on its head)
        crumble or advance, nets
(blades that cut up contradictions)
snare delicate wrists;
when the time comes, they need to be buried and these are
words, gestures, rites hastily carried out
between stone and sky;
these are rivers that have gone off with
the bones and returned as raging dust, and then
nothing. Nothing and no one is
waiting for them, not a soul,
not even a dog on the shadowy bank;
soul-ferrying jackal, expert of this fog,
you who carry them across the
blind pulsing
which has brought them as far as this side--
but there's only one side to this limbo.

...infine
    posizioni
            (si rovescia
il tempo)
        crollano o avanzano, reti
(lame che tagliano contraddizioni)

accalappiano polsi delicati,
e allora vanno seppelliti, e sono
parole, gesti, riti consumati
in fretta tra la pietra e il cielo, e sono
fiumi andati con gli ossi,
tornati polvere irosa, poi niente

e nessuno li aspetta non c'è un'anima
nemmeno un cane sull'argine d'ombra
sciacallo psicopompo
che li traghetti esperto delle brume
oltre il battito cieco
che li ha portati fino a questa sponda
--ha soltanto una sponda questo limbo

What counts in any action
is that almost carefree showing--
premeditated--mythical--
of your intention. You've got to
go back to the roots. Find the
most single-minded colors.
What strikes the eye straight off is
the polymorphic orchestration
of those colors' variety.

After all, even the senses have a soul.
Every fiber, every atom,
the root of our hair (meaning the brain),
the endings of our feet--
all of this had better take heed of
the slick floor of logic, the
stiff analogy of a ceiling.
The danger entices. Normality--that
deceiving, spotted animal--crouches everywhere,
ready to capture us.
We could almost die from it.

And it's death twice over when
those fanatic shadow-fighters
split their guts falling from the windows.

There--it's done? I adore you all.
You're my favorite monsters.

When a baby is born,
that's a girl who's become a mother.
And don't forget the roses:
it's their label; they're the most malicious,
most zealous symbols of
causality. Of course
there's no need to say
that we'll soon be back to gesturing,
an overrated theory
(as all theories are). In fact, given
the exceptional crop of theories this year
there's no need to say
anything. We are ungrammatical,
obscure sentences contemptuous of
the discerning glance of linguists.
And where there's meaning asleep
in arbitrary signs,
it's best not to wake it up. Otherwise...

Like that octopussy abbess,
charitable jellyfish who
nursing on a hot-air balloon
recognized orgasm and was canonized.

Essenziale, nel gesto,
è l'ostensione quasi casuale,
premeditata--mitica--
dell'intenzione. Bisogna
partire dalle radici. Si prendano

i colori più monomaniacali.
Balza subito all'occhio
l'orchestrazione polimorfa
della policromia.

Dopotutto, anche i sensi hanno un'anima.
Ogni fibra, ogni atomo,
l'etimo dei capelli che è il cervello,
la desinenza dei piedi,
tutto stia bene attento ai pavimenti
lucidi della logica, all'inflessibile
analogia dei soffitti.
Il rischio invischia. La normalità,
bestia bugiarda e maculata,
si acquatta ovunque, pronta a catturarci.
Si potrebbe persino morire.
E si muore due volte
quando dalle finestre si precipitano,
infrangendo le pance,
gli irriducibili pompieri dell'ombra.

Ecco fatto? Vi adoro.
Siete i miei mostri preferiti.

Quando nasce un bambino
è una ragazza che diventa madre.
E non scordate le rose:
è l'etichetta, sono i più maligni,
i più zelanti simboli
della causalità. Naturalmente
non c'è bisogno di dire
che torneremo nel gesto,
teoria troppo nota (come tutte
le teorie). Difatti
data l'annata eccezionale
di teorie, quest'anno
non c'è bisogno di dire

niente. Noi siamo periodi
oscuri, sgrammaticati, irridenti
alle occhiate sagaci dei filologi.
E quando il senso dorme
nell'arbitrio dei segni,
è bene non risvegliarlo. Altrimenti...

Come quella badessa polipaia,
medusa caritatevole che
poppando a un dirigibile
riconobbe l'orgasmo e fu canonizzata.

Remember the goose that
ended up in the office district
for some reason: etched, somehow, onto
the skyscraper with a graver--very

serious thing--and this highly personal way
of hers of watching her reflection in the windows
ah, burdensome liver and feather
and beak and antiquated symbol

darkness naturally
the long low
narrow blue room.

ricordi l'oca chissà come
capitata nel centro
direzionale: incisa, come,
nel grattacielo a bulino--gravissima

cosa--e quel modo
tutto suo di specchiarsi alle vetrate
ah gravura di fegato e piuma
di becco e di simbolo antico

il buio certo
la lunga
bassa
sottilissima camera azzurra

Sometimes, Doctor, I awake
in a night scene
in a white embrace and--
to put it briefly:
I find there's a huge deformed girl
with me.
Explain to me something about the theory of similars.
Tell me what it has to do
with the liver, with poor wine, with death.

Dottore, destandomi a volte
in un notturno,
in una bianca carezza
--per farla breve:
scopro
che una femmina immensa, deforme,
è meco.
Mi esponga
la teoria dei simili.
Mi dica cosa c'entra il fegato, il vinello, la morte.

The blades and slime, the limits,
and then the lights--of reason--
(flat cold if it weren't for love's rare vegetation)
crack the clock on my mind's bell tower.

Emptiness in the making--
deep, square traps for catching the
fantastical geometric progress of delirium--.

What shrill choruses, blue dizziness, colors.

I use pieces of glass and bits of childhood
but I like to think of mosaics as haphazardly inspired.
Have I really lived, when it comes down to it? Taking
stock, I guess I've read poppies, leafed through a few
newspapers.

Le lame e i limi, i limiti, e poi i lumi,
della ragione--piatto algore se non
fosse per rare vegetazioni d'amore--
rompono l'orologio del campanile mentale.

Il divenire del vuoto--quell'altro
tendere agguati cubici al fantastico
progedire geometrico del delirante--:
che striduli cori, vertigini azzurre, colori.

Dispongo di pezzi di vetro, frammenti d'infanzia,
ma dell'arte musiva m'è cara l'incuria.
Ho mai vissuto, tra l'altro? Credo, ripensandoci,
d'aver letto papaveri, sfogliato qualche giornale.

SILVIO GIUSSANI

Silvio Giussani was born in Novate Milanese, on the outskirts of Milan, in 1951. In the past he has taught middle school and tutored handicapped children; since 1990, he has worked as a coordinator in a center for the mentally ill. Giussani has also written essays and reviews for an Italian-Swiss newspaper and conducted a cultural program for the Italian State Radio (RAI). His prose poetry has appeared in numerous Italian literary reviews and translations of his work have been published in America and Great Britain.

In Giussani's work there is a curious interweaving of private obsessions and metaphysical observations--or better, there is a sense of both lurking in the imagery, when not in a strangely negated phase, or in the echo that the reader hears reverberating from one poem to the next. The matter-of-fact voice giving its rapid, objective-seeming description of settings and situations contrasts strongly with the repressed violence just under the surface. While his early prose poems can be compared to a strange flurry of photographs that halt an instant and make an object of it, his recent works extend for longer, "cinematic" sequences; moreover, he has switched from the present to the past tenses, giving stress to impersonal constructions (like "there was"), wherein memory intrinsically abides.

POETRY

Emmaus 1984
AA.VV. Sette Poeti del Premio Montale (The Seven Winning Poets of the Montale Prize) 1988
Madame Tusseaud 1994

Towards A Beginning

Trains go towards the fast bridge where in the darkness the wind fights sleep, towards the barking of dogs of which the hint of an instant name remains. Noumena stick to all the crevices that in my mind might be shadows.

An old song with holes here and there. Neighborhoods waiting for a certain moment to come or go. Now through the branches, the wind hisses the geographies of itself and of souls carried to those limits of the sight-line.

I'm outside any mind I believed I had, and beyond all its habits. Smiling, my father sits up in his coffin. Layers of sound hit against time made slow--the cavern towards which we return.

Verso l'inizio

I treni vanno verso il ponte veloce dove il vento lotta al buio col suo sonno, verso il latrare dei cani dei quali resta l'ombra di un nome istantaneo. Noumeni si attaccano a tutte le crepe della mia mente che potrebbero essere ombre.

Una vecchia canzone bucata qua e là. Quartieri che aspettano che un certo momento venga o se ne vada. Il vento, ora, sibila tra i rami geografie di sé e di anime portate a quei confini della vista.

Sono fuori da qualsiasi mente ho creduto d'avere, e da tutte le sue abitudini. Sorridendo, mio padre si è alzato a sedere nella sua bara. Strati di suono battono contro tempo divenuto adagio, che è la caverna verso cui ritorniamo.

In The Distance

There was a mute noise. The air of wheat when it allows itself to be watched. Dust from chalk, of fish from the Ice Age. In the wind the pigs sniffed the at-hand smell of their blood.

I envisaged ochre dunes, rain hitting with a light brown force. The nearly imperceptible weight of water, shivering embolus, yet it was heavy, setting on notebooks a past of hills and hard lunches.

Youths, heads followed by the beginnings of a neck.

Nella distanza

C'era un muto rumore. Un'aria della capacità di grano di lasciarsi guardare. Una polvere di gesso, di pesce dell'era glaciale. I maiali fiutavano, nel vento, l'odore prossimo del loro sangue.

Immaginavo dune ocra, la pioggia che s'abbatteva in un impeto castano. Il peso dell'acqua, embolia freddolosa, era quasi impercettibile, però pesava, posando sui quaderni un passato di colline e di merende dure.

Giovani, teste inseguite da un inizio di collo.

Hot and Cold

It's that hour when I empty my dreams of my existence in order to tell existence about this dream that is nothing if not myself. The wind outside goes barefoot, whistling to a dog of years ago. Dawn light filters across roofs into the dark garden. Its grass appears, damp with grey dew.

Herring fish swim about my room. Adventurers with tobacco come to the window to ask for a match. Moments of transcendence detour into oceans of hatred and fear, moonfish or phosphoric flashes at sea.

Caldo, freddo

È l'ora in cui comincio a far uscire dai miei sogni l'esistenza, alla quale racconto questo sogno nel momento in cui è me stesso. Il vento fuori passeggia scalzo, fischiando al cane di molto tempo fa. Luce d'alba arriva attraverso i tetti fino al buio giardino. L'erba ne emerge, impregnata di rugiada grigia.

Nuotano pesci nella mia stanza, aringhe. Avventurieri vengono alla finestra a chiedere fuoco per il loro tabacco. Momenti di trascendenza derivano verso oceani d'odio e paura, pesciluna o lampi di fosforo in mare.

The Aridness of Air

The sprinkler had come out on the road with a green hiss panning old peels and papers. As it dried, the water left a story like that of fresh melon. A spider swam in the branches on a day that established calm stillness like a pyramid on its tip. The fragile grass someone carried to the barn.

But where summer comprehends how much you hate biting a lemon as bitter as the world and the radio transmits a bouquet of sounds, geodetic signal no one understands, spiders aim only at existing quietly in what, as unlivable, is hounded by life.

L'aridità dell'aria

Sulla strada l'innaffiatrice era uscita col sibilo verde delle sue sventagliate su bucce e su giornali. L'acqua asciugandosi lasciava una trama come di fresca anguria. Un ragno nuotava sui rami, nel giorno che stabiliva la calma come una piramide sulla sua punta. Qualcuno portava la fragile erba alla stalla.

Ma dove l'estate comprende quanto si odia addentando un limone aspro come il mondo e la radio trasmette un mazzetto di suoni geodetico segnale che nessuno capisce, i ragni non si propongono altro che di stare tranquilli nel non vivibile di tutto ciò che vive scoperto dalla vita.

The Clothes Without the Monk

1.

Rooster nights with crests of screams; sleep that's gotten old. Smokestacks of machine shops, decapitated palms with smoking leaves. The mind moves towards a dry music, faded alarm sticking to the smell of grass. Owls blot their fat that goes from limb to limb with a green beak.

New buildings, unborn rooms. Cleaver sells guerilla warfare, stenography for illegitimate children. Thoughts send unpackaged thoughts into my mouth.

2.

There's a happening scratching its beat under the skin. The pockmarked paint of jeans grows into his pedestal of a time to come. Dawn already has the mint smell of the first smell, fluid mountains.

There are rooms with walls situated at a distance of years. Weight returns to weight in cold water. An hotel room returns from pitch-dark hills. A boat setting sail without crew returns in thirty years of snow.

L'abito senza il monaco

1.

Notte di galli con creste di urla; il sonno che diventa vecchio. Fumaioli d'officine, palmizi decapitati a fogliame di fumo. La mente si muove verso una musica secca, allarme avvizzito a cui s'incolla l'odore d'erba. Civette asciugano il grasso che va di ramo in ramo con becco verde.

Nuovi edifici, stanze che non sono nate.   Cleaver vende guerriglia, stenografia per figli illegittimi. Pensieri si mandano lingue non imballate dentro la bocca.

2.

C'è un avvenimento che graffia il suo battito sotto la pelle. L'intonaco di jeans crivellato cresce a lui piedistallo per un tempo a venire. Nell'alba c'è già l'odore di menta del primo suono, montagne fluide.

Ci sono stanze dai muri situate a distanza di anni. Pesi ritornano a pesi nell'acqua fredda. Una camera d'albergo torna da buie colline. Una barca salpa senza equipaggio ritornando in 30 anni di neve.

Abel and Abel

The Saint Bernards carry the food bowl, not him. Pasting relics on books, it's clear that at age seven he is learning about distances, beginning with his mother's knee.   On the grass, among things sitting like mail to be read, his father paints his testimony to an orderly world.

The evening is humid, in the air the leaves bite at thoughts. She's there in the shadows under the arch, lifting a dim lamp of a face, the white hair rolled back, the cheekbones almost free: old owl on a tree of ribs, who preaches from high up on her bones' scaffolding.

A tugboat in the harbor goes by launching its low note, risen from the lowest depths of the sea. A broom hisses over the asphalt like feet among leaves. John Wayne hovers in his sleep over blood-soaked terrain where the bodies of Marines collapse under the light of his hatred. It is destroyed in the neon, hung on the string of lights along the beach so that everyone can see and exercise caution: "The bottom is called obscurity, obscuring the obscurity is the way in."

Abele e Abele

I sanbernardo portano la ciotola, lui no. Incollando reliquie sui libri, si vede a sette anni che impara la distanza al ginocchio di sua madre. Nell'erba, tra cose sedute come posta da leggere, suo padre dipinge la sua testimonianza ad un mondo ordinato.

La sera è umida, nell'aria le foglie mordono pensieri. Lei se ne sta in ombra sotto l'arco sollevando la lampada fievole del volto, i capelli bianchi arrotolati indietro, gli zigomi quasi liberi: vecchia civetta su un albero di costole, che predica dall'alto dell'impalcatura delle sue ossa.

Un rimorchiatore nel porto passa lanciando la sua nota di basso, alzata dal più basso del mare. Una scopa sibila sopra l'asfalto come piedi tra le foglie. John Wayne fluttua nel sonno su terreni intrisi di sangue dove i corpi dei marines sprofondano alla luce del suo odio. È distrutto nel neon, appeso al filo di luci lungo la spiaggia, perché tutti vedano, e stiano attenti: "Il fondo si chiama oscurità, oscurare questa oscurità è l'entrata".

Vegetable Calendar

There's a woman who resembles a phrase. She has a spot of memory that moves language. Her children fall from insect lamps, pearls in the greyness.

There are memories everywhere. In the garden the ants tend to their black cows, dense foam that devours the juice of things green.

There's a spot out of which courses the information called desire. There are large remains of dark caverns, Comanche dynasties fleeing from the brain. In the blue coves inside the blue, mathematicians battle on the edge of freedom to close the too many doors that let in rain.

There is sometimes a note I can't explain. Sounded in voiceless air, it comes close to the echo of a beetle. A sparrow on the invisible wire of a dream. A verb sentenced to its literal meaning. In a dawn riddled with still corners I wait for those who put in the parentheses of ending.

Calendario vegetale

C'è una donna che assomiglia alla frase. Ha un luogo della memoria che muove il linguaggio. I bambini cadono dalle lampade d'insetti, perle nel grigio.

Ci sono ricordi ovunque. Nel giardino le formiche badano alle loro mucche nere, densa schiuma che divora il succo del verde.

C'è un luogo dal quale fluisce l'informazione che è desiderio. Vi sono grandi resti di oscure caverne, le dinastie dei Comanches in fuga dal cervello. Nelle spelonche d'azzurro dentro l'azzurro i matematici s'impegnano sull'orlo della libertà, per chiudere le troppe porte da cui cade la pioggia.

C'è talvolta una nota che non posso spiegare. Un'aria senza voce reggendola ne trae come l'eco di uno scarabeo. Un passero sul filo invisibile del sogno. Un verbo condannato al suo significato letterale. Nell'alba che è crivellata dagli angoli immobili aspetto coloro che mettono parentesi di fine.

Body Politic

1.
At this hour exiles look for sleep in pills. An ambulance descends the veins of the night, nightmares that drag us to the same address. Genny's in her childhood bed, then suddenly she's awake. Voices on the radio move from inside to out on the tongue, dervishes that leap ahead to the bounds of death.

His mother talks to him as if he were someone famous. Orlando nods, staring at the rust spreading over the branches of the chestnut tree. The clatter of a plate in a sink might be his: it's not much but it's all a man has to offer.

Giovanni's lips make a smacking sound. He's dammed up his blood and turned himself into a stone or dry wood. The living can't make these collect calls: the dead don't accept the charges and it's the living who pay.

2.
Nudity which is a smell in the hands of the air. A delta of arms pine for the water of a vision or for the opposite of every vision, husband to one word and wife to another.

Orlando falls silent suddenly to listen to the rain, drunkard
pissing in the cold dark. The dogs lie down suddenly and sniff
in the smoke of garbage that somebody's burning. The barking
penetrates with the smoke deeper and deeper into europe. Five
or six independent wars rage this morning; this thin blue smoke
comes from a bitter, white bread as it bakes.

Corpo comune

1.
È l'ora in cui gli esiliati cercano il sonno in compresse.
Un'ambulanza discende le vene della notte, gli incubi che ci
trascinano allo stesso indirizzo.   Genny è nel suo letto
d'infanzia.   All'improvviso, è sveglia.   Voci alla radio si
muovono dentro o fuori la lingua, dervisci che balzano avanti al
limitare della morte.

La madre gli parla come se fosse un uomo famoso.   Orlando
annuisce fissando la ruggine che invade i rami del noce.   Il
fracasso di un piatto in un lavandino potrebbe, forse, essere il
suo: non molto ma quanto un uomo può offrire.

Giovanni ha le labbra che fanno un rumore di frusta.   Ha
arginato il suo sangue, facendosi pietra o legno secco. I vivi non
possono chiamarli a loro spese: i morti non accettano il prezzo,
e a pagare sono i vivi.

2.
L'odore che è nudità nelle mani dell'aria, un delta di braccia
desidera l'acqua della visione o del contrario di ogni visione,
marito ad una parola e moglie ad un'altra.

Orlando s'interrompe di colpo per ascoltare la pioggia, ubriaco
che orina nel gelido buio.   I cani si sdraiano di colpo per
annusare, nel fumo dei rifiuti che qualcuno sta bruciando.
L'abbaiare si spinge con il fumo sempre più all'interno

dell'europa. Cinque o sei guerre indipendenti si combattono, ora, questa mattina, questo fumo blu leggero è d'un pane bianco e amaro che viene cotto.

MILO DE ANGELIS

Milo De Angelis was born in Milan in 1951 and recently moved back to Milan from Rome. He holds a degree in Italian Literature and has taught school off and on for years. From 1976 to 1979 he directed the literary magazine, *Niebo,* and today is one of the editors of the monthy review, *Poesia.* He has published translations from Spanish, French, and Classical Latin and Greek. Two anthologies of his work have been translated and published in France, and another was recently published in English by Sun and Moon Press of California.

Poems by De Angelis seem to contain a hidden spring of poetic sense from which the arduous and enigmatic may gush at times. Fairly frequently, in fact, an unexplained, almost magical image may appear out of nowhere, and while De Angelis ably manages to suggest some divine or transcendental origin for it, this image is--more pertinently--revealed to be a metaphor for whatever subject or occasion has inspired the poem. More than one critic has termed his work "phenomenological poetry" and underlined how the thrust and tension are maintained by the continual convergence of elements of prose narrative, lyricism, objective description and fantastical imagery.

POETRY

Somiglianze (Resemblances) 1976
Millimetri (Millimeters) 1983
Terra del viso (The Land of a Face) 1985
Distante un padre (Distant As A Father) 1989

FICTION

La corsa dei mantelli (The Cloak Race) 1979

ESSAYS

Poesia e destino (Poetry and Destiny) 1982

Every Metaphor

The same low sky
of ambulances and rain in the turmoil
and hands on the groin, summoned by the body
to fight off
a faint stupor at things
while outside, amidst traffic lights, europe
which invented the finite   stands firm
far from the animal, defending
real and irrelevant concepts
along its highways, linearly in time
towards some point
and eyes not shutting against things, fixed
where a millennium today hesitated
between giving in and not giving in
always an intelligent way of getting lost, always the delay.

Ogni metafora

Lo stesso cielo basso
di ambulanze e di pioggia, nel turbamento
e le mani sull'inguine, chiamate dal corpo
per opporre
uno stupore minimo alle cose
mentre fuori, tra i semafori, l'europa
che ha inventato il finito
resiste
lontana dall'animale, difende
concetti reali e irrilevanti
lungo le autostrade, nel tempo lineare
verso un punto
e gli occhi non si chiudono contro le cose, fermi
dove un millennio oggi ha esitato
tra cedere e non cedere
perdendosi sempre tardi, e con intelligenza.

Towards the Mind

Before the plums slept
and the real paper went blind
she retreated, feeling
hit and not recognizing
the dog in the water...
it was her father...
she ran out of the kitchen
made a gesture
where the sky happened to be
tearing up the carbon paper
washing the glasses with ashes
ducks like patriarchs
checking to see all is in order
she pulled out her bathing suit
and showed it to the night
scales run after scales
the bandage smells strongly
of chowder
and the apron stays locked up in her head
she waited in an elm tree for
a long thought to end
then she went to the window
and while the grass waited
nine days of June had passed.

Verso la mente

Prima che dormissero le mirabelle
e la vera carta diventasse cieca
indietreggiò sentendosi
colpita e non riconobbe
il cane nell'acqua...
era suo padre...
corse via dalla cucina

fece un cenno
dove capitò il cielo
stracciando la carta carbone
lavando i bicchieri con la cenere
anatre come patriarchi
sorvegliando che tutto sia in ordine
tirò fuori il costume da bagno
e lo mostrò alla notte
bilance rincorrono bilance
la benda odora forte di
zuppa di pesce
e il grembiule è rinchiuso nella testa:
attese sul platano che
un lungo pensiero finisse
poi si affacciò alla finestra
e mentre l'erba aspettava
erano passati nove giorni
di giugno.

The Main Idea

It came to mind (but by chance, suggested by the
whiff of alcohol and the bandages)
this pressing need to push on with plans
despite it all.
And once again, in front of everyone,
                                [a choice was being made
between actions and their meaning.
But by chance.
Despots were carelessly giving away the center,
                                [along with an X-ray,
and in dreams the menacing hiss of those in charge:
"if we take away everything that's not yours
you'll be left with nothing."

L'idea centrale

È venuta in mente (ma per caso, per l'odore
di alcool e le bende)
questo darsi da fare premuroso
nonostante.
E ancora, davanti a tutti, si sceglieva
tra le azioni e il loro senso.
Ma per caso.
Esseri dispotici regalavano il centro
distrattamente, con una radiografia,
e in sogno padroni minacciosi
sibilanti:
"se ti togliamo ciò che non è tuo
non ti rimane niente."

Reasons for the Beginning

There was a sunny interlude
and a yellow heat on the leaves
before the revelation of
a nitpicking smile

> *but you can't "look for"*
> *metamorphosis*
> *you are going through with an ill-prepared gesture*
> *no one can say*
> *what it was he loved the first time*

the slender body, propelled by wind,
goes down a street
she is permitted flowers, the waving grass
and the princess dream
in the room, the sweet certainty
that they are
not visible

it's incredible, you still believed that matter has
a center
and you cried because it was yours alone
and you wanted to say, to say
but there isn't any more time to make the moment

and the slight sweat on her neck
means "yes"
while the festive wind
slowly removes the tunic
without a gesture
and the spirits of the wind and air,
the river smell, the shout

    advancing in the darkness
    you may even find a body at the border
    it's happened many times
    within these complicated orders
    in a world revealed
    to whoever turns away

the hill is covered
with vineyards, while there is a right time for everything
and footsteps over the clods are slow
encouraging joy

    what comes out first is the only thing that counts
    and bad luck now doesn't win out over chance
    it's always late for specifying
    and so say it anyway, say that
    you're living, say it.

Le cause dell'inizio

C'è stato un intermezzo solare
e un giallo caldo sopra le foglie

e poi nasceva
il sorriso bizantino

> *ma non puoi "cercare"*
> *la metamorfosi*
> *compi un gesto impreparato*
> *nessuno può dire*
> *che cosa ha amato per la prima volta*

il corpo tenue, mosse dal vento,
percorre una strada
gli sono concessi fiori, l'erba che ondeggia
e il sogno della principessa
nella stanza, la dolce certezza
di non essere
visibili

> *è incredibile, credevi ancora al centro*
> *della materia*
> *e piangevi perché è solo tuo*
> *e volevi dire, dire*
> *ma non c'è più tempo per fare l'attimo*

e un delicato sudore sul collo
significa "sì"
mentre il vento festivo
toglie la tunica lentamente
senza un gesto
e gli spiriti dell'aria e dell'acqua,
l'odore del fiume, il grido

> *avanzando nella distanza*
> *si può anche trovare un corpo, al confine,*
> *quante volte è successo*
> *dentro questi ordini complicati*
> *nel mondo rivelato*
> *a chi si volta dall'altra parte*

la collina è coperta
di vigne, mentre tutto ha un tempo giusto
e i passi sopra le zolle sono lenti
a favore della gioia

conta solo ciò che esce per primo
e ora la sfortuna non sconfigge il caso,
è sempre tardi per precisare
e allora dillo pure, dillo che stai vivendo, dillo.

July Has Come For The Dead

July has come for the dead
who sense in the siege laid
by every flower
a remote justice.
And a paper noose
provides rebirth to more than I can say
in the history of the vast, steep earth,
things and things, clothes white and worm-eaten,
peasants hidden in the wheat. Or even
further inside, wherever chrysanthemums shout.
As it travels back and forth between the walls of
the head and a long-distance call,
this minute is being counted,
and the urn--another of the delightful
magnanimous mixtures--
has said: no more.

Giunge luglio per i morti

Giunge luglio per i morti
che sentono nell'assedio
di ogni fiore
una giustizia remota. E un

cappio di carta
rinasce a più non posso
nella storia
della terra, vasta, ripida,
cose e cose, vesti bianche e tarlate,
contadini nascosti
nel frumento. O ancora
più dentro, dovunque urlino
i crisantemi. Facendo la spola
tra i muri della testa e
una chiamata interurbana, questo minuto
viene contato;
e l'urna--delizia anch'essa
dei mescolati magnanimi--
ha detto basta.

There's A Hand That Nails Down

There's a hand that nails down
its grams
in a courtyard near Greece;
the numbers are increasingly chaste;
city of cotton and bronze
with a summer whose mouth faces north.
Bodies pass by here
(we surprise them)--proud
females in a brawl, or
else they keep quiet, or
else they are shadows, challenges, ties.
The stones know them well.

Them again, always
them again, like birthdays. Suddenly
a whirl of them returns up and down the spinal column
and they choose magic spells or forays,
a shrug of the shoulders or a type of nakedness;

the voice which had proclaimed itself
the twin-and-ball-and-teeth of twins
whizzes across its mountain
with the same life,
sworn to at once, just before dawn. They had given
her an almond
without sight-finder or space. But she
made up her mind at once and fired it!

Yes, that was
the circle of overly proud
foreigners, daydreaming about
a pact...I was there...look carefully...
I'd already been there...whirl and dirge of
the woman who has a child in her belly
and another making his way
into my archaic abode
you come,
minds full of light
with the rumbling of a lottery extraction,
every paradise knows the dizziness
of children downed and certain.

C'è una mano che inchioda

C'è una mano che inchioda
i suoi grammi
nel cortile vicino alla grecia
sono sempre più casti
i numeri
città di cotone e bronzo
con l'estate che ha una bocca a nord.
Qui passano dei corpi
che sorprendiamo femmine
orgogliose in baruffa. Oppure
tacciono;

oppure sono ombre, disfide, lacci. Le pietre
li conoscono bene.

Sempre loro, sono
sempre loro, come compleanni. Adesso
ritorna una bufera
lungo la colonna vertebrale e scelgono
il maleficio o l'incursione,
un'alzata di spalle o una nudità.
La voce che si era proclmata
gemella e sfera e denti di gemelli
scocca nella sua montagna
con la stessa vita
giurata subito, antelucana. Le hanno dato
una mandorla
senza mirino né spazio. Ma
ha deciso subito, ha tirato!

Sì, fu quello
il cerchio degli stranieri
dello smisurato orgoglio, che vaneggiano
un patto...ero lì...guarda bene...ero già lì...
bufera e nenia della donna
che ha un figlio in grembo e uno in salita
nel mio luogo arcaico
voi giungete
menti colme di luce
con il rombo di un'estrazione a sorte
ogni paradiso ha un capogiro
di figli falciati e certi.

IVANO FERMINI

Ivano Fermini was born in San Paolo, a small village near Bolzano, in 1948 and lives in Milan. He currently receives a small pension from the government due to his recurring episodes of mental illness. Encouraged back in the eighties by Milo De Angelis, who published some of his work in *Niebo*, Fermini has since published in numerous other reviews and is the author of two books of poetry.

Fermini's poems move at an erratic, contracted pace from one unforeseen, seemingly casual illumination to the next. His words might be compared to pieces of fall-out created by some internal Big Bang, which shoot off in every direction at varying speed thanks to Fermini's bending of the rules of Italian syntax to an extreme. (An "I" may suddenly become "you", then expand without warning to "they", to take one small example.) Clearly a translation doesn't--or can't--render this fundamental tension or "structural anguish" of his work. The juxtaposition of vivid images and "border line" mental states, however, comes through in English all the same.

POETRY

Bianco allontanato (Banished White) 1985
Nati incendio (Fire Births) 1990

that bound and tied they fled
(wherever gravel feathers the sea)
in June and a curve,
disciple-like opening,
whitened when it struck the ships;
in order to prepare myself a warmer stone;
and if I know it
they'll send me thin soldiers,
all the drops there are;
the nettle,
contemplating certain windows,
my heart dies in every grave of spring.

che legati fuggirono
in tutti i posti dove la ghiaia è la piuma del mare
a giugno e un tornante
l'apertura discepolo
colpì le navi diventando bianco
per prepararmi un sasso più caldo
e se io conosco
mi mandino soldati magri
le gocce che sono tutte
l'ortica
meditando certi vetri
col cuore io muoio in ogni tomba di primavera

The statue

It's like snow,
the leaves like
Zen on a rug;
spiked fingers play music
motions in every water from the sudden
                              [and gently unforeseeable
which words graze;

they are false, false.
It's true as young Laura
before the fall of the axe;
no tears over time,
just stand it there, the record plays,
I explode and the rags around me repel me,
pushing further off the small clouds,
mothers and fathers in hot-air balloons;
I am cured.

La statua

è come neve
le foglie
come zen sul tappeto
le dita suonarono a spiga
le spinte in ogni acqua dai dolci improvvisi
che le parole rasentano
sono false false
è vera
come lauretta prima della scure
non attraverso il tempo nessuna lacrima
solo appoggia il disco suona
io esplodo e gli stracci intorno mi respingono
allontano le nuvolette
padri e madri in mongolfiera
sono guarito

Waiting for sleep at the hair roots
one can't,
nor let amazement rot away in a sunlit glove.
But there will be other pony-tails,
other hardened elastics;
and let there be
the wild thunder you want of the one-handed poet.

attendendo il sonno alla radice dei capelli
non si può
né marcire lo stupore nel guanto assolato
ma ci saranno altre code
altri elastici induriti
e ci sia
tuono impazzito che vuoi del poeta senza mano

moments that hands without a vine...laughter...
.............thefinest crystals.........
as much as I dye the night,
a cut in breathing and
urn of names;
a clog holds
the tall slippery bodies

istanti che mani senza vigna...ridere...
...................cristallifinissimi..........
per quanto io tingo la notte
sforbiciando il soffio e
urna dei nomi
uno zoccolo tiene
i corpi alti e scivolosi

The wistaria-faced Visigoth
(the only pincers he owed
slipping away from the lightning)
is preserved in the snow
with shell-like hands and
words that blow on the dawn
till roots have tenderly risen,
and above ground, curled.

il visigoto dal volto di glicine
le sole tenaglie che doveva
defilando dal fulmine
viene
tenuto nella neve
con mani di conchiglia e
parole che soffiano sull'alba
finché radici teneramente si sollevano
inanellando
fuori

Detouring through the rooms were men and fumes,
a false circle,
yet I wonder about a fly to ascend
the route and the rust
like leaves, which in him
can barricade themselves and provide bread for the ribs;
what that see was
cries silently as I chain myself to the fire,
and when it's
a lily on my shoulder, my face will ache.

deviando per le stanze erano uomini e vapori
un cerchio falso
eppure mi domando una mosca per salire
rotta e ruggine
come le foglie che in lui
possono sbarrarsi e dare pane alle costole
cos'era quel seme
piange silenziosamente e io m'incateno al fuoco
e quando sarà
un giglio sulle spalle mi fa male il viso

The you I know is losing you

and the evil walnuts have won out;
further on,
the madmen wait for the heel beyond their dizziness.
It's night. That pounding may be lost again
in soft substance;
the head as well.

chi ti so perde che hai
e le noci malefiche hanno vinto
oltre
i pazzi attendono il tacco fuori dalla vertigine
è notte che si riperda il colpo nella sostanza molle
anche la testa

It descends rapidly under the twistable vine in the sky,
its brows a dark basin;
every change in temperature opens the
mouth, readying the anvil and blowing,
for this is the sea and afternoon and grey lantern,
small round soup that screams eyes.

si abbassa rapidamente sotto la vigna da torcere in cielo
ha un catino buio per le ciglia
ogni frattura delle colonnine apre
la bocca per formare l'incudine e soffiare
perché è mare e pomeriggio e grigio fanale
piccola tonda minestra che grida gli occhi

The first unexpected pain is beautiful.
I face you, I imagine with puppet-eyes that
I've come down from the rock;
I can jump;
you live the sun's reflections

one by one
and talk, woman, with a dished-up face,
and a sip that turns to snow;
walk, then look if
there's a stick to die with;
the fingers of thought
are here (I am dyed and all),
and over there, nibbling the air with brief detachment,
a thunderclap in the white room,
the stories of yesterday.

il primo dolore non previsto è bellezza
io di fronte a te
sono giù dalla roccia con l'occhio dei pupazzi
posso lanciarmi
i riflessi del sole
uno per uno vivi
mentre parli col tuo volto a scodellare
donna dal convertire in neve il tuo sorso
cammina poi guarda
se c'è un'asticciola per morire
il pensiero dita
è qua io sono tinto e tutto
e là mangiando l'aria con un breve distacco
un tuono nella stanza bianca
le storie di ieri

FRANCO BUFFONI

F ranco Buffoni was born in Gallarate in 1950 and is a professor of English Literature at the University of Cassino. He has translated the work of such poets as Auden, Spender, and Heaney. In 1988 he founded *Testo a fronte*, a specialized review dedicated to the theory and practice of literary translation.

Buffoni ably assembles pieces of our world into a small puzzle of reality only to take it apart it again. The flash images or moments contained in these mosaics do not preserve their original logic but are reordered in time and filtered. On occasion, the effect may be comical but underneath there lurks a certain uneasiness: the madness paraded in front of our eyes has little that's whimsical or fanciful about it, and it is only the poet's irony to protect against the tragic forms of nonsense.

POETRY

Nell'acqua degli occhi (Swimming in the Eyes) 1979
I tre desideri (The Three Wishes) 1984
Lafcadio 1987
Quaranta e quindici (Forty and Fifteen) (includes *Lafcadio*) 1987
Scuola di Atene (The School of Athens) 1991 (Sandro Penna Prize)
Pelle intrecciata di verde (Green-lined Skin) 1991
Suora carmelitana (Carmelite Nun) 1993
Adidas--poesie scelte 1975-90 (mini-anthology) 1993
Suora carmelitana e altri racconti in versi (Carmelite Nun and Other Poems) 1995

On Poetry

Haven't you already filled
the exercise book?
Like a root in a gravel bed
the real maze is to be found inside you,
and if it isn't called brain
it's called belly.
To put it bluntly:
History or the sweatshop?
But in the end even Alice's sister sees
the dream.

Perhaps you feel like a city or a street;
with your newspaper-wrapped pumpkin in hand;
well-covered by the chorus or by this broken crockery;
notable boundary between the animal and the vegetable;
leveled by the sea to a gumdrop between the rocks;
jellyfish that melts in the sun?

Di Poesia

Non hai forse già riempito
L'eserciziario?
Come radice nel suolo di ghiaia
Il vero labirinto ti sta dentro,
E se non ha nome cervello
Si chiama l'intestino:
In povere parole
Storia o sartoria?
Ma infine anche Alice's sister
Vede il sogno.

Ti senti forse una città una strada
Con la zucca in mano avvolta nel giornale
Ben coperto dal coro o questo coccio

Confine di riguardo tra animale e vegetale
Ridotto dal mare a una valda tra i sassi,
Una medusa che si scioglie al sole?

The Song of Diamond Eyes

Words can't ignite them nor
can blows from the brain,
for they have always lived in that yonder flame
and when they laugh they darken, shutting in,
against the light of the blade,
their fear of wounding too deeply.
Still, there's that taste for slow, black inflicting,
the pleasure in feeling moments light up
like the vaults of the mind when the fist in the
dagger with diamond blades traces
the song.

La canzone degli occhi di diamante

Che non possono infiammarsi alle parole
Né ai pugnali della mente
Perché vivono da sempre nella fiamma
Lì davanti, e se ridono si oscurano
E rinchiudono alla luce della lama la paura
Di ferire troppo in fondo.
Ma c'è il gusto di ferire nero e piano
C'è il piacere di sentire che le volte
Si son tutte illuminate come volte
Del pensiero quando il pugno costruisce
Con le lame di diamante nel pugnale
La canzone.

And those level fingernails of theirs.
At the service of ideology
on marble benches;
like Zachary's viper,
twisted about a stick
and stuffed forcibly into the bottle
of pure alcohol;
like cigarette burns
and occasional fractures
that a corrective view renders
in the true story of a six-year-old.
Paradox of a liar
who says it isn't worth it,
who says it is.

E quelle unghie uguali
Resi all'ideologia
Sui banchi di marmo;
Come la vipera di Zaccaria
Attorcigliata al bastoncino
Immersa a forza nella bottiglia
Dell'alcool puro;
Come le ustioni da sigaretta
E le fratture occasionali
Rese per mezzo di correzione
Dentro la storia vera a sei anni
Antinomia del mentitore
Che dice che non vale la pena
Che dice che vale la pena.

When he was far away from those evenings
it seemed natural
to forget the masquerade. His tires
were in good condition; there was
his sense of the city as solitude.

But when it got dark, and then still darker,
(and it was only a question of the doing:
to say tonight I don't feel like it
or for tonight I'll let it go.
Enough for an hour, but then for another),
and in the absence of the sun, desire returned
and empty was that need to climb on
the open stage in the center of the street.

Quando era lontano dalle sere
Gli sembrava tutto naturale,
Dimenticare il travestimento
Le gomme a posto, il senso
Della città d'essere solo.
Ma quando era già buio, e poi più buio
(E c'è soltanto il fare,
Dire stasera non mi sento
O per stasera lascio stare,
Basta per un'ora, ma poi l'altra).
Allora tornava senza sole
Il desiderio, vuoto il bisogno di salire
Sul palco aperto al cuore della strada.

De Pisis--Piacenza Papers

A spellbinding image,
for the special quality of those punished,
with their need of some Biblical verse
to put a match to that wicked-sinner formula.
An intricate affair
that in Italy brings to mind
the obscure crimes of Cranach's time.
Different perspectives.
Someone enters and sits in a corner of my life
where nothing was before;

the mirror confirms: if we weren't
men or women
we'd be perfect.

De Pisis--Cartella Piacenza

Un'immagine sortilegio
Per particolare qualità dei puniti,
Col bisogno di disporre di un passo biblico
Per infuocare l'equazione reo-peccatore.
È, sofisticato, un genere
Che richiama in ambiente italiano
I delitti opachi del tempo di Cranach:
Angolature diverse,
È entrato e si è seduto in un angolo della mia vita
Dove non c'era altro;
Ribadisce lo specchio: se non fossimo uomini
Né donne,
Saremmo perfetti.

And in the end, the entire earth may answer to a single name,
at rest on its knees with its content of bones,
offering the podium looks on the order of moderated segments--
and little curiosity of spirit.
Then, transforming all this into something ridiculous,
feeling a kind of faith in a pervasive death waiting
to be snatched, he can energetically flee this unanimous world
with its half-said things
old beyond comparison
in a diamond's flash.

Finché tutta la terra diviene un solo nome,
Giace inginocchiata con le ossa contenute
Offrendo al podio sguardi con segmenti moderati

E poco spirito di curiosità.
Poi, trasformando tutto ciò in ridicolo,
Sentendo qualcosa di fede alla morte intorno da strappare,
Sfugge con forza al mondo unanime
Con le sue cose accennate
Vecchie senza paragoni
Nel bagliore di diamante.

Partitions

Dry as the first of August,
Sing to me of the cedars of Lebanon
and pediments of hatred,
Pia of the automatic shutter.

I isolate myself in this moment
from all the babies crying
through open windows.
I isolate myself from all my babies.
And only in this white
vintage nineteen eighty-five
do I realize that
once you,
aunts and uncles of last century,
were alive.

Pareti

Asciutta come il primo agosto
Cantami di cederi del Libano
e di frontoni senz'astio,
Pia dell'autoscatto.

Mi separo in questo momento
Da tutti i babies che strillano

Dalle finestre aperte.
Mi separo da tutti i miei babies.
E solo in questo galestro
Bianco ottantacinque
Mi rendo conto
che siete stati vivi
Zii dell'ottocento.

To be soldiers together and allies
and coagulate in the saddle atop ploughs,
burying nests of pregnant field mice,
cradles, haze, rust on tombstones.

Knight and poet arrested by the Romans
when you are constrained by tears:
you are protecting those not your children,
when you pour oil into the metals of the sky.
And the city starts to function like an earring
For the dancing girl in the picture.

Essere soldati insieme ed alleati
E coagulare in groppa ad aratri
Seppellendo nidi di topine gravide
Culle foschia ruggine di lapide.

Cavaliere poeta arrestato dai Romani
Quando rimani stretto dalle lacrime:
Sei uno strumento di guardia ai non figli,
Versi l'olio nei metalli del cielo.
Poi la città si mette a far da orecchino
Alla danzatrice nel quadro.

ALESSANDRO CENI

Alessandro Ceni was born in Florence in 1957. He studied art before graduating from university in Italian Literature with a thesis on the collected works of Tommaso Landolfi. Today, besides writing poetry, he is a painter and a professional translator from English of such authors as E. A. Poe, J. Milton, S. T. Coleridge, R. L. Stevenson, and O. Wilde.

The evocative and magical aspects of language are underscored in Ceni's poems. Indeed, they are seen as constituting its intrinsic nature (and in this regard Ceni is similar to several of the poets included in the anthology, *La parola inammorata*). Poetry here is synonymous with Truth, a truth that is revealed by symbols, images, or objects which appear one after another in a seemingly illogical manner; in place of rational links, however, analogies and archtypes manage to suggest connections. There is often a faint hint of esoteric language in Ceni, in addition to allusions to mysterious rites of passage.

POETRY
I fiumi di acqua viva (Live-Water Rivers) (part of a mini-anthology of poets, *Poesia Uno*, published by Guanda) 1980
Il viaggio inaudito (The Incredible Journey) 1981
I fiumi (Rivers) 1985
La natura delle cose (The Nature of Things) 1991
Nel regno (14 passaggi) (In the Kingdom--14 passages) 1993
Nel regno (passages I-XXIV) 1995
Opere (collected works to date) scheduled for publication

ESSAYS
La sopra-realtà di Tommaso Landolfi (The Superimposed Reality of Tommaso Landolfi) 1985

Reconciled Flame

The fiery ball takes on oxygen, burning off
the clothes of the unwounded ready and packed for
their trip, turning into a grimace
the kiss sewn into a "*ciao*", and
the breath is a tomb in the crater of the lungs of those fallen.

Let me stay close by, in
the simple darkness, all night intent on
hearing the alarming jumble of beats
and the motives of the water
and the reason for the silence,
the performance climax to your work.

The flame striking the ball
gives oxygen to the buried man,
distracted by the bird as it disintegrates
within the fullness.
It's the still heart in the breaking vase,
or the firm wrist of relatives, zero air zero friction,
pushing the newcomer into the room.

Fiamma riconciliata

Il globo che urta d'ossigeno e fiammeggia
spela gli abiti degli illesi già
pronti con la valigia per il viaggio, smorfia
il bacio che in un ciao si cuce e
il fiato tomba nei crateri dei polmoni dei caduti.

Fammi restare accanto, nel semplice buio,
tutta la notte teso ad udire
il mucchio sconcertante dei battiti e
il motivo dell'acqua e
la ragione del silenzio,

la vetta recitante dell'opera tua.

La fiamma che urta il globo e ossigena
l'uomo sepolto distratto dall'uccello che
disintegra nel colmo,
il cuore immobile nel vaso che si spacca o
il polso fermo dei parenti, aria zero attrito zero,
spinge il nuovo venuto nella stanza.

The Key and The Tree

December at the feet of december,
the cries of patients in a moment of pardon,
naked to a rumble of glances, waking
in an empty shroud cicumcised of feeling and
sprayed, heartlessly, mercilessly,
with perfume;
from a cry of words to
a game of prayers,
hardened and rising,
returned to life by a close encounter;
the tree overturned in the darkness by
a sunstroke of men and of memories;
cries announce Mars will crash
due to the danger of light; due to those memories
the eyes will writhe with birth pain
and you will be welcomed in the
youngest oak in the youngest of woods.

La chiave e l'albero

Dicembre ai piedi di dicembre,
le grida dei pazienti nel perdono,
nudi a un fragore di sguardi svegliandosi
in un sudario vuoto

circonciso d'affetti e da profumo
cosparso senza pietà o amore,
dal grido di parole in
un gioco di preghiere
irriducibile salito,
rivoluto alla vita da un evitato incontro
l'albero capovolto nel buio da
un'insolazione d'uomini e di ricordi,
le grida gridano Marte precipiterà
per un rischio di luce, per quei ricordi
gli occhi infittiranno di doglie
e sarai accolto, la più giovane
quercia nel più giovane bosco.

With What Courage

With what courage
the birds remain on a
rim of air; in the distance, the fox changes
his call--it must be love--they advance
to dwell where you can see them,
resisting the guardian grown unsociable but
as yet fooled by his garden of whimsy.

Funneled off this morning,
half-formed, grey in the moment
before its summoning,
half-horse among men, almost and more;
at last the waters recede and,
out of an orifice of passion,

barely dry thunderheads--
without lightining--roam
round the room; the side of the hill
can be seen running at each hit,
dedicating the new moon

plus a quick new wife-and-the-sacred, one
who's risen during a harvest under lock
for a bridegroom with a treasure stock of keys
and the city, Lower Jerusalem--
lower still for its extreme desires--
though it's forbidden, a snake sheds its nest of stone
for the glory of its current victim;
it starts as an arrow and develops into dawn,
and oh look: the night is as long as the day.
The fear of both is without remedy.

Con quale coraggio

Con quale coraggio
rimangono gli uccelli
nell'orlo d'aria, il volpe cambia
lontano da qui il richiamo
significherà amore, avanzano perché risiedono
dove puoi vederli
opponibili al guardiano inselvatichito
ingannati dal suo giardino in estro,

a imbuto dal mattino
mezzo formati, grigio
un attimo prima che chiami,
semi cavallo tra uomo circa e ancora,
infine le acque si ritirano e
secchi appena
da un orifizio di passione molti

tuoni senza lampi girano
per la stanza il fianco della collina
si vede correre al colpo e dedicare
la luna
nuova più nuova rapida moglie e sacra,
innalzata tra i raccolti a serratura

per uno sposo con un bene di chiavi e la città,
Gerusalemme-sotto,

più sotto in voglie estreme,
sbuccia proibito da un nido di pietre
il serpente a gloria della sua
vittima in quel tempo,
nasce come freccia e si sviluppa aurora, e o
guarda: la notte ha la stessa durata del giorno,
temerli è irrimediabile.

Fragment

And it will be life to separate us, not death
described in all human measure: leagues, meters or millimeters--
but they're not enough, and I lash out with a kick,
like the remains of a snowball, and my
heart in a small magic circle,
its contours made of protests and words
scattered in the body hair of a god.
And these rooms have a sword;
shut inside them there's a germ like a bulldog on a chain--
and a multitude of boats, forests of painted humanity;
gentlemen, these are the twelve parts of a cactus,
and while here, multiplied among men,
I make the world go round,
even the sun launches
umbrella spokes in its own image.

Frammento

E ci separerà la vita non la morte
rappresentata con tutte le misure umane
leghe metri o millimetri non bastano,
e io scalcio come il resto

di una palla di neve il cuore
in un piccolo cerchio magico
con confini di proteste e parole
disperse tra i peli di un dio.
E queste stanze hanno una spada,
rinchiudono un germe come un mastino alla catena,
moltitudine di battelli, boschi d'umanità dipinta,
gentlemen, sono le dodici parti di un cactus,
e mentre qui, moltiplicato tra uomini,
faccio andare il mondo
anche il sole scaglia
stecche da ombrelli per immagine di sé.

Atrium

But at night, when there is most need,
when people huddle inside their houses,
a hatred comes to massacre us
with our guard lowered,
and the light off.

A terror of the door,
knowing you're there
with a trail of breath
gone numb between your lips:

Someone says something in the street below,
a few words while entering or leaving,
waves that the sea sets off,
moving your hand in the water.

"Alone in a single room,
I used to drive my car a lot,
all my children dead,
with the longest of hair
and tiny closed fists,

as if still behind the wheel
though having lost that pensive stance of drivers,"
but right then a window
cuts the speaker off from her voice.

The eye-pupils buzz, the heart's in neutral;
from a hook hangs the ceiling
and in a kitchen invaded by small flying insects
a woman dances with naked feet:
God eats with his hands.

Atrio

Ma di notte quando maggiore è il bisogno
e la gente si stringe e si sta in casa
viene a massacrarci un odio
abbassata la guardia
spento il lume

il terrore della porta
per saperti là
con un pennacchio di respiro
intirizzito tra la bocca:

qualcuno ha detto qualcosa di sotto
poche parole entrando e uscendo,
onde che il mare provoca
muovendo nell'acqua la mano

"Solo in una sola stanza
spesso guidavo la macchina,
tutti i miei figli morti
con lunghissime chiome
coi piccoli pugni stretti
come tuttora al volante
pur persa la posizione pensiva della guida",

ma subito una finestra
toglie la voce al parlante

le pupille ronzano col cuore in folle
dal gancio pende il soffitto e
danza una donna a piedi nudi in cucina
invasa da piccoli insetti volanti:
Dio mangia con le mani.

VALERIO MAGRELLI

Valerio Magrelli was born in 1957 in Rome, where he continues to live and work. He teaches French Literature at the University of Pisa and contributes articles to such national newspapers as *Messaggero* and *Unità*. For the publishing house Einaudi, Magrelli directs the trilingual series, *Scrittori tradotti da scrittori* (Writers Translating Writers); he himself has translated works by Valéry, Debussy and Verlaine. In addition to his poetry, Magrelli has authored an essay on Dadaism and a monograph on Joseph Joubert.

Already fairly well-known abroad, Magrelli writes poems about absence, the poet's absence from the world of objects, actions and even thoughts, which he observes like a ghost. His work seems suspended between imagery conveying the death-like silence in which all creation takes place--and where poetry originates--and that which renders the anxiety of not knowing enough about life's direction or course. In other words, a distinguishing feature of Magrelli's poetry is the penchant for nullity and negation--not in a judgmental sense but rather in the philosophical/mathematical sense of standing on the other side of the mirror.

POETRY

Ora serrata retinae 1980 (Mondello Prize)
Nature e Venature (Natures and Veinings) 1987 (Viareggio Prize)
Esercizi di tiptologia (Exercises in Typtology) 1992 (Montale Prize)

I prefer to come from silence to talk.
To set up a word carefully so that
it gets to its bank gliding docilely as a boat,
while the path of thought traces the curve.
Writing is a peaceful death:
the world goes luminious,
expands, and burns forever in one of its corners.

Preferisco venire dal silenzio
per parlare. Preparare la parola
con cura, perché arrivi alla sua sponda
scivolando sommessa come una barca,
mentre la scia del pensiero
ne disegna la curva.
La scrittura è una morte serena:
il mondo diventato luminoso si allarga
e brucia per sempre un suo angolo.

We go through life this way:
with the nervous tension of our table-mate
between courses that never come.
We eat a lot of bread and drink,
conversing at length about fabulous foods,
universes of oregano, forests of unheard of
flavors. It's getting late and
in a desert of crumbs of secret shapes
(and this, clearly, is a left foot),
a black Arabian death takes leave of us.

Così si percorre la vita,
con l'ansia del commensale
tra portate che non arrivano.
Si mangia molto pane e si beve,
molto si conversa di favolosi cibi,

universi d'origano, foreste
d'inauditi sapori. È già tardi
e sul limitare del pasto
in un deserto di molliche dalle segrete forme
(e questo è un piede sinistro, si vede),
la nera morte araba ci congeda.

Things have an admirable life.
Nothing comes to be known from their
impassible actions, foretold, chosen as
a sole and constant idea.
Absorbed priests,
they fill this room
for a mysterious chapter.

Ammirevole è la vita delle cose.
Nulla trapela dai loro gesti
impassibili, presagiti e scelti
come unica e costante idea.
Sono sacerdoti assorti
che occupano questa sala
per un misterioso capitolo.

Before the last curve of the day
I gather words to sleep with:
evening-time, they again wear their
heavy sagacious robes.
Their step is measured
and like aligned bricks they set themselves
in the white mortar of the page.
It's a wall that descends from above,
the slow passing of a sign.
There's no window nor opening,
just precious crammed-in

concern for a dense unifying.
I wish it were a single entity,
the bud still hard and closed that
the gardener picks for himself.

Prima dell'ultima curva del giorno
colgo delle parole con cui dormire:
nella sera esse riprendono
le vesti pesanti e accorte.
Il loro andare è misurato
e come mattoni allineati s'incastonano
nella bianca calce della pagina.
È un muro che scende dall'alto
il lento trascorrere del segno.
Non c'è finestra o spiraglio
ma preziosa e gremita
cura del fitto unire.
Vorrei fosse un'unica figura
la gemma che ancora dura e chiusa
il giardiniere stacca e si regala.

I have a brain populated by women.
My cranium must have caved in somewhere
and in my head gushes
and murmurs a fountain of love.
Through this shadowy region
I walk like a pilgrim
or like a monk.
Behind every curve
a silent face pops up,
white as a stone plaque.

Ho il cervello popolato di donne.
Da qualche parte

dev'essersi sfondato il cranio
e mormorando mi sgorga in testa
una fontana d'amore.
In questa regione d'ombra
cammino come un pellegrino
o come un monaco.
Dietro ogni curva
s'affaccia un viso silenzioso
bianco come una lapide.

I'm what is missing
from the world I live in,
the one who among all I will never
encounter.
Spinning round now I
coincide with
what I've been deprived of.
I'm my own eclipse,
the absence and the melancholy,
the geometric object
that I will have to make do without forever.

Io sono ciò che manca
dal mondo in cui vivo,
colui che tra tutti
non incontrerò mai.
Ruotando su me stesso ora coincido
con ciò che mi è sottratto.
Io sono la mia eclissi
la contumacia e la malinconia
l'oggetto geometrico
di cui per sempre dovrò fare a meno.

Like ground that's been walked over, it echoes

deep, hollow and abandoned
like quaking terrain,
this pale female body,
like a fallen animal, this back
made shiny by silent hands,
like stone polished
by the motion of other stone,
no perfume and no voice,
worn mouth weak as
an overused plant,
no shadow, handled all over,
jiggled everywhere, deserted field
without grass without tracks without borders
like the sad view of a blind man,
naked and suspended, accepted into
the circle of solitude
this is the last fruit of a love
that for itself preserves only
the disinhabited poverty of bone.

Come terreno calpestato, risuona
profondo cavo e abbandonato
come terra scossa,
questo corpo chiaro di donna,
come un animale battuto, questa schiena
fatta lucida da mani silenziose,
come pietra levigata
dal corso delle altre pietre,
senza profumo e senza voce,
bocca consumata e debole
come una pianta troppo usata,
senza ombra, ovunque toccata,
ovunque percossa, campo desolato
senza erba e senza tracce, senza margini
come la dolorosa immagine del cieco,
nuda e sospesa, raccolta

nel cerchio della solitudine,
questo è l'ultimo frutto dell'amore
che per sé trattiene soltanto
la disabitata povertà dell'osso.

The wood of my thoughts is on fire.
A spasm of light,
then ash covers the earth's evening
with bandages.
There's silence along the paths
leading to extinguished hotbeds.
Now I'll have to clear the ground
care for it, cultivate it, and wait
with affectionate wariness for new plants.
Then it'll be time to set a new fire.

Il bosco dei miei pensieri è in fiamme.
Dopo lo spasimo della luce
la cenere ricopre di bende
la sera della terra.
C'è silenzio lungo le piste
che portano ai focolai spenti.
Ora bisognerà liberare il suolo,
curarlo, coltivarlo ed attendere
con affettuosa cautela nuove piante.
Ora si dovrà preparare un nuovo incendio.

There are words that coast alongside thought
or that cross it at the same
sweet slant as tears.
Like forgotten guests they wander
secretly through the rooms,
touching every thing.
Their proceeding resembles the slow offering

of any fruit of the earth.

Esistono parole che costeggiano
il pensiero e lo attraversano
dolcemente oblique come lacrime.
Come ospiti dimenticati si aggirano
segrete per le stanze,
ogni cosa toccando.
Il loro andare sembra l'offerta lenta
di un frutto della terra.

PATRIZIA CAVALLI

Patrizia Cavalli was born in Todi, and since 1968 she has lived in Rome. She holds a degree in philosophy. She has worked for Italian state radio and television (RAI), primarily writing radio dramas, and has published numerous translations, including works by Shakespeare and Molière.

In Cavalli's work, there are echoes of classic Italian poets like Foscolo, the influence of Petrarch, and glimpses of the 17th century. Part of her originality, in fact, lies in the utilization of such recognizable sources (intended both as poetic forms and stylistic experiments) to express a contemporary sense of futility, anguish, or disillusioned combativeness. The focus of her poetry is Cavalli's own awareness of feeling dissatisfied with this troubled and troublesome world: "what sort of relationship am I to have with it?" seems to be her question.

POETRY

Le mie poesie non cambieranno il mondo (My Poems Won't Change the World) 1974
Il cielo e no (Not Only The Sky) 1981
Poesie (collection of previous poems, in addition to *L'Io navigatore proprio mio*--My authentic navigating self) 1992

In that small dark fever of every reawakening,
the sweat of sleep
turns brown, dripping over the windows
and the sky, though it's blue. And when
I emerge from the hissing of dreams, which has
left my dull ears buzzing with repetition,
and slowly regain gestures
that yield me a new position
(maybe if I put on a striped shirt and
white pants, I'll walk more quickly,
move more upright), where I'm not
some harmless fence enclosing terrors,
or the impresario of secret skirmishes
who winds up in love with his actors,
I find a mimosa, old gold, its
turn to shine now over;
a flock like a flat cloud moving over
the field without any fringe of lambs;
and the billy goat, leader with the bell round his neck,
by now used to believing
that what moves is sound.

Nella febbretta cuposa dei risvegli
il sudore del sonno si ingiallisce
e cola addosso alle finestre, al cielo
anche se è azzurro. E quando esco
dal sibilo dei sogni
che ha lasciato le mie orecchie ottuse
intossicate dalla ripetizione e riconquisto
lentamente i gesti
che mi portino a un'altra posizione
(forse metto una camicia a righe
e i pantaloni bianchi, camminerò più in fretta,
avrò un'andatura eretta) dove io non sia
il recinto inerme dei terrori,
l'impresario di scontri clandestini

che alla fine si innamora dei suoi attori,
trovo una mimosa oro antico
il suo turno di splendore ormai finito,
il gregge come una nuvola piatta e mobile
sul prato senza più la frangetta degli agnelli
e il caprone capo col campanaccio al collo
abituato ormai a credere
che muoversi sia il suono.

How pointless this straining,
this becoming more adult, more mature,
or taking interest in the many worldly fates
in the newspaper;
all the while exercising faulty senses to watch
vanishings and reappearances
within and without, and the miniscule gifts
of a memory gone sour
in boxes and tins.

È inutile fare sforzi
diventare più adulti più maturi
interessarsi alle tante sorti
del mondo nei giornali
e intanto guardare con sensi approssimati
scomparse e ricomparse
dentro e fuori minuscoli regali
della memoria inacidita
nelle scatole e nelle scatolette.

When I listen for the sound of
my ring against the railing
I am answered by dizziness.

(...so no more rings, then.

My hands return to their first birth-cry,
blanketed only in the inebriating ability
to settle on the chair-arm, on crossed knees.)

Quando ricerco il suono
dell'anello contro una ringhiera,
mi risponde una vertigine.

(...allora senza più anelli
le mie mani tornate al primo grido
della nascita, fasciate
della sola ebbrezza di potersi
posare sul braccio di una sedia,
sulle ginocchia incrociate).

Outside nothing's really changed:
it's my seasonal illness keeping me off the streets,
it's grown inside me, spoiled my eyesight and
all my other senses; and the world now
seems a citation.
It's happened and done with, but where was I?
When did my amazing distraction take place?
Where did the thread come loose, the
crevice open? Which lake lost its
waters, altered the landscape, messed up
my way?

Fuori in realtà non c'era cambiamento,
è il morbo stagionato che mi sottrae alle strade:
dentro di me è cresciuto e mi ha corrotto gli occhi
e tutti gli altri sensi: e il mondo arriva
come una citazione.
Tutto è accaduto ormai, ma io dov'ero?
Quando è avvenuta la grande distrazione?

Dove si è slegato il filo, dove si è aperto
il crepaccio, qual è il lago
che ha perso le sue acque
e mutando il paesaggio
mi scombina la strada?

I remember little of myself
though I've always thought about me.
From myself I disappear like an object
stared at too long.
I'll be back to tell
of my radiant vanishing.

Poco di me ricordo
io che a me sempre ho pensato.
Mi scompaio come l'oggetto
troppo a lungo guardato.
Ritornerò a dire
la mia luminosa scomparsa.

Who ever again will be able to say
that I lack courage, that
I never mix with others, that they never do me in?
Today I stood in line for nearly half an hour
at the post office; I moved up
through the line step by step, I
smelled the atrocious smells of
the old, of males, and even of women;
I felt hands on my ass, or
pushing on my side. I recognized my nausea
then left it there; my body filled with sweat,
I came close to catching pneumonia.
It's not love of self here but
a sense of self

founded on a horror for others.

E chi potrà più dire
che non ho coraggio, che non vado
fra gli altri e che non mi appassiono?
Ho fatto una fila di quasi
mezz'ora oggi alla posta;
ho percorso tutta la fila passetto
per passetto, ho annusato
gli odori atroci di maschi
di vecchi e anche di donne, ho sentito
mani toccarmi il culo spingermi
il fianco. Ho riconosciuto
la nausea e l'ho lasciata là
dov'era, il mio corpo
si è riempito di sudore, ho sfiorato
una polmonite. Non d'amor di me
si tratta, ma di orrore degli altri
dove io mi riconosco.

I don't have any seed to cast about the world.
I can't inundate urinals or mattresses.
My scarse female seed
is too trickly to offend anyone.
So what can I leave behind
in the streets, in houses, in
infertile wombs? Words,
lots of them,
but already they no longer resemble me,
they've forgotten the fury
and the cursing, they've become signorinas,
rather disreputable maybe,
but signorinas all the same.

Non ho seme da spargere per il mondo
non posso inondare i pisciatoi né
i materassi. Il mio avaro seme di donna
è troppo poco per offendere. Cosa posso
lasciare nelle strade nelle case
nei ventri infecondati? Le parole
quelle moltissime
ma già non mi assomigliano più
hanno dimenticato la furia
e la maledizione, sono diventate signorine
un po' malfamate forse
ma sempre signorine.

When, suddenly, you're hit with good health,
your gaze doesn't falter nor does it stick to anything;
it sits slightly spellbound, instead, on things at a standstill
and on the ferment. These sucked-up images
slip inside,
as into a cat, who narrows its eyes to greet me.

Noises come loose: shouts and sirens
are simply there. The crumbly texture of
smells registers things in their remoteness,
and memory, inventing sounds,
makes the voice sing a song
that makes headway through traffic and thorns.

It's clear we were born
for such consonance.
But living in the city,
there's bound to be--here and there--
some sudden stink of fried food to
send you running home.

Quando si è colti all'improvviso da salute

lo sguardo non inciampa,non resta appiccicato,
ma lievemente si incanta sulle cose ferme
e sul fermento e le immagini sono risucchiate
e scivolano dentro
come nel gatto che socchiudendo gli occhi mi saluta.

I rumori si sciolgono: i gridi e le sirene
semplicemente sono. La tessitura sgranata
degli odori riporta ogni lontananza
e la memoria, inventando i suoni, fa cantare
alla voce una canzone che avanza
fra il traffico e le spinte.

E certo noi eravamo nati
per questa consonanza.
Ma vivendo in città c'è sempre
qua e là una qualche improvvisa puzza
di fritto che ti rimanda a casa.

GIUSI BUSCETI

G iusi Busceti was born in Milan in 1955. She is a social worker by training, with certification in systemic therapy, but due to the ins and out of Italian bureaucracy, has been unable to work as such; instead, she works in the office of a Milanese elementary school. Since the eighties, when her work first appeared in *Alfabeta*, she has published poems in various Italian reviews. Giusi Busceti is part of editorial board of *Manocomete*, directed by Giancarlo Majorino.

Busceti is one of those poets that can say the most terrible of things softly. The poems themselves tend to crystallize into a small, hardened shout, like the one made at the end of a nightmare. And if there is a note of prophecy--of Cassandra lashing out--it captivates the reader precisely because not all is being said, because it must be accepted that revelations only happen once in a blue moon.

POETRY

Sestile (Sextile) 1991

An Exhausted Inconsistency Floats Here

An exhausted inconsistency
floats here,
half-sentences between a blender's teeth
or eyes widened by sudden circumstance.

The indifference
of the beetle advances here.

The return of the circle
to read the stele with three lights,
each is alien;
someone's sure to be pure, to have no
doubts about the verdict.
Memory finds itself alone and hesitates
at the edge of the bed linen,
the certainty of blood which has stopped:
nothing, not under this hail.

Vi galleggia un'esausta

vi galleggia un'esausta
inesistenza
mezzefrasi tra i denti
di un frullatore, o gli occhi
sbarrati da un'improvvisa

qui incede l'indifferenza
di un coleottero

torna il cerchio
per la lettura di una stele
dalle tre luci, ognuna è altro,
qualcuno è puro, non ha dubbi
sul verdetto. Sola

esita la memoria sulla sponda
del lino, certezza
del sangue che si è arrestato:
niente, sotto questa grandine.

One Hundred and Eighty

Whoever's seen them carries them in marble,
with a blast through an eardrum
that has no center nor expectations,
and no music, but is alone. He solicits
burning intimacy every fifteen minutes
and that hair, instantaneously on fire,
is the rite of ashes and cellophane.
Finally there is a celebration
of paradise and excrement
everywhere that they are sleeping and watching,
watching. These are the priests.

Centottanta

Chi li ha visti li porta nel marmo
con il fischio attraverso
un timpano che non ha centro
e attese, non ha musica, è
solo. Arrotola
un'intimità bruciante ogni quarto d'ora
e i capelli nel fuoco istantaneo
sono il rito di cenere
e cellophane. Finalmente si
celebra il cielo e l'escremento
ovunque, dove dormono e guardano,
guardano. Ecco i sacerdoti.

Dissonances

Speculate on anxiety, courtesy of midnight
and this after the magicians in costume
have bartered cloth with lusterful legends
and winter today is ecstatic.
Poets, absent from the perspective of red boulevard
--a vertical arrangement is what their station calls for--
fake knots in the cord, the fight is dying down:
I wasn't thinking about your face defenseless in strategy;
by minding the details I lose track of the intention;
I wasn't thinking about a kiss that can't remedy distances.
Inside the cloisters, you said, others know if I betrayed them.
But the step that sidesteps the rift opens onto the night
the window onto the lamp at home.

Dissonanze

Ansia speculare, cortesia della mezzanotte
al seguito dei magi travestiti:
barattano le stoffe con lucide leggende
ed oggi, estatico, l'inverno.
Poeti, assenti dallo scorcio del rosso viale
--allineati in verticale sono indizio di stazione--
falsi nodi nel filo, la lotta ora desiste:
non pensavo al tuo volto indifeso nella strategia
curando i particolari ignoro l'intenzione
non pensavo ad un bacio che non toglie le distanze.
Tra i chiostri, dicevi, altri sanno se ho tradito.
Ma il passo che elude il solco apre alla notte
la finestra sulla lampada della casa.

Suddenly on a day in July
appears an ocean-world of ashes, of sand;
buildings and cities disappeared--wrote a

certain world traveler--and there arose
city walls fortified by fire and windy death
mills where there will never be rest,
among the dunes sweet France sweet end,
from the fog emerges the flag
that says where I am, the sun always rises, amidst
laughter, the trip proceeds.
I don't even know
where I'm going, for this
departure comes when July goes berserk,
when berserk with pain and a
stomach on fire and a sour mouth
I we had seen
our springtimes, gone from
power drills to oxygen over the telephone to
umbrellas that meet and stop in Via Sforza, while
immortality, clearly, got entangled
in her hair; trembling this night--
they are young, they are shellings
in the sky that as fireworks every year resound
over the sea--
tent sail, muezim--let us pray--save us
for the wind carries it off, for we
die of bankruptcy in our hearts, of
blissful idling in the face of majesty.

Now the puppy paws this hand that
keeps me on the crest,
returning, walking
without radio, with a knowledge
lost to me, inside which I
grope for my thirst, a thirst
so dear to saints, who go where
the mule leads them and find fountains.

In un giorno di luglio d'improvviso
s'apriva il mondoceano di cenere, di sabbia
scrisse il grande viaggiatore, scomparvero
i palazzi le città comparvero le mura di città
fortificate a fuoco morte a vento
mulini dove mai sarà riposo
fra dune dolce francia dolce fine
nasceva dalla nebbia la bandiera
dove io sono sempre sale il sole
tra le risate si allargava il viaggio.
non so
neppure dove son diretta, perché
si parte ora che luglio impazza che pazza
di dolore e ventre in fiamma e bocca
amara fummo fui dai primavera
da trapano ad ossigeno a telefono
a ombrelli che s'incontrano e si
fermano in via Sforza, che è l'immortalità
si sa, le si è impigliata nei capelli,
tremando, questa notte--furono giovani, furono
granate nel cielo che i fuochi d'artificio
ogni anno riecheggiano sul mare--
tendavela, muezim--preghiamo--salvaci, che il vento
se la porta, che si muore
di bancarotta al cuore, di beati
gingilli dinanzi alla maestà: Ora

zampe di cucciolo mano che mi tiene
sul crinale tornando camminando
senza la radio senza più sapere
in cui spaurita sete vo cercando
sì cara a santi che vanno dove il mulo
li conduce e trovano fontane.

Eight Phases of Contemplation

I.

The happening,
your lips return to press the glass,
the heat blooms sparkling green, piazzas,
and holding hands and eyes
at rest on the asphalt,
here comes the honey of teacups;
between the lips some bread,
on the sound of a heel
it's summer.

II.

The breast that never stops
climbs steps, seizes
the last gleam, falters.
The smoke has rocks, bodies
it skims the day's veil of laughter
and for who opens it:
all turns silver.

III.

You couldn't silence
summer nor
the peace of grain, not at the sight of
golden festivities--
you couldn't, while hugging someone's stubborn head
inside the honey,
babble syllables and whiteness
and sunrays and
celebrate.

IV.

What he sees in her,
aside from markets and properties
where he loses her,
floats on a single horizon.
There's no thread
but an arc conducting him
through his solitary talk:
wandering away from derision
he opens his sky
and his hands, again, bread.

V.

A siege of nothing
drags with it a sandbank of wind;
the various leaves on the
temples obscure the joys of
last century, clay encircles the arms.
The present jingles,
unguarded letter of solitude, cry
that bends the sand and triumphs
in fires.

VI.

Pearls, where the Po flowed quickly,
perfect polygons in the aridness,
ragged clothes of a mother,
safe in the oak that grows,
every leaving a rainfall,
the rose of metals in your salt, desert of
dust and grain.

VII.

This line separates the
remaining wave of what's real
from who is watching and
has stopped distinguishing:
the green abyss helps, the
folding edge,
she's alive never concluding
in any of her directions.
Then whoever
advances through the ruins of loneliness--
humid plantations inside eyes--
its dark cloth, a peninsula.

VIII.

Empty Sunday of wind,
gods that stay awake,
an engrossed woman that slips in between the
Indian veils of the equator, but is actually a
leaf of turquoise. In a chorus
on the final gathering, reflection of
a huge hollow apple over the oceans;
who has the gift of God not to procrastinate, and
the only fitting form of
anguish draws these breaths into the hours at present.

Otto fasi di contemplazione

I.

Accadere ritorna--
connessione delle tue labbra al vetro--
fiorisce un caldo
al verde scintille, piazze

e per mano per occhi
adagiati al selciato
accade il miele
delle tazze, tra le labbra del pane
come il passo di un tacco è
l'estate

II.

il seno che non si è fermato
ha passi di scale, l'ultimo
bagliore afferrato, scivola.
Ha rocce il fumo ha corpi
del giorno sfoglia
il velo del riso e
chi apre, argento

III.

non potevi tacere
la pace del grano e
l'estate al cospetto
oro della festa. Non potevi
stringendo la testa caparbia
al centro del miele
gorgogliare di sillabe e il bianco
e le punte del sole e
celebrare

IV.

ciò che guarda in lei
senza mercati e averi
dove la perde,
galleggia sull'unica vista.
Non un filo,

un arco lo conduce nel solo
che parla:
vagando dall'iride
adempie il suo cielo
e le mani, ancora, il pane.

V.

un assedio di nulla
trascina una secca di vento, ha
foglie assorte alle tempie
oscurano gioie dal secolo scorso
argilla circonda le braccia.
Tintinna un presente un'incauta
lettera di solitudine, grido
che piega la sabbia e trionfa
nei fuochi.

VI.

dove il Po accelerava
perle, poligoni perfetti nell'arido
lacere vesti della madre
ferma nel tronco che sale
ogni partenza piove
la rosa dei metalli
al tuo sale, deserto di polvere
e grano.

VII.

questa retta disgiunge
l'onda che resta al reale
e chi guarda
e rinuncia al distinguere:
serve l'abisso del verde

confine di piega
lei, viva
mai conclusa nelle direzioni.
Poi, chi avanzava
tra le macerie dei soli
umide piantagioni negli occhi
lo scuro tessuto, una penisola.

VIII.

vuoto domenica dei venti
in veglia di dei l'assorta
che insinua tra i veli
grezzi d'equatore, ma è
foglia del turchese. In coro
sull'ultimo raduno
specchia la mela cava
agli oceani: chi ha in dono
di non rimandare e l'unica
angoscia adeguata
questi respiri conduce alle ore.

MAURIZIO CUCCHI

Maurizio Cucchi was born in Milan in 1945 and still resides there. He graduated from the University of Milan with a specialization in modern Italian literature in 1971. He works as a Public Relations consultant and as a free-lance editor for Mondadori; he has written for several national newspapers, including a column on Milan's neighborhoods for *La Repubblica*. Over the years he has translated such French authors as Flaubert, Villier de l'Isle-Adam, Lamartine, and Mallarmé.

Cucchi's poetry explores the idiosyncrasies of a middle-class existence that he acknowledges as his own yet describes with disenchanted detachment. The voice in these poems seems torn between the desire for a peaceful, quiet life and the dizzy realization that there will inevitably come an irrepressible explosion of the world's titanic vitality surrounding him. This tension is manifested in the style as well: Cucchi compensates with self-control, not only tempering his tone but also hinting at an attitude towards life--what he calls "the hysterical patience of the spider."

POETRY

Il disperso (The One Missing) 1976
Le meraviglie dell'acqua (The Wonders of Water) 1980
Glenn 1982 (Viareggio Prize)
Il figurante (The Stand-in) (anthology of poems from 1971-1985, with notes by Cucchi) 1985
Donna del gioco (The Woman in the Game) 1987 (*includes Glenn*)
Poesia della fonte (Poetry from the Source) 1993 (Montale Prize)

THEATRE

the poetic text for *Nel tempo che non é più e che non é ancora* (1989), later published as *La luce del distacco* (The Light of Detachment) 1990

OTHER

Poeti dell'Ottocento (an anthology of poets from the 1800s) (edited) 1978
Dizionario della poesia italiana (A Dictionary of Italian Poetry) 1983

Like the Chinese, I too am going to
paint the flower's death;
a light dabbing on the candid whiteness
of the clay cup: a last mechanical

effort...but maybe tomorrow we'll
enjoy even fresher hopes. There's
an hour during the day or in winter--
believe me--when the eyelids close briefly

at the coming to light of calmer waters:
I put no more than my foot in where
the darkness begins
and it sucks me all up!

Dipingerò come il cinese anch'io
la morte del fiore sulla terracotta
con un tratto lieve sul bianco candido
della tazza: ultimo meccanico

approccio...ma forse godremo domani
di ancora più fresche speranze: c'è un'ora
del giorno o dell'inverno--credimi--
in cui le palpebre si abbassano

dinanzi all'affiorare di un'acqua
più serena: ho messo solo un piede
dove comincia l'ombra
e mi ha succhiato tutto!

Hibernation

1.

The great pleasure of laziness...as it slides,

forming a ball in the decanter; contemplating, perhaps,
the marvels on a glass slide,
                    [the goings-on of life during hibernation,
during vacation...

Rather suddenly, I'm putting myself on the same level as other
people.

2.

The usual ice cream,
thick, repulsive, and sickening sweet...

I remember the magnificence of the metro:
"But beware"--someone told me--
"it'll break down before long and leave you stranded..."

3.

Maybe you, woman, were my enemy on account of those
disturbing signs...

the hell with your catty simpering (I attack you in
my partisan way, certainly cowardly)...at the table
you'd been making eyes at some fellow
and that sort of thing...

I'm writing about you.

4.

Puny monstrous driver...arrogant and hateful;
those few hairs of a straggly red beard...
I'd been strolling back and forth;
after its stop, the boat set off again;
a question of a minute and my solitary excursion,

its destination still a mystery, went up in smoke.

5.

Ruling from his hiding place is an invisible,
compassionate mysterious observer: he'll have figured out
our typical, essential phases:
how in the human body there's that long lying-almost-immo-
bile...

identical visions,
possible, gratuitous metaphors...
internal juices, slimy stagnating food
to assimilate, distribute, expell.

6.

Get exercise, this was the advice...

I'm speaking with the voice of an outsider, of
a friend... Faces that tend to disintegrate, to merge;
the number of intruders increases, ruffians,
those multiple ambiguous features...

Animalesque, monkey-like, sudden thickening of
eyebrows on his forehead, small harmless C.,
overly mature, that look, that smile
already idiotic, timorous...

7.

Beyond those mountains
are other mountains--he said--and still others:
bare, awful, uninhabited; with untouched pines...
and the roaring of torrents...from valley
to valley: nothing but my steps, my sandals.

8.

I manage to keep my writing steady,
controlled by my hand on each letter,
proudly...

I waver uncertainly
between the inward and outward: the hero...the ant...
the ages-old epistolary profundities...

9.

A few glimpses: a light striped lady's suit, a
certain voluptuous taste in the mouth
that's half-open, softened, swelling...

the word "ending" isn't enough upon wakening;
some satisfaction's got to be there during sleep;
full gratification...

It's hard to decide, to get going and finally leave,
what with the milk and the filth in the Grasselli gardens...

10.

He started running, running...he swang through the fields,
                                           [the farm,
increasing in importance and dimension...feeling the effort now;
he moved, convulsed close-up and almost in relief, reeling, so
much as to suffocate me, fall on top of me...

Then, for better or worse, he'd straighten up.

(On the peak
it's still undefined territory, a no man's land...further on--
but the night would grant the fighters new strength--
it's like rolling towards the sea, plunging in...)

Letargo

1.

il gran piacere dell'accidia...scivola, si appallottola
nella boccia di vetro; magari contemplando
le meraviglie del vetrino, lo svolgersi della vita nel letargo
nella vacanza...

quasi di colpo mi sto portando a pari degli altri.

2.

quel solito gelato ripugnante,
denso; quella crema dolciastra...

ricordo lo sfarzo della sotterranea:
"ma non fidarti--mi diceva uno--
presto si ferma, ti lascia a metà strada..."

3.

mi eri forse nemica per turbati segni...

al diavolo le moine del gatto (ti aggredisco
fazioso, certo vilmente)...a tavola
strizzavi l'occhio a un tizio
e via di questo passo...
ti scrivo.

4.

mostriciattolo d'autista...arrogante, odioso;
quei pochi peli di una barbetta rossiccia...passeggiavo
su e giù; dopo la sosta, ecco il battello andarsene:
solo per poco in fumo la mia gita solitaria,
nel mistero ancora la destinazione.

5.

domina nascosto, invisibile,
il pietoso, sconosciuto osservatore: ne dedurrà
le fasi essenziali, tipiche:
nel corpo umano quel lungo giacere quasi
[immobile...

l'identità delle visioni,
possibili metafore gratuite...
i succhi interni, pappa vischiosa che ristagna,
da assimilare, distribuire, espellere.

6.

fare del moto, questo il consiglio...

parlo per voce di un estraneo, un amico...
facce che tendono a scomporsi, fondersi; gli intrusi
si moltiplicano...i ruffiani, ambigue
fisionomie multiple...

belluino, scimmiesco, folto di sopracciglia
d'improvviso sulla fronte, l'innocuo, piccolo C.,
cresciuto a dismisura, lo sguardo, il sorriso,
già ebete, pauroso...

7.

oltre quei monti
sono altri monti--disse--e altri ancora:
nudi, tremendi, inabitati; d'intatti abeti...
e lo scrosciare dei torrenti...di valle in valle:
null'altro che i miei passi, i sandali.

8.

riesco a tenere ferma la scrittura,
controllata nella mano sulla lettera,
fieramente...

oscillo incerto
tra dentro e fuori: l'eroe...la formica...
l'antica profondità epistolare...

9.

pochi barlumi: un tailleur chiaro a righe, un certo
sapore voluttuoso nella bocca, socchiusa, ammorbidita,
gonfia...

non basta la parola fine nel risveglio;
soddisfazione occorre già dal sonno;
appagamento pieno...

difficile decidersi, muoversi e andare,
tra latte e sporcizia, nel verde dei Grasselli...

10.

prendeva a correre, a correre...veniva su tra i prati,
                                        [la cascina,
crescendo d'evidenza, dimensioni...con maggiore affanno: mosso
convulso in primo piano, quasi in rilievo, tanto
da soffocarmi, annaspando, cadermi addosso...

bene o male, poi, si sarebbe ridestato.

(sulla cima
è ancora zona indefinibile, terra di nessuno...più in là
--ma i lottatori, dalla notte,
avrebbero ripreso nuove forze--

è come rotolare verso il mare,
immergersi...)

I wouldn't know what it's like to be a pawn,
those exploding inner mechanisms, synchronized
sensitivity skills, squares of water.
A silent glimmering, the pop-up geometry of footsteps
a ripping of the felt-like or vitreous design,
green surface leading to the den. From the
spider's hysterical patience to a
reacquired flow, intense intact control of
energies; we are so interpenetrated as to already
be dissolving and destroying ourselves,
a spider who follows, thanks to the
work of an intervening hand, some ideal course.

Ignoro il senso delle piccole pedine,
sprizzanti meccanismi, allineate
abilità sensibili, quadrati d'acqua.
Un muto bagliore, la scattante
geometria dei passi; fendere la felpata
o vitrea tracciata superficie verde
alla sua tana. Dalla pazienza isterica
del ragno a un riacquistato flusso, acuto
controllo intatto di energie, compenetrandosi
fino già a sciogliersi, sbranarsi; seguendo,
opera della mano, un suo ideale corso.

You said: it's hot tonight,
let's protect the entrance; solitary types
follow the dead leaves found on paths.
He pounded on the window pane but
calmly said: au revoir
au revoir monsieur, I'm no thief,

I've lost my way, it's pouring
and I fear the myrtle's groan.
At present I await the lucid anxiety of daytime
which individuates death.

Dicevi: è una notte calda
proteggiamo l'entrata, i solitari
viaggiano sulle foglie morte
nei sentieri. Picchiava nel vetro
ma placido diceva: au revoir
au revoir monsieur non sono un ladro
ho smarrito la via diluvia
e il mirto cigola che fa paura.
Aspetto l'ansia lucida del giorno
che seleziona la morte.

Every season has its dead
roots...look outside: the noble couple
of oaks and silver poplars stand watch.
Nothing existed

before a mind or gaze created it.
I think roses, a column...
a fitting recompense--you seemed to be asking me--
the quiet wait in a dreamy illusion

where absurdity disappears. My fate, however, is
to know the shifting, uncontainable energy of
winds. Still, calm down now: there's no one
invading our rooms.

Ogni stagione ha le sue morte
radici...osserva là fuori in vedetta
la nobile coppia delle querce e i pioppi

d'argento: nulla era già compiuto

prima che mente o sguardo lo creasse.
Penso le rose, la colonna...
La giusta ricompensa--sembravi chiedermi--
l'attesa quiete nel sognato illuso

dileguarsi dell'assurdo. Mi tocca
invece l'energia più varia incontenibile
dei venti. Eppure càlmati
nessuno invade le nostre stanze.

It's over now, the time for observation, for
penetrating, impotent, inventive study...it's
my fault: look...can we, almost weightless, leave
this place and get to know the world?
But the striding will dissolve these efforts,
it'll carry me off: I'll have a
slipping veil and an immense black plastic hood.

The workings of relationships numb and dull...here
comes the dilation, the interaction of all layers, and then...

there's no more to the story left, nor evolution.
The gestures repeat. They ice over.

È terminato il tempo dell'osservazione,
dello studio acuto, impotente, fantasioso...
è colpa mia: guarda...potremo
uscire...leggerissimi, conoscere il mondo?
ma la falcata dissolverà lo sforzo,
mi porterà lontano: avrò un velo cadente e un gran
                                        [cappuccio
di plastica nero.

La meccanica dei rapporti intorpidisce...ecco
il dilatarsi, l'interagire degli strati e poi...

non c'è più storia, evolversi. I gesti
si ripetono, si ghiacciano.

MICHELANGELO COVIELLO

M ichelangelo Coviello was born in 1950 in Agropoli (Salerno). As a boy he lived in Tuscany and then in Como, before moving definitively to Milan. In 1974 he graduated with a degree in philosophy, and a thesis on Parmenides, from the University of Milan. He worked briefly as an assistant lecturer in Ancient Philosophy before becoming a copy writer in advertising. He has written for the theatre, radio, and film, and has published translations of poems by Homer and Ezra Pound. In 1984 he founded the small literary press *Corpo 10*, which published more than 50 titles of poetry, prose poetry, and experimental fiction before closing in 1992. At more or less the same time he opened a bookshop, *Buchmesse*, in Milan which hosted art exhibits, readings, and debates. In 1985 Coviello launched the magazine *Scrivere*, a more commercial venture which printed monthly the best of what its subscribers had to offer by way of poems or stories; he organized courses on creative writing and on writing for advertising during this same period. In 1993 Coviello's collages were featured in a one-man show at the Mudima Art Gallery in Milan.

One of the few practitioners of prose poetry in Italy, as previously mentioned, Coviello is capable of taking those sudden wing-tips or nosedives which characterized his earlier work in the "reinvented" genre of rhyming poetry. A certain tension may accumulate in a word or phrase, then erupt with force, making its final repetition into something on the order of a giant rift of color and light. In the cycle of prose poems entitled *Caravaggio*, (we include *Self-Portrait* here), Coviello uses the form of dramatic monologue (or dialogue) to superimpose his own concerns on those of the hounded, sixteenth-century artist;

he does much the same, blending his voice with that of the city of Milan, in the excerpt from *The Well of Clouds*.

POETRY

Pin Pidin (poems for children, with those of other poets) 1975
Indice (Index) 1976
Grossomondo (Hefty World) 1982
Tempo reale (Real Time) 1985
Dobbiamo vendere il cielo (We Have To Sell The Sky) 1992

ESSAYS

Caravaggio (with an introduction by Enzo Siciliano) 1987

THEATRE

Un milione di domani (A Million Tomorrows) 1980
Farsi bello (Looking Good) 1986

OTHER BOOKS

Il mestiere del copy (How to Be a Copywriter) 1987
Viceverso: antologia di prosa poetica (anthology of prose
   poetry edited by Coviello) 1989

from the series entitled **Caravaggio**

Self-Portrait

This tumultuous life is nothing for me but the sound of a flute, the subtle seduction of a viola or the music of the sea gone to sleep between the arms of a shell become an echo. Even I don't know why blood is born from the striking of a head or sword, its hissing victorious and I with it.

It's strange no one ever told me that man's brain could contain both the skies of heaven and of hell. There is nothing I can't cope with: stolen money, the silence of the body, the tedium of love and also its voice. My voice is true wisdom. Lotus petals, ballad in the wood.

There is no peace under the light of day full of other light where even the soul flies uncertain from limb to limb or enters by chance in a lily cup or else makes the shepherd stumble while gathering the hyacinth's warm blue. It seems to me that here in this world that never rests, in this world down here I've sworn the pledge.

And though regret trails me like a shadow in the shade, always there to strike me, I am happy to have loved and to think about the whole of the sun and the whole of the moon. In my eyes I look for what has revealed the violence of reason, the excess of passion and of kisses never given. Of singing never done.

Strike my youth with the weapons of despair, exhibit the gaudy faith of these times, leave to wealthier hands my only work, have my soul imprisoned in a beauty net. I swear I don't like all this. It's you who want me to get bigger and then pettier, following your teaching. You force me to accept the sameness, the imitation of a name. Satiated with lost wandering, I don't want to adopt your rules in vain. That's why I'm selling you to the first one who comes along, like dawn somewhere ordinary.

Da **Caravaggio**

Autoritratto

È questa vita tumultuosa per me non altro che suono di flauto, la sottile seduzione della viola o la musica del mare addormentato tra le braccia di una conchiglia nel suo astrarsi nell'eco. Non so neanch'io perché nasce il sangue da un colpo di testa e di spada, il suo sibilo vittorioso ed io con lui.

È strano nessuno me lo aveva mai detto che il cervello dell'uomo potesse racchiudere il cielo del paradiso e quello dell'inferno. Non c'è nulla che io non possa affrontare: il denaro rubato, il silenzio del corpo, il tedio dell'amore, la sua voce. La mia voce è vera sapienza. Petali di loto, canzonetta nel bosco.

Non vi è pace sotto la luce del giorno piena d'altre luci dove anche l'anima vola incerta di ramo in ramo o entra a caso nel calice di un giglio oppure fa oscillare il passo del pastore mentre coglie il tiepido azzurro d'un giacinto. Qui mi pare, in questo nostro mondo che non conosce riposo, quaggiù io feci giuramento.

E benché il rimorso mi segua come un'ombra nell'ombra sempre pronto a colpirmi, io sono felice d'aver amato e penso a tutto il sole e a tutta la luna. Cerco nei miei occhi ciò che ha rivelato la violenza della ragione, l'eccesso delle passioni e di baci mai dati. Di canti mai cantati.

Pugnalare la mia giovinezza con le armi della disperazione, esibire la sgargiante fede di quest'epoca, lasciare nelle mani più abbiette il mio solo lavoro, avere l'anima prigioniera nella rete della bellezza. Giuro che non amo tutto questo. Sei tu che vuoi che diventi più grande e poi più meschino secondo i tuoi insegnamenti. Mi costringi all'uguaglianza all'imitazione del nome. Sazio di smarrimento non voglio invano seguire le tue orme. Così ti vendo al primo che si offre come un'alba di un posto qualunque.

from **The Well of Clouds**

...This hour is made of iron grates where the underground
trains appear in hot volumes of air vibrating fast messengers of
zeal virtue omnipresence of work. Other grates exhibit the
sewer's subtle architecture, the lead encasements sealing the
city's fluid excrement, from the manholes rises a white dense
smoke like a signal, a warning of another life in us, inside us or
underneath. Towards the middle of the planet, under the hot
crust, faces the city, Milano Milano, rough absent plain, at the
foot of the Matterhorn I'd say to travelers. This hour exclaims
and without a voice sings out the route bulletin to navigators
who have left for the rich mountain, a distant island and then
the shipwreck, the wind, empty-handed return, the Turks the
Turks were also defeated by ships, girlfriends pausing for a
betrayal, peace to privateers, peace to history, to the seas, they
are coming home those dear sons who have remained
adventureless fishermen. Skimming the sidewalk you can't
exclaim, the city is vulgar (I'm on my way home now, too).
Stone lane or serpentine path, uninterrupted place where
language has no peace, where nothing is safe from the nightly
refusal of rest, even dawn passes unobserved by the frigid
sequence of thoughts designated to round up the errors of life,
the falterings of the will, the frigid morning gets rid all of this
even in August, gets rid of the weight that accelerates that
opaque rhythm of the heart that often goes unheard, like life,
like everything. (The roadbed on the other hand is neat and
clean, as clean as it needs to be, shiny river slowly flowing).
(Now he's the one asking, he wants--without being the conscious
subject) (Desire, that is to say without love). And the image in
fact speaks for itself, especially to those who are no judge. The
wind rises in a silent gathering fight, surprising the city rum-
maged by such a fast hand, by such a provident circumstance so
important to the extremely riled, that which was here before is
no longer here, it stirs, moves the first steps towards the sky
fighting against gravity (this hour has no time), for this general
catharsis substance lightens, can be docilely pushed to rise

upwards. *Libeccio* or icy mistral, wind of revolt, spirit of rebellion, flight and velvet, what else in order to name a ransom for what was simple, now worthless. Free; like an unsupported body, even a jar, violates every law and rises, other flights to follow, from the skimming flights of the newspapers to the long skips of cans open on one side, crushed tales, ships, sails in the wind directing the prow towards their own objective. Pindaric height, free-motion vertical shower, air compression and motion that results, keep it up!

Rain, things, leaves, everything is capsized, outstretched to follow the most loquacious clouds towards the heart of fire, the horizon's flame, and even he (it's me it's me) has ended up on the ground for having stumbled or taken ill and notes the relative launch towards the highest highest life contact of life where muscle recedes but not one's glance, fast messenger.

(I saw above the buildings the coming of things in chorus from the bottom of the earth, but a duty-free zone where slings, tops, marbles and other games drew a boundary line, one over and beyond me, child who had come to flaunt in the face of memory another flight, a warm farewell.)

(It seems to be light that sustains me; if without a source, still rigorous in how it touches me, entering and pushing that flight to the bitter end towards the bright path of the spirit that knows and doesn't hold back, and which allows such dead weight to press against the open thoughts born to the splotchy pure intimate part of man (it's me it's me) (hovering high in a plunge to contemplate this flying sky that gathers everything to it.)

(Oh! end of the line sky, even the trams at this hour and the iron tracks) (run windy sky) (trot gallop my soul blow) (wish it'd take me away, too) (earth of memories, you too!) (enough, enough!) (danger of falling mass) (run flow) (friend brother) (if only you'd fall, too) (oh! love) (it's me it's me) (oh! you) (it's me it's me) (a well of clouds).

Da **Il pozzo delle nuvole**

...Quest'ora è fatta di grate di ferro da cui il treno sotterrraneo si manifesta con caldi volumi d'aria vibranti veloci messaggeri di solerzia virtù ubiqua del lavoro. Altre grate al passante mostrano la sottile architettura degli scarichi, i materiali al piombo a sigillare i fluidi escrementi di città, dai tombini s'alza un fumo bianco e denso quasi un segnale, un avvertimento di un'altra vita in noi, dentro di noi o sotto. Verso il centro del pianeta, sotto la crosta calda punta la città, Milano Milano, rozza assente pianura, ai piedi del Cervino direi a chi venisse da lontano. Quest'ora esclama e senza voce canta la rotta ai naviganti, partiti verso la montagna ricca, un'isola lontana e poi il naufragio, il vento del ritorno a mani vuote, i Turchi i Turchi anch'essi vinti da navi amiche in sosta a tradimento, pace ai corsari, pace alla storia ai mari, tornano a casa dai cari figli rimasti pescatori senz'avventura. Radente al marciapiede non si può esclamare, la città è volgare (ora torno a casa anch'io). Viottolo di pietra o porfido sentiero ininterrotto luogo dove il linguaggio non ha pace, dove niente è inviolabile dal rifiuto notturno del riposo, perfino l'alba passa inosservata dalla gelida sequenza dei pensieri posti a rastrellare gli errori della vita, i cedimenti della volontà, sgombrasse tutto il gelido mattino anche in agosto, sgombrasse il peso che accelera del cuore quel ritmo opaco che spesso non si sente, come la vita, come tutto. (Il letto della strada invece è lindo, pulito quanto basta, lucido fiume che lento scorre). (Ora è lui che chiede, vuole senza essere il soggetto che si pensa). (Desiderio, cioè senza amore). E infatti l'immagine parla chiaro, soprattutto a chi non se ne intende. Si alza il vento con volo silenzioso e radunato, sorpresa è la città frugata da così veloce mano da tale circostanza provvida cara ai più agitati, ciò che prima stava ora non sta più, si scuote muove i primi passi verso il cielo, contro la gravità si lotta (quest'ora che non ha tempo), per catarsi generale la materia s'assottiglia, docile alla spinta che verso l'alto innalza. Libeccio o gelido maestrale, vento di fronda, spirito di ribellione, volo e velluto cos'altro per nominare un riscatto di ciò che prima semplice, senza più valore. Gratis, anche un barattolo come corpo cui manchi l'appoggio sospende ogni legge e s'alza, altri voli a seguire, dai radenti sorpassi dei giornali ai balzi lunghi di scatole di lato aperte sfiancate novelle navi vele nel vento la prua dirigendo al proprio scopo. Pindarica altezza, doccia verticale in moto libero, compressione d'aria e moto che risulta, forza!

Pioggia, cose, foglie, tutto è ribaltato proteso ad inseguir le nubi più ciarliere verso il cuore del fuoco fiamma d'orizzonte e anche colui (son io son io) finito per terra per aver incespicato o per malore avverte il relativo slancio verso l'altissimo contatto della vita dove il muscolo recede ma non lo sguardo veloce messaggero.

(Vedevo sopra gli edifici il venire degli oggetti in coro, dal basso della terra non più reale reperto carico di senso ma zona franca in cui fionde trottole palline ed altri giochi segnavano un confine un al di là di me bambino venuto ad esibire in faccia alla memoria un altro volo, un caldo addio.)

(Mi pare luce tutto ciò che mi sostiene sebbene senza fonte ma rigorosa nel suo toccarmi entrare e spingere quel volo a oltranza verso la via luminosa dello spirito che sa e non trattiene tale zavorra poiché preme sui pensieri aperti nati al variegato puro intimo dell'uomo) (son io son io) (librato alto in tuffo a contemplare questo cielo volante che tutto porta in sé.)

(Oh! cielo capolinea, anche i tram a quest'ora e il ferro dei binari) (corri ventoso cielo) (trotta galoppa anima mia soffia) (portasse via anche me) (terra di memoria, anche tu!) (basta, basta!) (pericolo caduta) (corri scorri) (amico fratello) (cadessi anche tu) (oh! amore) (son io son io) (oh! tu) (son io son io) (pozzo delle nuvole).

LELLO VOCE

L ello Voce was born in Naples in 1957. From 1990 to 1992 he was at the University of Geneva on a post-graduate fellowship; since then, he has lived in Treviso, where he teaches Italian Literature in a secondary school. Among the founders of **Gruppo 93**, he co-directs the literary review, *Baldus*, with Biagio Cepollaro. His work has been published in numerous reviews and anthologies both in Italy and abroad.

Voce's poetry has a rebellious, argumentative tone to it, for he openly questions the insignificant role of poetry in our world and takes offense at what is presumed to be its uselessness. His work also communicates a sense of anger, impotence, and bewilderment in its "carefully deconstructed" flow of language, which springs from an uncountable number of sources (one neologism or citation after another) yet which by the saving grace of its form--a dialogue between two voices--remains comprehensible. Humanity is depicted as a swarming yet uniform species whose folly appears to have no limit or end. Voce's sort of linguistic collage technique--switching from one language to another constantly--makes much of his work impossible to translate.

POETRY

Singin' Napoli cantare (Singin' Naples Singing) 1985
(*Musa!*) (Muse!) 1992

from **Variation III (on love and more...)**

"When he had made an end, the thief exclaimed,
raising his hands with both the figs on high:
take thou them, God; at thee, at thee they are aimed."
                    (*Inferno*, XXV, 1-3)

your eyes stolen
    (in a puff!)
    arms thighs
    (in a puff
starved   breathless
    your eyes chomped on
cannibalistic metaphor of love
    (of the usual love-death
    LesbiamyLesbia
                    down there...
(down there in your
    wombsuitcase
    my marsupial love
    giving birth to me anew
devouring your insides
    ("and still called to them who were two days dead.
    Then fasting did what anguish could not.")
and young men and women
    --To the gallows! to the gallows!
and old people and passersby
    (and merchants and smiths (fabbri!..Ezra..
    and peasants and anuses
    and quivering peasanuses
(mais non tu quoque
    --To the gallows! to the gallows!
and then...

immobile here, nailed to the
    years squeezed mouth-to-the-ground strangling time
        suffocating the dying century

(To the cliff! to the cliff
     these posthumous and infantile years
(I speak of this my

     posthumous love, my sweet,
but hold me tight in your pouch, Lesbia,
     and douse the fear

     ("If I were water, if I were wind,
     if I were fire, love,
     I'd set the world ablaze"
whilst the unhappy Jo:Starace was stoned,
wounded, pierced, sliced, dismembered, and dragged,
and his flesh sold by the piece"

para comida
     and los trabjadores
          "yet they had not the least stitch of compassion"
          remember,Lesbia, the damned ice pick
               between Trotsky's eyes?
          (but love going at a loss isn't worth it
               and a posthumous love
          is the lost-orientation of desire
          the compass corrected
               of the sell-out of Reason,
          the imperfect logic of a glance
          that squirms away like cat-rat-fish
               that burns nostrils into the palms,
               that consumes, Lesbia,
          ("most of the time human flesh was served,
          flaying secretly the dead bodies
          and of that meat making mash"
"the dead he said we have transferred them
               to storage
               so much for psalms and banners"
          "I'd like to see more fire than water or land,
          and earth and sky in plague, war and famine.

"All grows old, Gentlemen, all grows
old, old, and so very fast, Gentlemen".
and then if by posthumous you intend
    the defeat of losing a little
        of your past
    then that means a little more useless future, Lesbia,
    who will avenge me?
Remember, Lesbia?
    Berryman's river,
    Mayakovsky's revolver, Villon's rope,
        your sword drawn against the horror;
        Michel'Angelo, Berni's poison;
    the rifles at Lorca's back, the cage
    the cage!
Ezra in the glass cage suspended
    from the fortified walls of the Empire's capital
(seven years, love, seven years in Sant'Anna)
    or a little simpler and more defined:
    backwards hometown
    that tough alley
the descending and ascending by another stairway
"and yet not appeased by this,
at every street they dismembered him,
and so dead they dragged him
with great shame and dishonor"

        (...)

    but for how long still
    Lesbia
we remain looking at each other
tasting the other's body   diffident
for how long, love
    the questions will elude
    the answers and what's poetry
    worth, love?
to what end do those words chase after

things?
for how long still, Lesbia, will
   the border be the only place
(I wanna wolf you, please, let me
     wolf you...
"He sells their flesh while yet alive
   then kills them like old cattle
--many a head of life, himself of honor to deprive.
Bloody he comes forth from the wood of dread;
   he leaves it such that hence a thousand years
'tis not to its first state reforested"
     (I wanna wolf you, please, let me
        wolf you...
because writing poetry does not help, Lesbia,
   to determine reasons (to show the different
   roads)
   but rather to recognize yourself in a sign--
   the gender of angels and
   its lost meaning
      the severed clot that reveals
   the blind ghost attending
      to the vanishing of possibilities
   at the intersection, love, of life
   with that viewing of God's deep bow.

da **Variazione III (d'amore, d'altro)**

> "Al fine de le sue parole il ladro
> le mani alzò con amendue le fiche,
> gridando: --Togli, Dio, ch'a te le squadro!"
>   (*Inferno*, XXV, 1-3)

:volarti via gli occhi
     (in un soffio!)
   le braccia le cosce

   (in un soffio
affamato affannato
   masticarti gli occhi
metafora cannibalica d'amore
   (del solito amore-morte
   LesbiamiaLesbia
      in fondo...
(in fondo al tuo
   ventrevaligia
   mio marsupiale amore
   per partorirmi a nuovo
per divorarti dentro
     ("e due dì li chiamai, poi che fur morti.
     Poscia, più che 'l dolor, poté il digiuno"
e giovani uomini e donne
    --Alla forca! alla forca!
e vecchi e passanti
    (e mercanti e *fabbri* (fabbri!...Ezra...
   e contadini ed ani
   e frementi contedani
(mais non tu quoque
    --Alla forca! alla forca!
e poi...

:immobile, qui, inchiodato agli
   anni stretto boccalsuolo a strangolare il
      tempo a
   soffocare il secolo che muore
   (Alla rupe! alla rupe
    questi anni postumi e infantili
   (parlo di questo mio

    amore postumo, mia dolce,
  ma stringimi al marsupio, Lesbia,
   e spegni la paura
   ("s'io fossi acqua, se fossi vento
   s'io fossi fuoco, amore,

io arderei lo mondo"
"intanto che l'infelice Gio: Starace fu lapidato
ferito, trafitto, smembrato, e strascinato,
e le sue carni a pezzi vendute"
para comida
   e los trabajadores
     "pur non l'ebbero punto di compassione"
     ricordi, Lesbia, la picconata maledetta
     tra gli occhi di Trotskji?
        (ma un amore in perdita non vale
        ma un amore postumo
     è l'orientamento smarrito del desiderio
     la bussola rettificata
        dal commercio di Ragione la
     logica imperfetta dello sguardo
     che sguatta via come gatto-topo-pesce
        che brucia le nari ai palmi
        che consuma, Lesbia,
     ("il più delle volte delle carni umane si servivano
     scorticando secretamente i corpi morti
     e di questo fattone pastoni"
"i morti disse li abbiamo trasportati
     in magazzino
     altro che salmi e bandiere"
     "vorrei veder più fuoco ch'acqua o terra
     e il mondo e 'l cielo in peste e 'n fame e 'n guerra"
     "tutto invecchia, Signori, tutto invecchia, invecchia
     e così in fretta, Signori.
e se poi per postumo intendi
     la sconfitta di perdere un po'
        del tuo passato
     un po' d'inutile futuro in più, allora, Lesbia
        chi mi farà vendetta?
:ricordi, Lesbia? il fiume di
     Berryman la pistola di
     Majakovskji la corda di Villon la spada
        tua sguainata sull'orrore

Michel'Angelo il veleno del Beri
i fucili alla schiena di Lorca la gabbia la
gabbia!
Ezra nella gabbia di veto sospesa
    alle mura della capitale dell'Impero
(sett'anni, amore sett'anni in Sant'Anna)
        o un più semplice e definito
        natìo borgo selvaggio
        il duro calle
lo scendere e 'l salir per l'altrui scale
"e pur non sazj di questo
per ogni contrada lo smembravano
e così morto lo strascinarono
con gran vergogna e disonore"

            (...)

        ma per quanto ancora
        Lesbia
resteremo a guardarci ad
assaggiarci il corpo   diffidenti
per quanto, amore
        le domande eluderanno le
        risposte e la poesia
        a che vale, amore
a che le parole che inseguono le
        cose
per quanto ancora, Lesbia, l'unico luogo
        sarà il confine
(I wanna wolf you, please, let me
        wolf you
"vende la carne loro essendo viva;
        poscia li ancide come antica belva;
molti di vita e sé di pregio priva
sanguinoso esce de la trista selva;
        lasciala tal, che di qui a mille anni
ne lo stato primaio non si rinselva"

(I wanna wolf you, please, let me
    wolf you
chè scrivere poesie non serve, Lesbia
    a stabilire le ragioni (ad indicare
    strade
    è identificarsi in un segno
    il sesso degli angeli il senso
    disperso
        il grumo diviso che dice
    la fantasima orba che attende
        al vanire delle possibilità
    all'angolo, amore, tra vivere e vedere lì
    sull'acuto piegarsi di Dio.

BIAGIO CEPOLLARO

Biagio Cepollaro was born in Naples in 1959. He has a degree in philosophy and teaches in a secondary school in Milan. A leading exponent of the now-disbanded **Gruppo 93**, he has participated in the founding and direction of more than one literary review; at present he co-directs *Baldus*. His poems have appeared in various magazines and anthologies both in Italy and abroad.

What stands out about Cepollaro's poetry is the rich and varied mix of archaic and modern Italian, dialect, slang, and technological or specialized terms--a blend that fuses convincingly into a sort of musical kaleidoscope, in which given words and sounds may repeat, creating allusions and associations at a still more subtle level. A myriad of literary periods and historical epochs is also there between the lines, meaning that each word conveys not only a principal poetic sense but also the history of its usage by poets of other times, as well as the particular connotations it once lent to humanity's essential experiences. An additional consequence of this "simultaneous approach" is that a reader is free to either appreciate the poem as an orderly progression from start to finish or in a profoundly random fashion, fixing only on brief sequences or strophes.

POETRY

Le parole di Eliodora (In Eliodora's Words) 1984
Scribeide 1993
Luna persciente (Moon of Total Knowledge) 1993

OTHER

Poesia in Campania (anthology of poets from Compania) 1990

Requiem in C

for Cecilia T.

But then, flaking off bit by bit, it dissolves--this
waiting upon dampness that slumps the shoulders
                              [and hugs the middle

you become a poor thing, your eyes unstuck and lost
underfoot, hard-to-believe tininess and helplessness,
                              [so natural and naked,

hanging from two threads but such uncertain ones, so
like mirrors, so ready to get entangled if the wind
blows and there's not even a bit of shelter for the eyes

no rejoicing if a live man forgets, gets drunk, then
goes anyway
swinging out from every cliff because he's got
a secret in his toes,

not to be put down anywhere,
so he stays standing and hunched over in his movements
for it's the wisdom of a mouse confronted with water
and I don't need the sea much for...

but a rule, a way out, the old sex urge propelling
you to make that poor thing your lover--
so much blank space around this word! Believe it or not,
this thing
in front of you
speechless
unanswered
whose story doesn't play any film tricks on you:

        --I was there and so was...--
        --that fellow who was looking...--

--I got surprised...--
--and then I made a sudden decision...--

what a surprise, what a decision, and
where have you been, woman, and where
who is talking has never decided but only
been as if churned up at who knows what altitude

does the air get thin and can you see what's down there?

but all at once she looks like a companion to me
I'm shaken undone dazed
I'm speechless
disheveled, incapable of making a poem of this shambles
I'm thrown out of bounds
lost and voiceless
stunned like a live one who's had his arm cut off

while the dead are just a little colder and nicer
they're in your bed, far away and yet near, and for
the last time they show you the way, you who don't
understand a thing and yet hope to discover it under your skin
only it isn't there
it isn't anywhere
and nothing gets shared
neither the heat nor the cold
and he isn't afraid if they cut off the electricity
he isn't afraid of suffocating underground
and he isn't tired of standing still
because he isn't here anymore; he's truly scattered into pieces
without strings, unstrung pearl by pearl, thought by thought,
in the crazy whirlpool, from house to house, from the
truck in the dirt, between falling rock, and I'm not
there you realize, you have your picnic (a thousand table)feature
you look like a man, not a mouse, for there isn't water nor the
sea nor...
but that bit of flesh on the bones

even before the skin becomes a face
and the face becomes words and glances
and the words become thought and that's to say
                     [universal foolishness
that lines our ruin with a message--
weakness beauty lawfulness honesty of fads and customs
faithfulness magnanimity temperance and prudence
the science of motions and halts
the stakes involved and damned-blasted rubbings
leads, loads, overland aqueducts, cereal grains
and helmets, narrow passageways, inspections,
spies and elementary educations.

but that bit of flesh on the bones
the end to this waiting
upon dampness
and the poor thing
two eyes
speechless
unanswered
hampered
momentarily lost to all the--"I was there..." and:

    --I got surprised...--and
    --I made a sudden decision...--whether you believe it or not

hers the wisdom of the mouse confronting water
without film tricks   without a story line
in the middle of a landslide, she herself a pebble
in air that's gotten thinner
the shoulders she slumps as she hugs her middle
without strings, she's unstrung pearl by pearl,
                    [thought by thought
no rejoicing if the live man, if I forget
and wordless
unanswered
he clings.

Requiem in C

per Cecilia T.

Ma poi che scrostandosi a poco a poco si scioglie st'attesa
d'umido ca le spalle fa scendere e stringere i fianchi ca sei

la povera cosa degli occhi scollati e dispersi tra i piedi e
mai creduto così piccola e inerme così sciolta e nuda appesa

a due fili ma così incerti così specchi così pronti a torci
gliarsi se tira vento se non c'è er poco de riparo all'occhi

non è tripudio se il vivo se dimentica s'embriaca e va
comunque
sbilicando de scoglio en scoglio ca c'ha nella punta
dei piedi er segreto

de non poggiare
e resta all'impiedi e curvo ner suo movimento ed è saggezza
de topo coll'acqua de fronte ca me basta poca de mare per

ma na regola na scappatoia che la foia te ricorda è
fare de quella povera cosa cumpagna
quanto de bianco ntorno a sta parola! ce credi e no sta cosa
davanti a te
sanza vucabulo
sanza resposta
sanza quel trampolo de film che te gioca er racconto:

    --sono stata e c'era...--
    --quell'altro che guardava...--
    --rimasi sorpresa...--
    --e poi decisi all'improvviso...--

che sorpresa e decisione e dove sei stata e dove chi parla
ha mai deciso ed è stato dove se mescolato a quale altezza

l'aria se fa rada e se pò vedé che cesta sotto?

ma di botto mi si cumparsa come na cumpagna
i'tragliato sfatto straliniato
i' sanza vucabulo
incomposto incapace de fare tutto er macello testo
i' fora campo
sperzo e non voce
ncoglionito come pò uno ca ce tagliano vivo er braccio

mentre i morti sono solo un po' più freddi e gentili sono
nel letto allontanati e vicini e per l'ultima volta ti fanno
strada a te ca nun capisci e pensi a scovarlo sotto la pelle
e nun c'è
nun c'è da nessuna parte
e niente spartisce
né er freddo né er caldo
e non ha paura se staccano la luce
non ha paura de soffogà sotto la terra
e nun se stanca de sta fermo
pecché nun ce sta più s'è sparpagliato veramente sperso
senza fili sfilato via perla a perla pensero a pensero
en mulinello pazzo de casa en casa de camion en mezzo
alla terra tra le petre ca franano e manco te ne accorgi
ca fai er pic-nic cor tavolino nmezzo alla natura
ca sembri n'omo e non un topo ca non c'è l'acqua né mare per

ma la poca carne sopra le ossa
ancor prima ca la pelle se fa viso
e il viso se fa parola e occhiata
e la parola fa pensero e quindi la minchiata universale
ca reveste de testo l'affossatura
la debiltà la beltà la liceità l'onestà dei modi e dei costumi
la fedeltà la magnanimità la temperanza e la prudenza

la scinza dei moti e delle soste
le poste in gioco e le sfrottenze
le piste le portanze gli acquedotti continentali le spighe
e gli elmetti gli stretti ed i controlli
le spie e le istruzioni elementari

ma la poca carne sopra le ossa
sciogliendosi st'attesa
d'umido
e la povera cosa
degli occhi
sanza vucabulo
sanza resposta
tutta stretta
per il momento spersa da tutti i-sono stata...--e

          --rimasi sorpresa...--e
          --decisi all'improvviso...--ce credi o no sta cosa

fatta saggezza de topo de fronte all'acqua
sanza trampulo de film sanza racconto
nmezzo a na frana essa stessa piccola petra
coll'aria ca s'è fatta un po' più rada
le spalle fa scendere e stringere i fianchi
sanza fili sfilata perla a perla pensero a pensero

non è tripudio se er vivo se dimentico
e sanza vucabulo
sanza resposta
s'avvinghia

INDEX